Recommended

WAYSI

COUNTE

GW00493055

of Britain 2000

A Selection of Hostelries of Character
for Food and Drink and, in most cases,
Accommodation

with

The  Supplement
for Pet-Friendly Pubs

and

Family Friendly Pubs
Supplement

FHG Publications
Paisley

The Cornish Arms

16th Century Coaching Inn

Pendogett, Port Isaac,
North Cornwall PL30 3HH
Tel: 01208 880263
Fax: 01208 880335

Situated in the small rural village of Pendogett, just one mile from the coast. Anyone who makes the Cornish Arms a base for exploring the area will not be disappointed by the attractive accommodation or the warmth of welcome extended. Whilst retaining the character of a traditional coaching inn, The Cornish Arms offers all modern amenities in every bedroom: colour and satellite TV, telephone, tea and coffee making facilities etc.

The highly recommended restaurant specialises in locally caught seafood and an extensive range of other dishes. Complement your meal with wine from the extensive cellars of the Cornish Arms. Pendogett Special Bitter is famous for its strength – the locals won't touch it – it's so strong. With Bass straight from the barrel, together with other real ales, you will see why it is worth visiting the Cornish Arms.

ETB ♛♛♛ Commended   RAC ★★   Les Routiers

QUEEN'S HEAD HOTEL
ETC ♛♛♛ Commended AA ★★

The 16th century Queen's Head, set in the traffic-free village of Hawkshead on the edge of Esthwaite Water, has a wonderful atmosphere, with low oak-beamed ceilings, panelled walls and a warm log fire whenever necessary. The friendly bar and separate dining room are noted for high quality food, with many locally and organically produced ingredients and a comprehensive wine list. Beer is hand-pulled from the wood. The attractive en suite bedrooms, some with four-poster beds, have colour television, tea and coffee making facilities, hairdryer and telephone.

Hawkshead Village was the home of Beatrix potter and is an excellent centre for fishing, bowling, riding, water-ski-ing, cycling and walking.

QUEEN'S HEAD HOTEL, HAWKSHEAD, CUMBRIA LA22 0NS
TEL: 015394 36271 FAX: 015394 36722 FREEPHONE: 0800 137263
E-mail: enquiries@hawkshead-queens.demon.co.uk
Website: www.hawkshead-queens.demon.co.uk

SUN HOTEL

and Coaching Inn

Family-run Hotel in idyllic location with stunning views of the fells. Offering quality meals both in the Restaurant and our own rustic 16th Century Inn accompanied by a selection of fine wines and traditional ales.

Open all year for a warm welcome in comfortable surroundings. Gardens and terrace open during the warmer months with open fires and lounge to help while away the winter nights. Most rooms en suite with excellent views and all comfortably fitted, offering TV, telephone and beverage facilities. Direct access to walking routes at the side of the Hotel. Two minutes' walk from the main village and ten minutes' walk from the Lake. Party bookings, weddings etc. catered for. Telephone for reservations.

Coniston, Cumbria LA21 8HQ

Telephone: 015394 41248 • Fax: 015394 41219
E-Mail: p.elson@binternet.com

THE BLACKSMITHS ARMS

Talkin Village, Brampton, Cumbria CA8 1LE
Tel: 016977 3452 • Fax: 016977 3396

The Blacksmith's Arms offers all the hospitality and comforts of a traditional country inn. Enjoy tasty meals served in the bar lounges, or linger over dinner in the well-appointed restaurant. The inn is personally managed by the proprietors, Anne and Donald Jackson, who guarantee the hospitality one would expect from a family concern. Guests are assured of a pleasant and comfortable stay. There are five lovely bedrooms, all en suite and offering every comfort. Peacefully situated in the beautiful village of Talkin, the inn is convenient for the Borders, Hadrian's Wall and the Lake District. There is a good golf course, walking and other country pursuits nearby.

THE POACHERS INN

Piddletrenthide, Near Dorchester DT2 7QX
01300 348358; Fax: 01300 348153

Country Inn set in the heart of lovely Piddle Valley. Within easy reach of all Dorset's attractions. All rooms en suite with colour TV, tea and coffee, telephone; swimming pool (May-September). Riverside garden, restaurant where Half Board guests choose from à la carte menu at no extra cost.

Bed and Breakfast – £27.50 per person per night.
Dinner, Bed and Breakfast – £41 per person per night. 10% discount for seven nights.

Low Season Breaks – two nights Dinner, Bed and Breakfast – £82 per person per night.
Third night Dinner, Bed and Breakfast – FREE. Send for brochure.

AA
QQQQQ
Premier Selected

SILVER AWARD
1999

Ashley
Courtenay

THE WOODFALLS INN

The Ridge, Woodfalls, Hampshire SP5 2LN
Tel: 01725 513222 • Fax: 01725 513220
E-mail: woodfalls@aol.com • Website: www.trad-inns.co.uk/woodfalls

Nestling on the northern edge of the New Forest, on an old route to the cathedral city of Salisbury, this award-winning inn has provided hospitality to travellers since 1870.

Ideal for visiting the New Forest, Stonehenge, Romsey and Winchester.

After recent refurbishment, all ten bedrooms are tastefully and individually decorated, with en suite facilities (some with four-poster beds).

There is an award-winning restaurant and a bar serving food and real ales.

String of Horses
Country House Hotel

String of Horses

Unique, secluded hotel set in two acres in the heart of the New Forest. Friendly, relaxed atmosphere with service, cuisine and accommodation of the highest standard. Eight Luxurious double bedrooms each with its own en-suite Jacuzzi and shower plus full facilities including remote controlled TV, telephone and hospitality tray. Four-poster bed and mini bars are a special feature in several rooms. Romantic dining 'francais' in the oak beamed award winning 'Carriages Restaurant'. Heated swimming pool in tranquil gardens. Close to yachting resorts, golf, riding stables and cycle hire. Smoke free common areas. Regrettably No Children or Pets.

ETC ★★★ AA ❀ **Mead End Road, Sway, near Lymington. Hampshire SO41 6EH**

Tel: 01590 682631 • E-Mail: relax@stringofhorses.co.uk • Web page: www.hotelregister.co.uk/hotel/stringofhorses.asp

---

The Strawbury Duck Hotel
Overshores Road, Entwistle,
Near Bolton, Lancashire BL7 0LU
Tel: 01204 852013

Small and cosy and bursting with old-fashioned charm, this welcoming free house sits comfortably by the Manchester/Blackburn railway line and offers four nicely furnished guest bedrooms to the weary traveller, three with four-poster bed and all with full en suite facilities and tea/coffee making. Bar fare ranges from sandwiches to genuine Aberdeen Angus steaks served on a hot sizzle plate. Also a choice of vegetarian dishes and a wide range of authentic Indian and Balti cuisine. Pub renowned for fine selection of hand-drawn real ales (weekly guest beers).

THE FALCON HOTEL
Castle Ashby, Northamptonshire NN7 1LF
Telephone:(01604) 696200. Fax:(01604) 696673

The Falcon Hotel is on the estate of the Marquess of Northampton who lets it to resident proprietors Michael and Jennifer Eastwick on some kind of feudal arrangement known only to marquesses.

The Falcon is a magnificent inn and is four hundred years old, though as Michael points out there's no-one around to disprove it. It started life as a farm, then got mixed up in religious pop festivals and now has the Silverstone motor racing circuit within handy distance. If this sounds pretty mixed up, don't wait up at night to see Arthur the ghost. Michael invented him. Michael and Jennifer organise painting weekends, though this is not believed to be a way of getting guests to decorate their own bedrooms.

Sixteen bedrooms. • Double room – £95.50 • Single Room – £79.50
2 Conference rooms available • Compton Room holds 40 people • Ashby Room holds 10 people.

The Red Lion Hotel
East Haddon, Northamptonshire NN6 8BU
Tel: 01604 770223 Fax: 01604 770767

This traditional, stone-built inn sits snugly in the charming village of East Haddon, just eight miles from Northampton. Golf, fishing, squash, swimming and snooker are all available locally. Those wishing to make the most of a relaxing weekend break will find comfortable, spick-and-span bedrooms with full en suite facilities, television, etc. Good English cooking is the basis of the carefully balanced à la carte menu and a comprehensive range of gourmet bar food is available at lunchtime and in the evening in the brass and copper bedecked bars, accompanied by one's choice from the well-kept ales, beers, wines and other refreshments.
Egon Ronay, Good Food Guide.

The Castle Hotel

Porlock, Somerset TA24 8PY
Tel: 01643 862504
Fax: 01643 862504

The Castle Hotel is a small, fully licensed family-run hotel in the centre of the lovely Exmoor village of Porlock. It is an ideal holiday location for those who wish to enjoy the grandeur of Exmoor on foot or by car. The beautiful villages of Selworthy and Dunster with its castle are only a short distance away.

There are 13 en suite bedrooms, all fully heated, with colour TV and tea/coffee making facilities.

The Castle Hotel has a well-stocked bar with Real Ale. Draught Guiness and Cider. A full range of Bar Meals are available at lunchtimes and Evenings or dine in our Restaurant.

Children and pets are most welcome. Family room available, cots available on request.

❖ ❖ ❖ *Special Breaks available* ❖ ❖ ❖
Extremely low rates *Please contact Mr Bickerstaff on 01643 862504*

The
HOOD ARMS
Kilve, Somerset TA5 1EA
Tel: 01278 741210 • Fax: 01278 741477

17th Century Coaching Inn on the edge of Exmoor.

THE HOOD ARMS nestles in the heart of the Quantocks in an area which is totally unspoilt. A traditional black and white 17th century coaching inn owned by Barry and Vanessa Eason, it is set in landscaped lawns, with a spacious walled garden. The comfortable bars have distinct character created by old beams, large fireplaces with roaring log fires in season, and candlelight for evening dining. The extensive and varied menus will satisfy the heartiest of appetites, with a comprehensive wine list to complement your meal. The five double bedrooms are fully en suite, with television, trouser press, hairdryer and hospitality tray. Two cottages adjacent to the Inn are available for weekend or longer breaks and are ideal for families. Resident managers Matthew Haggett and Brian Pook look forward to welcoming you.

AA QQQQQ • EGON RONAY • GOOD PUB GUIDE • WHICH PUB GUIDE

A perfect example of the traditional English hostelry, the Chequers Inn stands at the end of a quiet lane in this delightful village in the Vale of Evesham. Those seeking accommodation will find beautifully kept en suite guest rooms, some with balconies, some with open rural views, and all well equipped with colour television, radio, telephone, and tea trays. Even if time precludes one staying a while in this charmed area, the Chequers is still worth a flying visit for its fine fare. A carvery is provided Thursday, Friday and Saturday evenings and Sunday lunchtime; bar meals and an à la carte menu are available daily. Golf breaks available, details on request.

Chequers Lane, Fladbury, Pershore WR10 2PZ
Tel: 01386 860276/860527 Fax: 01386 861286

—THE—
CHEQUERS INN
♔♔♔
COMMENDED

Please mention Recommended Wayside and Country Inns when enquiring

New Inn Hotel

Clapham, 'Jewel of the Dales'

A comfortable hotel in the
Yorkshire Dales National Park

New Inn Hotel, Clapham, near Settle LA2 8HH
Tel: 015242 51203   Fax: 015242 51496

BUILT in 1776, The New Inn is set in the magnificent Yorkshire Dales National Park with its dramatic peaks, delightful dales, rivers, waterfalls and caves. It is situated in the centre of the charming village of Clapham.

Keith and Barbara Mannion and family have owned the New Inn since 1987. During this time they have lovingly and carefully refurbished with a fine blend of old and new to retain the characteristics of this eighteenth century coaching inn, where you can experience a warm and friendly welcome.

The New Inn has superb accommodation, all bedrooms having full central heating, bathroom, colour television, telephone, hairdryer, tea and coffee tray and ample writing space – all designed to make your stay a "home from home".

Excellent facilities are provided with a residents' lounge situated on the first floor, first class restaurant and two bars.

Enjoy excellent food prepared by our resident chefs, either in the restaurant or from our extensive bar menu.

Being a true Free House, a variety of hand pulled beers may also be sampled in the comfort of either bar, (each with open fire), where traditional pub games of pool, darts and dominoes can be enjoyed.

English Tourist Board ♔♔♔ *Commended*   *Inns of Tradition*

AA   ETC ♦♦♦   RAC

Local attractions include historic town of Richmond (3 miles), Catterick Racecourse (2 miles) Croft Motor racing Circuit (6 Miles), Yorkshire Dales within easy reach.

Vintage Hotel & Restaurant

Scotch Corner North Yorkshire DL10 6NP
Tel: 01748 824424 / 822961 • Fax: 01748 826272

Very conveniently situated for a meal/overnight stop on A66, just 150 yards from Scotch Corner Junction(A1). Family-run with rustic Spanish-style Bar and Restaurant with picture windows overlooking open countryside. All bedrooms with central heating, double glazing, TV, telephone and tea and coffee making facilities.

Open all year except Christmas, New Year and Sunday evenings.
Room rates from £25 single; £35 double.
2 night break (Monday to Saturday inclusive.) from
£30 per person per night, Dinner, Bed & Breakfast.

Available from most bookshops, the year 2000 edition of
The GOLF GUIDE covers details of every UK golf course – well over 2500 entries – for holiday or business golf.
Hundreds of hotel entries offer convenient accommodation, accompanying details of the courses – the 'pro', par score, length etc.
Holiday Golf in Ireland, France, Portugal, Spain, The USA and Thailand. In association with GOLF MONTHLY
Including the Ryder Cup Report.

£9.95 from bookshops or £10.50 including postage
(UK only) from FHG Publications,
Abbey Mill Business Centre, Paisley PAI ITJ   FHG

THE BUCK INN

Delightful Country Inn overlooking cricket green in quiet
Wensleydale village. Relax in our comfortable en suite
bedrooms, enjoy superb home cooked food and drink
from our selection of five real ales. Ideal centre for
exploring Herriot country. Private fly fishing available
on River Ure and six golf courses within 20 minutes'
drive. Good Pub Guide. CAMRA Good Beer Guide,
Room at the Inn, Good Pub Food Guide, British Cheese
Board Recommended.
**Thornton Watlass, near Bedale
Ripon, North Yorkshire HG4 4AH
Tel: (01677) 422461 Fax: (01677) 422447**

Delightful 18th Century
Coaching Inn.

Excellent à la carte Restaurant,
Bar meals, and
hand pulled beers.

Seven en-suite bedrooms.

The Star Inn

Ideal for walking, rambling and touring.

ETB ♛♛♛♛ *Commended*

For more details contact Keith or Jo.

★ **Warter Road, North Dalton, East Riding of Yorkshire YO25 9UX** ★
Tel: 01377 217688; • Fax: 01377 217791

*The Hawk
& Buckle Inn*

WTB ★★★ INN

Every 20th century comfort is to be found at this welcoming seventeenth century
village inn. All the en suite guest rooms in the tasteful extensions are equipped with
telephones, tea/coffee making facilities and televisions; trouser press and hairdryer
available. Furnishings are comfortable and pleasing to the eye. Local game, pork,
lamb and freshly caught
salmon and trout are imaginatively served in the inn's popular restaurant, and
varied and substantial bar snacks are offered at lunchtimes and evenings. Closed
lunchtimes (except Wednesday and weekends) between October 1st and May 1st.
Hosts Robert and Barbara Pearson will happily supply a wealth of information on
the area. Visa and Access accepted. Egon Ronay, Ashley Courtenay.

**Llannefydd, Near Denbigh LL16 5ED
Tel: 01745 540249; Fax: 01745 540316**

PUBLISHER'S NOTE

While every effort is made to ensure accuracy, we regret that FHG Publications
cannot accept responsibility for errors, omissions or misrepresentations in our
entries or any consequences thereof. Prices in particular should be checked
because we go to press early. We will follow up complaints but cannot act as
arbiters or agents for either party.

FHG

Recommended

WAYSIDE & COUNTRY INNS

of Britain 2000

FHG Publications
Paisley

Editorial Consultant, Peter Stanley Williams

Other FHG Publications

Recommended Short Break Holidays in Britain
Recommended Country Hotels of Britain
Pets Welcome!
B&B in Britain
The Golf Guide: Where to Play/Where to Stay
Farm Holiday Guide England/Scotland/Wales/Ireland & Channel Islands
Self-Catering Holidays in Britain
Britain's Best Holidays
Guide to Caravan and Camping Holidays
Bed and Breakfast Stops
Children Welcome! Family Holiday and Attractions Guide

Acknowledgement

We thank The Clarendon Hotel & Wight Mouse Inn, Chale. Isle of Wight
for the use of their pictures on our Outside Front Cover.

Cover design: Oliver Dunster, Link House Magazines

ISBN 185055 301 7
© IPC Magazines Ltd. 2000
No part of this publication may be reproduced by any means or
transmitted without the permission of the Publishers.

Cartography by GEO Projects, Reading
Maps are based on Ordnance Survey maps with the permission of
Her Majesty's Stationery Office, Crown Copyright reserved.

Typeset by FHG Publications Ltd. Paisley.
Printed and bound in Great Britain by William Clowes, Beccles, Suffolk

Distribution. Book Trade: WLM, Unit 11, Newmarket Court, Newmarket Drive, Derby DE24 8NW
(Tel: 01332 573737. Fax: 01332 573399).
News Trade: Market Force (UK) Ltd, 247 Tottenham Court Road, London WIP 0AU
(Tel: 020 7261 6809; Fax: 020 7261 7227).

Published by FHG Publications Ltd., Abbey Mill Business Centre,
Seedhill, Paisley PA1 ITJ (Tel: 0141-887 0428 Fax: 0141-889 7204).
e-mail: fhg@ipc.co.uk

US ISBN 1-55650-875-1
Distributed in the United States by
Hunter Publishing Inc., 130 Campus Drive, Edison, N.J., 08818, USA

Recommended Wayside & Country Inns is a Link House publication, published by
IPC Country & Leisure Media Ltd, part of IPC Magazines Group of Companies.

Recommended
Wayside & Country Inns
OF BRITAIN

CONTENTS

ENGLAND

SCOTLAND

WALES

Recommended

WAYSIDE & COUNTRY INNS OF BRITAIN 2000

PUBLISHER'S FOREWORD

Many people enjoy touring around the countryside, admiring the beautiful scenery and visiting stately homes and gardens – especially in Spring or early Autumn. *Recommended Wayside & Country Inns* is the ideal companion on such journeys, and this edition for the year 2000 contains a comprehensive selection of inns, pubs and small hotels, all over the country, where you can drop in for a meal or just to quench your thirst – and maybe even learn something about local history and customs at the same time.

Should you decide to continue your explorations next day, most of our entries offer comfortable, sometimes luxurious, accommodation and you can be sure of a warm and friendly welcome and a hearty breakfast to set you up for the day ahead.

Our selection of pubs, inns and small hotels is 'recommended" on the basis of reputation, written descriptions, facilities and long association rather than through personal inspection and as usual we have included the separate 'family-friendly' and 'pet-friendly' supplements which we hope will prove useful. We cannot accept responsibility for errors, misrepresentations or the quality of hospitality but we are always interested to hear from readers about their own experiences. Fortunately complaints are few, and rarely serious, but if you do have a problem which cannot be settled on the spot (the best solution, by the way), please let us know. We cannot act as intermediaries or arbiters, but we will record your complaint and follow it up with the establishment.

As far as we can establish, the details for all our entries are accurate as we go to press. We do suggest, however, that you confirm prices and other specific points while you are making enquiries and bookings.

Please mention RECOMMENDED WAYSIDE & COUNTRY INNS when you make enquiries or bookings. Whether this latest edition is your touring companion, a source of holiday ideas or a handy outings guide, we hope that you will find high quality fare, good value and a warm welcome.

Anne Cuthbertson
Editor

Berkshire

THE DUNDAS ARMS,
Station Road, Kintbury,
Berkshire RG17 9UT

Tel: 01488 658263/658559; Fax: 01488 658263
e-mail: info@dundasarms.co.uk
website: www.dundasarms.co.uk

5 bedrooms, all with private bathroom; Free House with real ale; Children welcome; Bar meals, restaurant evenings only; Non-smoking areas; Hungerford 3 miles; S££££, D£££.

The inn's lovely position between the River Kennet and the canal makes it a most pleasant spot to stop for refreshment, and indeed for an overnight stay or weekend break. The comfortably furnished bedrooms are fully equipped with private bathroom, television and tea-making facilities, and enjoy relaxing views over the river. If your visit here is purely for refreshment, you will be delighted by the excellent bar food menu, which features really interesting "specials" alongside traditional favourites such as ploughmans and steak and kidney pie, and by the range of well kept real ales. For more leisurely dining, menus in the restaurant make full use of fresh local produce, and there is also an excellent wine list. *CAMRA.*

THE COMPTON SWAN HOTEL,
Compton, Near Newbury,
Berkshire RG20 6NJ

Tel: 01635 578269
Fax: 01635 578765

5 bedrooms, all with private bathroom; Real ales; Pets welcome; Bar meals; Streatley 5 miles.

Situated in the heart of the Berkshire Downlands, the hotel has five bedrooms with en suite bathrooms, television, beverage facilities and telephones. There is an extensive menu with traditional, exotic, vegetarian, and special diets catered for. Our home-cooked meals are a speciality. Downlands Healthy Eating Award winner. Large walled garden where we have al fresco eating; barbecues. We are near the famous ancient Ridgeway National Trail and are an ideal base for walking, horse-riding, and golf. Stabling and horsebox available. Real ales and bar meals available. *CAMRA Good Beer Guide and Good Pub Guide.*

The **£** symbol when appearing at the end of the italic section of an entry shows the anticipated price, during 2000, for full Bed and Breakfast.

Normal Bed & Breakfast rate per person (in single room)		Normal Bed & Breakfast rate per person (sharing double/twin room)	
PRICE RANGE	CATEGORY	PRICE RANGE	CATEGORY
Under £25	S£	**Under £25**	D£
£26-£35	S££	**£26-£35**	D££
£36-£45	S£££	**£36-£45**	D£££
Over £45	S££££	**Over £45**	D££££

This is meant as an indication only and does not show prices for Special Breaks, Weekends, etc. Guests are therefore advised to verify all prices on enquiring or booking.

Buckinghamshire

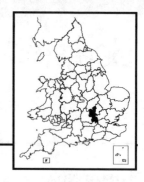

THE PLOUGH,
Hyde Heath, Near Amersham,
Buckinghamshire HP6 5RW

Tel: 01494 783163

No accommodation; Real ale; Children and pets welcome; Bar meals; Chesham 2 miles.

In a tranquil position on the gentle slopes of the Chiltern Hills and actually in the famed Chiltern Hundreds, this homely inn is only a mile or so west of Chesham and a leisurely drive from the urban hassle of Greater London. The Plough is just the place to recharge the batteries through the medium of excellent refreshment and good company. There is a most interesting and varied selection of dishes on offer at lunchtime and in the evening, all of which are home-cooked to order using only fresh produce. After satisfying ourselves in style and at surprisingly moderate cost, we found the return to the concrete jungle something of a penance. *CAMRA.*

GEORGE HOTEL,
73 Wycombe End, Beaconsfield,
Buckinghamshire HP9 1LZ

Tel: 01494 673086
Fax: 01494 674034

11 bedrooms, all with private bathroom; Free House; Historic interest; Children and pets welcome; High Wycombe 5 miles; D££££.

This lovely old 15th century coaching inn is unusual in that it was originally built around a living oak tree which today forms the pivot of the spiral staircase leading to the bedrooms in the main concourse. These rooms are individually decorated and richly furnished with antiques and have private bathrooms with power showers and satellite television. There are three charming family cottages overlooking the garden and also special suites for honeymooners; self-catering accommodation is also available. There are many places of interest to visit nearby, including Windsor Castle, Ascot and the leafy banks of the River Thames; London is just 30 minutes by train. The hotel is totally non-smoking. *AA* ◆◆◆◆

PLEASE MENTION THIS GUIDE WHEN YOU WRITE

OR PHONE TO ENQUIRE ABOUT ACCOMMODATION.

IF YOU ARE WRITING, A STAMPED,

ADDRESSED ENVELOPE IS ALWAYS APPRECIATED.

Cambridgeshire

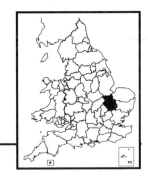

THE RED LION,
47 High Street, Stretham, Ely, Cambridgeshire CB6 3JQ

Tel: 01353 648132
Fax: 01353 648327

12 bedrooms, all with private bathroom; Free House; Historic interest; Children and pets welcome; Restaurant meals; Non-smoking areas; Cambridge 12 miles, Ely 4; S££.

The Red Lion is a 17th century coaching inn which has been carefully renovated and offers comfortable accommodation in en suite bedrooms with colour television and tea/coffee making facilities. The inn is situated in a commanding position in the centre of the village of Stretham, ideal for visiting Ely, Cambridge and Newmarket, plus a host of historic houses and places of interest such as Duxford Air Museum. A large variety of individually cooked meals, including special salads, are available each lunchtime and evening, and vegetarians are catered for. Credit cards accepted. 👑 *Approved.*

ELEPHANT & CASTLE FREEHOUSE & MOTEL,
The Green, Wood Walton, Near Huntingdon, Cambridgeshire PE17 5YN

Tel: 01487 773337
Fax: 01487 773553
http://members.aol.com/Ghewlett/index.htm

All bedrooms with private bathrooms; Free House; Pets welcome in motel complex; Huntingdon 6 miles; S£, D£.

Conveniently situated in a quiet village just two miles from the A1(M), the Elephant & Castle Freehouse and Motel offers comfortable accommodation in eight country-style units. Rooms are on the ground floor and are all en suite with 20" Teletext TV, dual alarm clock radios and drink-making facilities. Set amongst a wealth of nature reserves and animal sanctuaries, it lies directly between Cambridge and Peterborough with easy access to all major motorway links and airports. There is also standing for up to 16 tourist caravans or campers, with facilities. An extensive bar meal menu is available. Your hosts, June and Glynne Hewlett, will be pleased to welcome you.

NAGS HEAD HOTEL,
2 Berkley Street, Eynesbury, St Neots, Cambridgeshire PE19 2NA

Tel: 01480 476812
Fax: 01480 391881

8 bedrooms, all with private bathroom; Free House with real ale; Children and pets welcome; Bar meals evenings, restaurant by arrangement; Non-smoking areas; Huntingdon 8 miles; S£££, D£.

Merely a stone's throw from the busy A1 and A428, this is a much respected port of call, either as a refreshment break or as a rewarding overnight stop. Originally a small inn with a history dating back to the 15th century, the 'Nags Head' was completely renovated in 1990 and a new guest wing added with four of the eight rooms being on the ground floor; all have en suite facilities, colour television, direct-dial telephone and tea and coffee-makers. There is a large car park and, with a popular bar, this is a friendly and well-favoured family hotel where guests of all ages are warmly welcomed.

Cheshire

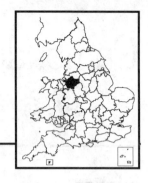

THE EGERTON AT ASTBURY,
Astbury Village, Near Congleton,
Cheshire CW12 4RQ

Tel: 01260 273946
Fax: 01260 277273

6 bedrooms, 2 with private bathroom; Robinsons House with real ale; Historic interest; Children welcome; Bar and restaurant meals; Non-smoking areas; Congleton 1 mile; S£, D£.

Visitors to Brereton Country Park, Jodrell Bank Science Centre and Little Moreton Hall, the most perfect timber-framed house in the country, would do well to call in at this pleasant 16th century inn, situated in the beautiful village of Astbury. Family-run under the personal supervision of Allen and Grace Smith (who welcome children with well-behaved parents!), excellent, freshly-prepared lunches, dinners and snacks are served every day, including vegetarian dishes as well as Robinson's real ale. A friendly port of call, the 'Egerton' offers good overnight accommodation in comfortable, well-furnished bedrooms, all with colour television, radio and tea and coffee-making facilities. *AA* ◆◆◆

HAND AND TRUMPET INN,
Main Road, Wrinehill, Crewe,
Cheshire CW3 9BJ

Tel & Fax: 01270 8200

6 bedrooms, all with private bathroom; Free House with real ale; Children welcome; Bar and restaurant meals; Non-smoking areas; Crewe 9 miles; £.

A friendly little inn in a picturesque rural setting, the family-run 'Hand and Trumpet' stands in pleasant gardens by the A531, a most convenient centre for the Potteries. Traditional beers and bar meals are served in warm and congenial surroundings and the grill room has established a reputation for its quality fare. Neat, tidy and attractively-furnished throughout, the inn welcomes residential guests who have the choice of centrally-heated single, double or twin rooms, all with bath or shower en suite, colour television, direct-dial telephone and tea and coffee-making facilities. The spruce Kingfisher Suite is a popular venue for a variety of functions. 👑👑👑 *Commended.*

CHURCH HOUSE INN,
Church Street, Bollington, Macclesfield,
Cheshire SK10 5PY

Tel: 01625 574014
Fax: 01625 576424

5 bedrooms, all with private bathroom; Free House with real ale; Children welcome; Bar meals; Non-smoking areas; Macclesfield 3 miles; S££, D£.

Convenient for Chester and Manchester and for the unspoiled scenery of the Peak District National Park, this charming hostelry makes the most of an tranquil and relaxing situation. Delightfully decorated and efficiently run by hosts, Stephen and Julie Robinson, the inn provides good food, ale and company in a warm, unhurried atmosphere, a subtle amalgam of Victorian values and modern practicality. All food is freshly cooked to order; generous portions beautifully presented and at the most reasonable prices, too! En suite bedrooms are tastefully furnished, each with tea/coffee facilities, television and trouser press. 👑👑👑 *Commended, Egon Ronay.*

THE PHEASANT INN,
Higher Burwardsley, Tattenhall,
Cheshire CH3 9PF

Tel: 01829 770434
Fax: 01829 771097

10 bedrooms, all with private bathroom; Free House with real ale; Historic interest; Children welcome; Bar and restaurant meals; Non-smoking areas; Chester 9 miles; S£££££, D£££.

For 300 years the lovely half timbered and sandstone Pheasant Inn has stood atop the Peckforton Hills, gazing out over the Cheshire Plain to distant Wales. Panoramic views are to be enjoyed from most of the nicely decorated bedrooms, which are complete with en suite bathroom, colour television, radio alarm, hairdryer and beverage making facilities. Accommodation is in the beautifully converted barn, tucked quietly away from the convivial bar with its huge log fire, and the Bistro Restaurant which enjoys a well-deserved reputation for fine fare, well presented and served with cheerful efficiency. Weekend mini-breaks are a popular feature of this commendable establishment. 👑👑👑 Commended, AA**.

Other specialised

FHG PUBLICATIONS

• Recommended COUNTRY HOTELS OF BRITAIN   £4.95

• Recommended WAYSIDE & COUNTRY INNS OF BRITAIN   £4.95

• PETS WELCOME!   £5.25

• BED AND BREAKFAST IN BRITAIN   £3.95

• THE GOLF GUIDE Where to Play / Where to Stay   £9.95

Published annually: Please add 55p postage (UK only)
when ordering from the publishers

FHG PUBLICATIONS LTD
Abbey Mill Business Centre, Seedhill,
Paisley, Renfrewshire PA1 1TJ

Cornwall

OLD FERRY INN,
Bodinnick-by-Fowey,
Cornwall PL23 1LX

Tel: 01726 870237
Fax: 01726 870116

12 bedrooms, 8 with private bathroom; Free House with real ale; Historic interest;Children welcome; Bar food, restaurant evenings only; Non-smoking areas; Liskeard 15 miles, Looe 10; S££, D£/££.

Under the supervision of Royce and Patricia Smith, this 400-year-old hostelry, fully licensed, combines the charm of a past era with modern comfort. Rooms are well-appointed, and several bedrooms have private bathrooms. A reputation has been rapidly gained for fine food and wine. This free house stands in a quiet sheltered position facing south, overlooking the beautiful Fowey estuary. Bodinnick is a splendid centre for sailing, boating and fishing; Fowey, easily reached by car ferry, has a famous yachting harbour. There are lovely coastal walks in the vicinity.

THE WELLINGTON HOTEL,
The Harbour, Boscastle,
Cornwall PL35 0AQ

Tel: 01840 250202; Fax: 01840 250621
e-mail: vtobutt@enterprise.net
website: www.enterprise.net/wellington-hotel

17 bedrooms, 16 with private bathroom; Free House with real ale; Historic interest; Pets welcome; Bar meals, restaurant evenings only; Non-smoking areas; Tintagel 3 miles; S££, D££.

This historic 16th century coaching inn is situated by the Elizabethan harbour and is surrounded by National Trust countryside. It is ideally situated for walking, touring and golfing holidays and close to glorious sandy beaches, beautiful wooded valleys and dramatic moorland.The Wellington Hotel is a free house, and offers real ales, pub grub, open fires and beams; the fine Anglo-French restaurant specialises in regional cuisine and seafood. There are 10 acres of private woodland walks and pets are very welcome. *AA and RAC **.*

THE EARL OF ST VINCENT,
Egloshayle,
Cornwall PL27 6HT
Tel: 01208 814807

No accommodation; St Austell Brewery House with real ale; Bar meals; Bodmin 7 miles.

Dating from the Middle Ages, this friendly pub is named after Sir John Jervis, the Earl of St Vincent, who was Lord Nelson's commanding officer. Among many attractive features are colourful floral displays and a collection of old clocks. A comprehensive menu is available lunchtimes and evenings.

THE HALZEPHRON INN,
Gunwalloe, Helston,
Tel: 01326 240406
Cornwall TR12 7QB
Fax: 01326 241442

2 bedrooms, both with private bathroom; Free House with real ale; Historic interest; Children and pets welcome; Bar and restaurant meals; Non-smoking areas; Helston 4 miles; S£, D££

Although the name 'Halzephron' comes from the Old Cornish for 'Cliffs of Hell', visitors to this pub on the unspoilt Lizard Peninsula will be warmly welcomed. We are renowned for our fresh food, using local produce. The menu includes local fish, meat, shellfish and vegetarian items, with dishes such as lemon sole, Dover sole, scallops, fresh crab, steak, and our speciality 'Halzephron Chicken'. The restaurant is open lunchtimes and evenings. Comfortable accommodation is available.

THE HALFWAY HOUSE INN,
Tel: 01752 822279; Fax: 01752 823146
Fore Street, Kingsand, Near Torpoint,
e-mail: david.riggs@virgin.net
Cornwall PL10 1NA
website: www.connexions.co.uk/halfway/index.htm

Accommodation available; Free House with real ale; Bar and restaurant meals; Children welcome; Torpoint 5 miles; S£, D£.

This traditional low-ceilinged pub on the Coastal Path is still the official border between the conservation fishing villages of Kingsand and Cawsand (hence the name) even if no longer the border between Devon and Cornwall. The award-winning restaurant specialises in seafood but may also include chicken supreme, venison casserole, and lamb noisettes with rosemary and redcurrant sauce. Single and double accommodation is available. To find the inn, follow the brown tourist signs to Mount Edgcumbe, and turn in to Kingsand/Cawsand.

GLOBE INN,
3 North Street, Lostwithiel,
Cornwall PL22 0EG
Tel: 01208 872501

3 bedrooms, all with private bathroom; Free House with real ale; Historic interest; Children welcome; Bar and restaurant meals; Bodmin 5 miles; £/££.

Excellent home-cooked food is just one of the attractions of this delightful 13th century inn beside the River Fowey. Situated on the A390, this is a fine centre for touring the county. There is plenty of choice and prices are extremely reasonable. The inn is homely and warmly welcoming; excellent en suite accommodation is available – but limited, so book early! All rooms have television, radio and tea and coffee-making facilities. Evening meals are served in a pleasant restaurant and summer days will find the beer garden well patronised. Lostwithiel, the ancient capital of Cornwall, is a lovely old town with several historic sites, including Restormel Castle, home of the Black Prince. Good opportunities exist nearby for golf, sailing and salmon and trout fishing.

When making enquiries or bookings,
a stamped addressed envelope is always appreciated.

SHIP INN,
Lerryn, Lostwithiel,
Cornwall PL22 0PT

Tel: 01208 872374
Fax: 01208 872614

4 bedrooms, all with private bathroom; Free House with real ale;
Children and pets welcome; Restaurant meals; Lostwithiel 3 miles; £.

This charming and traditional Cornish country inn can be found in what must surely be the prettiest riverside village in Cornwall. The wooded river banks were the inspiration for Kenneth Grahame's *The Wind in the Willows*. Popular with walkers and sailors alike, it offers a warm welcome to all. A log fire and central heating ensure year round comfort and make this a cosy choice for an out of season break. The attractive guest rooms all have en suite bathrooms, beverage-making facilities, colour television and radio. One bedroom is on the ground floor, making it ideal for elderly or disabled visitors. Excellent home-cooked fare is available in the restaurant lunchtimes and evenings, when you can choose from our extensive menu which also includes a good choice for vegetarians; an extensive wine list will complement any meal. The bar offers a choice of real ales and a large selection of malt whiskies. Conveniently situated for the coast, valleys and moors of central and east Cornwall. *Good Pub Guide.*

TREWELLARD ARMS HOTEL,
Trewellard, Pendeen, Near Penzance,
Cornwall TR19 7TA

Tel: 01736 788634

3 bedrooms, all with private bathroom; Free House with real ale; Historic interest;
Children and pets welcome; Bar and restaurant meals; Non-smoking areas; St Just 2 miles; S£, D£.

Silent witness of Cornwall's industrial past, the friendly Trewellard Arms plies its popular trade alongside the B3306 coast road a few miles north of Land's End and close to the famous Levant Mine and Geevor Tin Mine Heritage Centre. Christine and Martin Barnett welcome guests to this historic mining country and provide an appetising selection of home-cooked food and real ales in the long bar of this recommended free house. There are spectacular views of the restless Atlantic to be had from nearby coastal paths and those enchanted by the mystic grandeur of the area may book excellent en suite accommodation here. *ETC* ★★★

CRUMPLEHORN MILL,
Polperro,
Cornwall PL13 2RJ

Tel: 01503 272348; Fax: 01503 272914
e-mail: AndrewCrumplehorn@msn.com
website: www.crumplehorn-inn.co.uk

14 bedrooms, all with private bathroom; Free House with real ale; Historic interest; Children and pets welcome; Bar meals, restaurant evenings only (Oct –July); Liskeard 6 miles; S££, D££.

A complex created out of old farm buildings in 1972, the hotel, bars, restaurant and self-catering facilities exhibit character and an enlightened appreciation of the worthwhile things of life. Crumplehorn Mill has, in part, been transformed into a most attractive free house with a notable à la carte restaurant and traditional bar snacks. Food is freshly prepared and represents excellent value for money. Many are the fascinating stories featuring the inn, especially of the days of 'Good Queen Bess' when a tally of treasures acquired by privateers from France and Spain was counted here. The hotel provides luxurious accommodation in suites and bedrooms, matched only, perhaps, by the splendid self-catering flats and penthouse apartment. ♛♛♛, *CAMRA*.

LUGGER HOTEL,
Portloe, Truro,
Cornwall TR2 5RD

Tel: 01872 501322
Fax: 01872 501691

19 bedrooms, all with private bathroom; Free House; Historic interest; Bar lunches, breakfasts/dinners in restaurant; Non-smoking areas; Mevagissey 6 miles; S££££, D££££.

On the very water's edge of a picturesque fishing village, itself part of the beautiful Roseland Peninsula, this delightful 17th century inn was once the haunt of local smugglers. Indeed, one of its landlords, Black Dunstan, was hanged for smuggling in the 1890's and the inn ceased trading. After a variety of uses, it was re-opened in 1950 and under the loving care of three generations of the Powell family, has evolved into a delectable little hotel of immense character. Modernisation has not spoilt its unique atmosphere and today's guests are assured of excellent food and accommodation, all bedrooms having full en suite facilities, half-tester beds, remote-control television, radio, direct-dial telephone and tea and coffee-makers. ♛♛♛♛ *Highly Commended.*

The Cornish Arms

THE CORNISH ARMS,
Pendoggett, Port Isaac,
North Cornwall PL30 3HH

Tel: 01208 880263
Fax: 01208 880335

7 bedrooms, 6 with private bathroom; Free House with real ales; Historic interest; Children welcome; Bar and restaurant meals; Non-smoking areas; Wadebridge 8 miles, Polzeath 6, Port Isaac 1; S£££, D££.

A delightful 16th century Coaching Inn in the small rural village of Pendoggett, just one mile from the coast. Anyone who makes The Cornish Arms a base for exploring the area will not be disappointed by the attractive accommodation or the warmth of welcome extended. Whilst retaining the character of a traditional coaching inn, The Cornish Arms offers all modern amenities in every bedroom; colour and satellite TV, telephone, tea and coffee making facilities, etc. The highly recommended restaurant specialises in locally caught seafood and an extensive range of other dishes. Complement your meal with wine from the extensive cellars of The Cornish Arms. Pendoggett Special Bitter is famous for its strength – the locals won't touch it, it's so strong. With Bass straight from the barrel, together with other real ales, you will see why it is worth visiting The Cornish Arms. 👑👑👑 *Commended, RAC**, Les Routiers.* **See also Colour Advertisement on page 2.**

DRIFTWOOD SPARS HOTEL,
Trevaunance Cove, St Agnes,
Cornwall TR5 0RT

Tel: 0187-255 2428/3323

9 rooms, all with private facilities; Free House with real ale; Historic interest; Children welcome; Bar and restaurant meals; Newquay 12 miles, Truro 8, Redruth 7; ££.

Situated only a hundred yards from the beach, the building which is now the popular Driftwood Spars Hotel is over 300 years old and has seen active service as a tin miners' store, a chandlery, a sailmaker's workshop and a fish cellar. But nowadays the emphasis is strictly on providing guests with good food, ale and atmosphere. There are three bars – one has a children's room – serving a selection of real ales, including a weekly guest beer, and appetising home-cooked food; there is also an upstairs dining area. Driftwood Spars offers nine bedrooms, all with private facilities, colour television, telephone, tea-making equipment and sea views. Open all day during the holiday season. Please telephone or write for brochure.

THE CROOKED INN,
Trematon, Saltash,
Cornwall PL12 4RZ

Tel: 01752 848177
Fax: 01752 843203
e-mail: crooked.inn@virgin.net

19 bedrooms, 16 with private bathroom; Free House with real ale; Children and pets welcome; Bar and restaurant meals; Non-smoking areas; Saltash 2 miles; S£££, D££.

Turn left off the busy A38 about two miles past the imposing Saltash bridge into an enchanted land of leafy lanes that most tourists, hell-bent for Looe, Polperro and all points west, scarcely realise is there. The paradise we found many years ago is but six miles from Plymouth and the time has come to share our secret. The Crooked Inn is set above the glorious Lynher Valley, peaceful and seemingly remote, yet within easy reach of a variety of secluded beaches and the moors. Tony and Sandra Arnold are hosts at this truly delightful inn which has an attractive timber-beamed bar with an open log fire. An extensive range of home-cooked meals, complemented by a good choice of real ales, fosters a relaxed and happy mood and children are genuinely welcomed. En suite bedrooms across the yard offer the choice of centrally heated double, twin or family rooms; each has its own private bathroom, remote-control colour television, bedside radio alarm, hair dryer and tea and coffee-making facilities. This is a superb place for carefree family holidays. Guests with young children may take their meals in the comfortable family room upstairs which, like the spacious beer garden, enjoys beautiful country views. Outside, as well as a heated pool available to guests, children may work off excess energy in the playground and make friends with Mimi the sheep, Misty the goat, and pigs, Daisy and Penny. For golfers, the famous St.Mellion course is only three miles away .AA ◆◆◆.

THE MILL HOUSE INN,
Trebarwith Strand, Tintagel,
Cornwall PL34 0HD

Tel: 01840 770932/770200

8 bedrooms; Children welcome; Non-smoking areas; Tintagel 2 miles; S££, D££.

Formerly a corn mill, the Mill House Inn now provides accommodation throughout the year. It is situated in the dramatic Trebarwith Valley in seven acres of unspoilt woodland with a small trout stream flowing past. The inn has eight letting bedrooms, most en suite, all with central heating, tea/coffee making facilities and television. Home-cooked food is served in the bar, and there is a beer garden and a patio. Winter breaks are especially popular and you can book three nights for the price of two from November to March excluding Bank Holidays. Please write or phone for an information leaflet. *Tourist Board Listed Approved.*

MOLESWORTH ARMS HOTEL,
Wadebridge,
Cornwall PL27 7DP

Tel: 01208 812055
Fax: 01208 814254

16 bedrooms, 14 with private bathroom; Free House with real ale; Children welcome; Bar food, restaurant evenings only; Non-smoking areas; Bodmin 6 miles; S££, D££.

Cars have now replaced the coaches and carriages that once clattered across the cobbled courtyard of this 16th century coaching inn. Rich panelling, beamed ceilings, cheerful log fires and traditional Cornish hospitality are reminders of those days, although the splendid facilities now to be found at this welcoming hostelry would be well beyond the ken of guests of former years. Under the kind supervision of hosts, Nigel and Shelley Cassidy, the inn is elegantly furnished; two bars invariably buzz with amiable conversation, some guests no doubt studying the comprehensive selection of bar meals. For formal dining, the Coach House Restaurant is justly popular, especially for its fresh local seafood. Excellently appointed overnight accommodation is available. 🏆🏆🏆 *Commended, AA**.*

Please mention *Recommended Wayside & Country Inns*

when enquiring about accommodation featured in these pages.

THE WENDRON NEW INN,
Wendron,
Cornwall TR13 0EA
Tel: 01326 572683

No accommodation; Free House with real ale; Historic interest; Children and pets welcome; Bar and restaurant meals; Non-smoking areas; Helston 2 miles.

Shire brasses collected over the years adorn both bars of this 200-year-old village inn. The menu features duck, game, and vegetarian dishes, all locally produced, and the inn is also famed for home-made pies, and strawberries with clotted cream. Bar meals are available lunchtimes and evenings and there is a full à la carte restaurant. To find this free house, leave the A30 at Redruth, take the B3297 to Helston; Wendron is two miles before Helston, and the pub is next to the church.

FOR THE
MUTUAL GUIDANCE
OF GUEST AND HOST

Every year literally thousands of holidays, short breaks and overnight stops are arranged through our guides, the vast majority without any problems at all. In a handful of cases, however, difficulties do arise about bookings, which often could have been prevented from the outset.

It is important to remember that when accommodation has been booked, both parties – guests and hosts – have entered into a form of contract. We hope that the following points will provide helpful guidance.

GUESTS: When enquiring about accommodation, be as precise as possible. Give exact dates, numbers in your party and the ages of any children. State the number and type of rooms wanted and also what catenng you require – bed and breakfast, full board etc. Make sure that the position about evening meals is clear – and about pets, reductions for children or any other special points.

Read our reviews carefully to ensure that the proprietors you are going to contact can supply what you want. Ask for a letter confirming all arrangements, if possible.

If you have to cancel, do so as soon as possible. Proprietors do have the right to retain deposits and under certain circumstances to charge for cancelled holidays if adequate notice is not given and they cannot re-let the accommodation.

HOSTS: Give details about your facilities and about any special conditions. Explain your deposit system clearly and arrangements for cancellations, charges etc. and whether or not your terms include VAT.

If for any reason you are unable to fulfil an agreed booking without adequate notice, you may be under an obligation to arrange suitable alternative accommodation or to make some form of compensation.

While every effort is made to ensure accuracy, we regret that FHG Publications cannot accept responsibility for errors, omissions or misrepresentations in our entries or any consequences thereof.

Prices in particular should be checked because we go to press early. We will follow up complaints but cannot act as arbiters or agents for either party.

Cumbria

NEW DUNGEON GHYLL HOTEL,
Great Langdale, Near Ambleside,
Cumbria LA22 9JY

Tel: 015394 37213
Fax: 015394 37666

Fully licensed; 16 bedrooms, all with private bathrooms; Children and pets welcome; Conference facilities; Ambleside 4 miles; S£/££, D£.

Pack up all your cares and woe – and escape to a magic land of majestic fells and sparkling lakes, where you can relax and feel refreshed whether you choose to take to the hills in your walking boots or simply soak up the peace and tranquillity of the surrounding countryside. Such an idyllic retreat is this attractively appointed hotel which has a spectacular setting at the head of the picturesque Langdale Valley. Sheltered, secure, the hotel stands in lawned grounds, whilst inside, open log fires, superb food and friendly service add up to a recipe of utter contentment. And at the end of the day, retire to a delightful room with en suite facilities, colour television, direct-dial telephone and tea and coffee-makers. ♚♚♚ *Highly Commended, Johansens.*

THREE SHIRES INN,
Little Langdale, Ambleside,
Cumbria LA22 9NZ

Tel: 015394 37215; Fax: 015394 37127
e-mail: ian@threeshiresinn@clara.co.uk
website: www.threeshiresinn.com

10 bedrooms, all with private bathroom; Free House with real ale; Historic interest; Children welcome, pets in public bar only; Bar meals, restaurant evenings only; Non-smoking areas; Ambleside 5 miles; S££, D££.

The three shires in question are the old counties of Cumberland, Westmorland and Lancashire, and for over a century the inn has provided a welcome resting place for travellers in this most scenic area. True peace and relaxation can be found here, the roar of traffic and the bustle of city and town but a distant memory. However long or short one's stay, the warm welcome accorded to all visitors will ensure lasting memories - and a heartfelt desire to return at the earliest possible opportunity! The prettily furnished bedrooms afford delightful views over the valley, and guests can also relax in their own television lounge and lounge bar. Appetites large and small are amply catered for in the restaurant and public bars, and a wide range of traditional ales, wines and spirits are dispensed with friendly courtesy. ♚♚♚ *Commended, AA.*

TOWER BANK ARMS,
Near Sawrey, Ambleside,
Cumbria LA22 0LF
Tel and Fax: 015394 36334

*3 bedrooms, all with private bathroom; Free House with real ale; Children lunchtimes only,
pets welcome; Bar meals, restaurant evenings only; Hawkshead 2 miles; ££.*

Popular with summer tourists visiting Beatrix Potter's farmhouse, Hill Top, which adjoins the inn, this appealing cream and green hostelry is particularly recommended for out-of-season visits, when one can relax and savour its tradtional country atmosphere. Real ale is always available and food ranges from soup, filled rolls and quiche at lunchtimes to more substantial evening menus which feature local fish and game in season. Those wishing to indulge in Lakeland pursuits such as fishing (the inn has a licence for two rods a day on selected waters), walking, sailing and birdwatching will find delightful bedrooms, all en suite, with colour television and lovely views of the village. *Listed Commended, CAMRA.*

THE BLACKSMITH'S ARMS,
Talkin Village, Brampton,
Cumbria CA8 1LE
Tel: 016977 3452

Fax: 016977 3394

*5 bedrooms, all with private bathroom; Free House; Historic interest;
Bar and restaurant meals; Non-smoking areas; Carlisle 9 miles, Brampton 3; S££, D£.*

The Blacksmith's Arms offers all the hospitality and comforts of a traditional country inn. Enjoy tasty meals served in the bar lounges, or linger over dinner in the well-appointed restaurant. The inn is personally managed by the proprietors, Anne and Donald Jackson, who guarantee the hospitality one would expect from a family concern. Guests are assured of a pleasant and comfortable stay. There are five lovely bedrooms, all en suite and offering every comfort. Peacefully situated in the beautiful village of Talkin, the inn is convenient for the Borders, Hadrian's Wall and the Lake District. There is a good golf course, walking and other country pursuits nearby. **See also Colour Advertisement on page 4.**

QUEEN'S ARMS INN & MOTEL,
Warwick-on-Eden, Carlisle,
Cumbria CA4 8PA
Tel: 01228 560699

Fax: 01228 562239

*6 bedrooms, all with private bathroom;Thwaites House with real ale; Children and pets welcome;
Bar meals, restaurant evenings only; Non-smoking areas; Carlisle 4 miles; S££, D£/££.*

Situated four miles east of Carlisle and only a few minutes' drive from the M6, the Queen's Arms is an ideal base for exploring Hadrian's Wall, the Scottish Borders, the Lake District and the rolling Cumbrian Fells. All the tastefully furnished bedrooms are en suite, with television, radio/alarm clocks, central heating and tea/coffee making facilities. A cosy restaurant offers an excellent choice, and an extensive bar snack menu is also available (served in the garden in fine weather). Parents will be pleased to note that there is a modern adventure playground where children can play safely while they relax. Sporting activities available locally include fishing, golf and walking.

Please mention
Recommended WAYSIDE & COUNTRY INNS
when seeking refreshment or accommodation
at a Hotel mentioned in these pages.

GRAHAM ARMS HOTEL,
Longtown, Near Carlisle, Cumbria CA6 5SE

Tel: 01228 791213; Fax: 01228 792830
Web-site: www.cumbria.com/hotel

14 bedrooms all with private bathroom; Free House with real ale; Pets welcome; Bar meals;
Carlisle 8 miles; S££

A warm welcome awaits you at this 180-year-old former coaching inn. Situated six miles from the M6 (Junction 44) and Gretna Green, the Graham Arms makes an ideal overnight stop or perfect touring base for the Scottish Borders, English Lakes, Hadrian's Wall and much more. 14 comfortable en suite bedrooms, including four-poster and family rooms, with television and radio. Meals and snacks are served throughout the day. Friendly local bar serving real ale and a fine selection of malt whiskies. Secure courtyard parking for cars, cycles and motorcycles. Pets are welcome with well-behaved owners. Special breaks on request. *RAC***.

BARBON INN,
Barbon, Via Carnforth, Lancashire LA6 2LJ

Tel and Fax: 015242 76233

10 bedrooms, 7 with private bathroom; Free House with real ale; Historic interest;
Children and pets welcome; Bar meals, restaurant evenings only; Non-smoking areas;
Kirkby Lonsdale 3 miles; S££, D££.

If you are torn between the scenic delights of the Lake District and the Yorkshire Dales, then you can have the best of both worlds by making your base this friendly 17th century coaching inn nestling in the pretty village of Barbon. Individually furnished bedrooms provide cosy accommodation, and for that extra touch of luxury enquire about the elegant mini-suite with its oak four-poster bed. Fresh local produce is featured on the good value menus presented in the bar and restaurant, and the Sunday roast lunch with all the trimmings attracts patrons from near and far. A wide range of country pursuits can be enjoyed in the immediate area, and the helpful staff will be happy to give information.

SHEPHERD'S ARMS HOTEL,
Ennerdale Bridge, Cleator, Cumbria CA23 3AR

Tel & Fax: 01946 861249

8 bedrooms, all with private bathroom; Free House with real ale; Children and pets welcome;
Bar meals, restaurant evenings only; Non-smoking areas; Whitehaven 8 miles; S££, D££.

Although one of the smaller lakes, Ennerdale can fairly claim to be the most beautiful. From here, valley paths, forest tracks and lake shores offer a variety of rewarding walks suitable for all ages and capabilities. Other activities available include fishing, canoeing, bird watching and pony trekking. With an informal and relaxed atmosphere on one of the most attractive stretches of Wainwright's Coast to Coast footpath, this splendid small hotel presents first-rate food and accommodation. Several real ales are served and there is an extensive bar menu including daily 'specials'. Traditional comforts are very much in evidence and bedrooms have private facilities, central heating, remote-control colour television and tea and coffee-makers.

SUN HOTEL AND COACHING INN

Coniston,
Tel: 015394 41248; Fax: 015394 41219

Cumbria LA21 8HQ
e-mail: p.elson@btinternet.com

11 bedrooms, all with private bathroom; Free House with real ale; Children and pets welcome; Bar food, restaurant evenings only; Non-smoking areas; Ambleside 6 miles; S£££.

Family run hotel in an idyllic location with stunning views of the fells. Offering quality meals both in the restaurant and our rustic 16th Century Inn accompanied by a selection of fine wines and traditional ales. Open all year for a warm welcome in comfortable surroundings. Gardens and terrace open during the warmer months with open fires and lounge to help away the winter nights. Most rooms are en suite and most with excellent views, all comfortably fitted offering television, telephone and beverage facilities. Direct access to walking routes at the side of the Hotel. Two minute walk from the main village and ten minute walk from the lake. Party bookings, weddings catered for. Telephone for reservations. ☜☜☜ *Commended.* **See also Colour Advertisement on page 3.**

BOWER HOUSE INN,

Eskdale, Holmrook,
Tel: 019467 23244

Cumbria CA19 1TD
Fax: 019467 23308

24 bedrooms, all with private bathroom; Free House with real ale; Historic interest; Children welcome; Bar meals, restaurant evenings only; Car park (60); Gosforth 6 miles; £££.

A 17th century inn of considerable character, the Bower House is as popular with the locals as it is with tourists, always a good recommendation for any establishment. Decor and furnishings throughout are tasteful and designed with an eye to comfort as well as style, and all guest rooms have private facilities, colour television and telephone. Cuisine is of a consistently good standard, with fresh produce from nearby farms featuring extensively in skilfully prepared and well presented dishes, and the wine cellar should satisfy the most demanding palate. Mature gardens make a fine setting for this gem of an inn. *AA **.*

GRASMERE RED LION HOTEL,

Red Lion Square, Grasmere,
Tel: 015394 35456

Cumbria LA22 9SS
Fax: 015394 35579

36 bedrooms, all with private bathroom; Free House with real ale; Historic interest; Children and pets welcome; Bar meals, restaurant evenings only; Non-smoking areas; S££££,££££,D££££.

Situated in Grasmere village, made famous by Wordsworth, this 200 year old coaching inn offers 36 delightfully refurbished en suite rooms, many with jacuzzi baths and exquisite views of the surrounding fells. Enjoy dinner in the Courtyard Restaurant or lunch and afternoon snacks in the Easdale Bar and Conservatory. For pub meals there's the Lamb Inn and buttery, serving meals lunchtimes and evenings. Visit our own Lilliput's fitness centre with mini gym, sauna, solarium, steam room and jacuzzi, or enjoy free membership of a nearby luxury Leisure Club for swimming and squash. Whatever your reason to visit, a warm, friendly welcome is assured at The Grasmere Red Lion Hotel. ☜☜☜☜ *Commended, AA and RAC ***.*

QUEEN'S HEAD HOTEL,
Main Street, Hawkshead, Cumbria LA22 0NS

Tel: 015394 36271; Freephone: 0800 137263
Fax: 015394 36722

e-mail: enquiries@hawkshead-queens.demon.co.uk   website: www.hawkshead-queens.demon.co.uk

13 bedrooms, all with private bathroom; Hartleys House with real ale; Historic interest; Children welcome; Bar and restaurant meals; Ambleside 4 miles; ££.

The 16th century Queen's Head, set in the traffic-free village of Hawkshead on the edge of Esthwaite Water, has a wonderful atmosphere, with low oak-beamed ceilings, panelled walls and a warm log fire whenever necessary. The friendly bar and separate dining room are noted for high quality food, with many locally and organically produced ingredients and a comprehensive wine list. Beer is hand-pulled from the wood. The attractive en suite bedrooms, some with four-poster beds, have colour television, tea and coffee making facilities, hairdryer and telephone. The village was the home of Beatrix Potter and is an excellent centre for fishing, bowling, riding, water skiing, cycling and walking. *ETC* ★★, *AA* ***. **See also Colour Advertisement on page 2.**

COLEDALE INN,
Braithwaite, Near Keswick, Cumbria CA12 5TN

Tel: 017687 78272

12 bedrooms, all with private shower/WC; Free House with real ale; Children and pets welcome; Bar and restaurant meals; Non-smoking areas; Carlisle 30 miles, Cockermouth 10, Keswick 2; S£, D££.

A friendly, family-run Victorian Inn in a peaceful hillside position above Braithwaite, and ideally situated for touring and walking, with paths to the mountains immediately outside our gardens. All bedrooms are warm and spacious, with en suite shower room and colour television. Children are welcome, as are pets. Home-cooked meals are served every lunchtime and evening, with a fine selection of inexpensive wines, beers and Coledale XXPS and Yates real cask ale. Open all year except midweek lunches in winter. Tariff and menu sent on request. 👑👑👑.

The £ symbol when appearing at the end of the italic section of an entry shows the anticipated price, during 2000, for full Bed and Breakfast.

Normal Bed & Breakfast rate per person (in single room)		Normal Bed & Breakfast rate per person (sharing double/twin room)	
PRICE RANGE	CATEGORY	PRICE RANGE	CATEGORY
Under £25	S£	**Under £25**	D£
£26-£35	S££	**£26-£35**	D££
£36-£45	S£££	**£36-£45**	D£££
Over £45	S££££	**Over £45**	D££££

This is meant as an indication only and does not show prices for Special Breaks, Weekends, etc. Guests are therefore advised to verify all prices on enquiring or booking.

PHEASANT INN,
Casterton, Kirkby Lonsdale,
Cumbria LA6 2RX

Tel and Fax: 015242 71230
e-mail: pheasant.casterton@eggconnect.net
website: www.pheasantinn.co.uk

10 bedrooms, all with private bathroom; Free House with real ale; Historic interest;
Bar meals, restaurant evenings only (not Mon.); Non-smoking areas;
Children and pets welcome; Kirkby Lonsdale 1 mile; S£££, D£££.

Perfectly located between the Lake District and Yorkshire Dales, this lovely old country inn has a peerless reputation for its outstanding cuisine, from the hearty Cumbrian breakfast to start the day to the superbly-presented dishes served in the beautiful panelled restaurant. May and Melvin Mackie are convivial hosts and are to be congratulated on the high standards of decor and appointments. Hand-pulled beers and appetising meals are on offer in the welcoming bar or the non-smoking Fox Room, which is also suitable for small private parties. A fine touring base, the inn has delightfully furnished guest rooms, all with en suite bath or shower, colour television, direct-dial telephone and tea and coffee making facilities. ☙☙☙ *Commended.*

BAY HORSE INN,
Winton, Near Kirkby Stephen,
Cumbria CA17 4HS

Tel: 017683 71451

3 bedrooms, all with private bathroom; Free House with real ale; Historic interest; Bar food;
M6 (Junction 38) 11 miles, Appleby 10, Brough 3, Kirkby Stephen 1; S£, D£.

A warm and welcoming little inn situated on the western side of the scenic Cumbrian Pennines, and ideally placed as a stopping-off point on your journey north or south on the nearby M6. Resident proprietors Sheila and Derek Parvin offer the warmest of welcomes to all guests, with the finest of traditional ales, good food and comfortable accommodation. Lying as it does in the picturesque Eden Valley, the Bay Horse is also ideal as a touring base for those wishing to stay longer in this lovely part of the country. Open all year.

WHITE LION HOTEL,
Patterdale, Penrith,
Cumbria CA11 0NW

Tel: 01768 482214

7 bedrooms, all with private bathroom; Real ales; Children and dogs welcome; Bar meals;
Windermere 12 miles; S£££, D£££.

This old world country inn with a friendly atmosphere is situated on Lake Ullswater, near Helvellyn, an ideal centre for walking, fishing and sailing. The seven cosy letting bedrooms are mostly en suite with all facilities. Traditional beers and good home-made food are served. Whatever the reason for visiting the White Lion, you will always leave with the memory of a good time. Open all year. *ETC* ◆◆◆.

QUEENS HEAD INN,
Tirril, Near Penrith,
Cumbria CA10 2JF

Tel:01768 863219; Fax:01768 863243
e-mail: bookings@queensheadinn.co.uk
website: www.queensheadinn.co.uk

7 bedrooms, 5 with private bathroom; Free House with real ale; Historic interest; Children welcome,
pets in bars only; Bar and restaurant meals;, Non-smoking areas; Penrith 2 miles; S££, D£.

This privately-owned free house dates from 1719 and has a wealth of beams, brasses and four traditional open fireplaces where one may sit snugly, drink in hand, in cool weather. Over the years, this old inn has been extended to take in the adjoining stable block and cottages which now form the restaurant. Here, home-cooked food of the highest calibre is presented, the à la carte menus featuring such widely-acclaimed local delicacies as Ullswater trout, Solway salmon and Cumbrian farmhouse cheeses. Adjacent to the inn is the Tirril Brewery, a lure for real ale buffs who congregate here for the Cumbrian Beer and Sausage Festival held each August. Just 2½ miles from Ullswater, this well recommended hostelry offers splendid accommodation. *ETC* ◆◆, *CAMRA.*

RUSLAND POOL HOTEL, Haverthwaite, Ulverston, Cumbria LA12 8AA

Tel: 01229 861384; Fax: 01229 861425
e-mail: enquiries@rusland-pool.ndirect.co.uk
website: rusland-pool.ndirect.co.uk

18 bedrooms, all with private bathroom; Free House with real ale; Historic interest; Children welcome; Bar and restaurant meals; Newby Bridge 2 miles; S£££, D££.

Ideally situated between Morecambe Bay and the Lake District, this beautifully decorated hotel exudes hospitality in the age-old traditions of the English coaching inn. On the A590 and just within the confines of the Lake District National Park, the hotel takes its name from a stream which rises in Grizedale Forest and meanders through green fields and woods from Lake Windermere to the sands of Morecambe Bay. The rewards of a visit to this well-organised retreat are the cameraderie of the cosy Saddle Bar, mouthwatering food and, for those who so easily fall in love with the place, superb accommodation. Bedrooms are handsomely appointed with an en suite bath and/or shower, colour television, direct-dial telephone, radio, hair dryer and beverage-makers. ☗☗☗ *Commended.*

MORTAL MAN HOTEL, Troutbeck, Windermere, Cumbria LA23 1PL

Tel: 015394 33193
Fax: 015394 31261
e-mail: The-Mortalman@btinternet.com

12 bedrooms, all with private bathroom; Free House with real ale; Children and pets welcome; Bar and restaurant meals; Windermere 3 miles; S££££, D£££.

Gazing across a panorama of rugged fells to Lake Windermere, this popular Lakeland inn in the lovely Troutbeck Valley has offered hospitality and inspiration since the late 17th century. The ideal place to get away from it all and relax, the Mortal Man has a cosy bar made even cosier by log fires in winter whilst accommodation is of the highest calibre, each guest room being superbly equipped with en suite bath and shower, television, radio and direct-dial telephone, to say nothing of stunning views. Good reputations are jealously-guarded attributes and the à la carte cuisine here reflects flair and meticulous attention to detail with a variety of good wines to complement one's choice of dish. *ETC* ★★ *and Silver Award.*

Key to Tourist Board Ratings

 The Crown Scheme

The English Tourism Council (formerly the English Tourist Board) has joined with the AA and RAC to create a new, easily understood quality rating for serviced accommodation. **Hotels** will receive a grading ranging from **one to five STARS** (★). Other serviced accommodation such as **guest houses** and **B&B establishments** will be graded from **one to five DIAMONDS** (◆). These ratings represent Quality, Service and Hospitality not just facilities. *NB.Some properties had not been assessed at the time of going to press and in these cases the publishers have included the old CROWN gradings.*

♀ **The Key Scheme**

The Key Scheme covering self-catering in cottages, bungalows, flats, houseboats, houses, chalets, etc remains unchanged. The classification from **One to Five KEYS** indicates the range of facilities and equipment. Higher quality standards are indicated by the terms APPROVED, COMMENDED, HIGHLY COMMENDED AND DE LUXE.

Derbyshire

BENTLEY BROOK INN & FENNY'S RESTAURANT,
Fenny Bentley, Ashbourne,   Tel: 01335 350278
Derbyshire DE6 1LF   Fax: 01335 350422
e-mail: bentleybrookinn@btinternet.com   website: www.btinternet.com/#.bentleybrookinn

9 bedrooms, 7 with private bathroom; Free House with real ale; Children welcome,
pets by arrangement; Bar and restaurant meals; Non-smoking areas; Ashbourne 2 miles; S££, D££.

One of the most attractive hostelries in the Peak District National Park, this is the home of the Leatherbritches Brewery, brewers of CAMRA award-winning, cask-conditioned ales which attract connoisseurs from far and wide. This is an interesting port of call just two miles from Dovedale, with a bar arranged around a central log fire. From noon to 9.30pm, informal, home-cooked meals are served to eat in the bar or garden whilst, in the restaurant, the chef and his dedicated team prepare dishes of the highest quality in both traditional and exotic style. A lively venue in which to find good company and refreshment (maybe at the garden barbecue), the inn has splendidly appointed en suite accommodation. 🏆🏆🏆, AA.

BERESFORD ARMS HOTEL,
Station Road, Ashbourne,   Tel: 01335 300035
Derbyshire DE6 1AA   website: www.beresford-arms.demon.co.uk

12 bedrooms, all with private bathroom; Free House with real ale; Historic interest;
Children welcome; Restaurant meals; Non-smoking areas; Derby 13 miles; S£££,.D££.

Situated at the gateway to the Peak District, this family-run hotel is ideal for visiting such places as Alton Towers, Carsington Water and Dovedale, as well as many historic buildings. Built at the turn of the century, it offers a warm welcome in a pleasant environment of olde worlde charm. The comfortable en suite bedrooms have colour television, direct-dial telephone and tea/coffee making facilities. The hotel has a restaurant and two bars, and there is parking for guests' use. Outdoor children's play area. Open Christmas and New Year. 🏆🏆🏆.

THE DOG AND PARTRIDGE COUNTRY INN,
Swinscoe, Ashbourne,   Tel: 01335 343183
Derbyshire DE6 2HS   Fax: 01335 342742

29 bedrooms, all with private bathroom; ; Free House; Historic interest; Children welcome;
Bar and restaurant meals; Non-smoking areas; Ashbourne 3 miles; S££, D££.

Mary and Martin Stelfox welcome you to a family-run seventeenth century inn and motel set in five acres, five miles from Alton Towers and close to Dovedale and Ashbourne. We specialise in family breaks, and special diets and vegetarians are catered for. All rooms have private bathrooms, colour television, direct-dial telephone, tea-making facilities and baby listening service. It is ideally situated for touring Stoke Potteries, Derbyshire Dales and Staffordshire moorlands. The restaurant is open all day, and non-residents are welcome.Open Christmas and New Year.

THE WHEATSHEAF,
Nether End, Baslow,
Derbyshire DE45 1SR

Tel: 01246 582240
Fax: 01246 583648

5 bedrooms, 3 with private bathroom; Mansfield Brewery House with real ale; Historic interest; Children welcome; Bar and restaurant meals; Non-smoking areas; Bakewell 3 miles; S££, D£££.

On the very fringe of the Chatsworth House estate, this traditional English wayside inn provides excellent Bed and Breakfast accommodation in beautifully furnished rooms, ideal for family parties intent on exploring the possibilities of the delightful Peak District National Park. Family accommodation is enhanced by an extensive children's play area adjoining the hostelry. An appetising range of home-cooked dishes is available, meals being served in the friendly surroundings of the lounge bar. There is a straightforward menu featuring tried and trusted favourites (for children as well!) and prices are most reasonable. Knowledgeable ale drinkers will be in their element here for the hotel is run by the Mansfield Brewery, a recommendation in itself! *ETC* ◆◆◆, *AA, Les Routiers.*

STRINES INN,
Mortimer Road, Bradfield Dale, Sheffield,
Derbyshire S6 6JE

Tel: 0114 285 1247

3 bedrooms, all with private bathroom; Free House with real ale; Historic interest; Children and pets welcome; Bar meals; Non-smoking areas; Sheffield 6 miles; S££, D££.

Full of character, this old inn overlooks the Strines Reservoir which is appropriate as 'strines' is an old English word meaning 'meeting of water'. People in the know also meet here to enjoy excellent home-made food and drink and to escape from urban bustle to a tranquil oasis amongst the sweeping moors of the Peak District National Park. Built as a manor house in 1275, transformation into an inn took place in 1771. Look it up on the map but don't be fooled. Although appearing to lurk in Sheffield's shadow, the old hostelry could be a world away! Three en suite, four-poster bedrooms await discerning guests with the bonus of breakfast served in one's room.

THE CHARLES COTTON HOTEL,
Hartington, Near Buxton,
Derbyshire SK17 0AL

Tel: 01298 84229
Fax: 01298 84301

16 bedrooms; Free House with real ale; Historic interest; Children welcome; Bar and restaurant meals; Non-smoking areas; Ashbourne 9 miles; ££.

The Charles Cotton is a small comfortable hotel lying in the heart of the Derbyshire Dales, pleasantly situated in the village square of Hartington, with nearby shops catering for all needs. It is renowned throughout the area for its hospitality and good home cooking. Pets and children are welcome; special diets are catered for. The Charles Cotton makes the perfect centre to relax and enjoy the area, whether walking, cycling, pony trekking, brass rubbing or even hang-gliding. Open Christmas and New Year. *Tourist Board Listed.*

THE CASTLE HOTEL,
Castle Street, Castleton, Hope Valley,
Derbyshire S33 8WG

Tel: 01433 620578

Fax: 01433 622902

website: www.peakland.com/thecastle

9 bedrooms, all with private bathroom; Real ale; Historic interest; Children and pets welcome; Bar and restaurant meals; Non-smoking areas; Sheffield 16 miles; S£££, D£.

A delightful blend of 17th century character and 20th century comforts, the Castle is an ideal base for a relaxing break in the heart of the Peak District National Park. This is just how one imagines the perfect English country inn – low beams, cheerful log fires, friendly conversation and good ales – and the management and staff take great pride in upholding the noble traditions of English hospitality. Food is good and plentiful, and can be enjoyed all day every day. Should accommodation be required, a choice of delightfully furnished bedrooms is available, each en suite and with a full range of amenities. This splendid establishment is within convenient reach of many sporting activities and places of interest. Our vision: to be consistently consistent in our excellent guest care and our passion for fantastic food. *AA ****.

THE MANIFOLD INN
Hulme End, Hartington,
Derbyshire SK17 0EX

Tel: 01298 84537

5 bedrooms, all with private shower/toilet; Free House with real ale; Bar meals and dining room; Non-smoking areas; Buxton 10 miles, Ashbourne 10, Bakewell 10, Leek 8; S££, D££.

The Manifold Inn is a 200-year-old coaching inn now owned by Frank and Bridgette Lipp. It offers warm hospitality and good pub food at sensible prices. This lovely mellow stone inn nestles on the banks of the River Manifold opposite the old toll house that used to serve the turnpike and river ford. All guest accommodation is in the old stone blacksmith's shop in the secluded rear courtyard of the inn. The bedrooms have en suite showers, colour television, tea/coffee making facilities and telephone. 👑👑👑 *Commended.*

MILLSTONE INN,
Sheffield Road, Hathersage,
Derbyshire S30 1DA

Tel: 01433 650258

Fax: 01433 651664

website: millstoneinn.co.uk

7 bedrooms, all with private bathroom; Free House with real ale; Historic interest; Children and pets welcome; Bar meals, restaurant evenings only; Non-smoking areas; Bakewell 8 miles; S££, D££.

For over 100 years, the homely and attractively decorated bar of this splendid hostelry has reverberated to the buzz of friendly conversation between valley walkers and locals, maybe before an open fire; this concourse animated at times in appreciation of the creative offerings of the Millers Restaurant, meals being available seven nights a week. Originally a coaching inn, the Millstone has undergone many changes and improvements over the years and its excellent modern facilities are the pride of the scenic Hope Valley of which there are breathtaking views. Delightfully appointed en suite guest rooms have power showers, colour television and tea and coffee-makers. *AA* ◆◆◆

THE WATERLOO HOTEL,
Taddington, Near Buxton,
Derbyshire SK17 9TJ

Tel: 01298 85230

*Bedrooms with private facilities available; Robinson's House with real ale; Bar and restaurant meals;
Children welcome; Bakewell 5 miles.*

Margaret and Norman Whitelaw welcome you to the Waterloo Hotel, which has real open fires. The
hotel offers lunches and dinners; private parties and group parties catered for. Restaurant and bar
service seven days a week, 12 to 2.30pm and 7 to 9pm. Every Thursday is pie night, all home-made;
traditional Sunday Lunch and Sizzlers our speciality. En suite accommodation available. The perfect
place for every occasion.

GEORGE HOTEL,
Tideswell,
Derbyshire

Tel: 01298 871382
Fax: 01298 872408

*4 bedrooms; Historic interest; Bar and restaurant meals;
Non-smoking areas; Chatsworth 10 miles, Buxton 9, Bakewell 8; £.*

The church of this ancient market town is known as the "Cathedral of the Peak" and visitors come
from far and wide to see it. Next door, the George offers tourists to the Peak District hospitality in
keeping with its history as an old coaching inn dating from 1730. A four-poster suite is available for
honeymoons or other special occasions. All meals are served every day of the week and a wide range
of appetising snacks are also obtainable over the bar. Live 60s music every Friday evening. Used in
the TV series "Yesterday's Dreams" set in this "best kept" Derbyshire village.

FHG

The
GOLF GUIDE
*Where to Play
Where to Stay*
2000

Available from most bookshops, the 2000 edition of
THE GOLF GUIDE covers details of every UK golf course
– well over 2500 entries – for holiday or business golf. Hundreds
of hotel entries offer convenient accommodation, accompanying
details of the courses – the 'pro', par score, length etc.

*In association with 'Golf Monthly' and including the Ryder Cup
Report as well as Holiday Golf in Ireland, France, Portugal,
Spain, The USA and Thailand .*

**£9.95 from bookshops or £10.50 including postage
(UK only) from FHG Publications,
Abbey Mill Business Centre, Paisley PAI ITJ**

Devon

THE SHIP INN,
Church Street, Axmouth,
Devon EX12 4AF

Tel: 01297 21838

No accommodation; Real ale; Bar food; Seaton 1 mile.

Especially pretty on summer evenings, this fine, creeper-clad Inn extends a warm welcome at any time of year and guaranteed Devonshire hospitality. Extensive menu mornings and evenings hot, and cold, with the emphasis on local fish and game using home-grown salads, herbs and fruit. Jane Chapman, her husband Christopher and son Paul often take in injured birds (including owls) to convalesce in the back garden (enquire about visiting hours!).

THE SWAN,
Station Road, Bampton,
Devon EX16 9NG

Tel: 01398 331257

6 bedrooms, 2 with private bathroom; Free House with real ale; Historic interest; Children and pets welcome; Bar and restaurant meals; Tiverton 6 miles; S£. D£.

A 15th century building retaining much of its old character, the Swan was originally built to house the stonemasons who built the church which stands next to the hotel. Today, it is a small, award-winning, family-run hotel offering warm hospitality and high standards of food, accommodation and service. Bedrooms are very comfortable and some are available with en suite facilities; all have colour television, washbasins, and tea and coffee makers. Meals in the oak-beamed candlelit dining room may be complemented by wine chosen from a comprehensive list. On the edge of Exmoor and with both coasts easily accessible, this is a perfect base for exploring the scenic South West. *Les Routiers.*

The £ symbol when appearing at the end of the italic section of an entry shows the anticipated price, during 2000, for full Bed and Breakfast.

Normal Bed & Breakfast rate per person (in single room)		Normal Bed & Breakfast rate per person (sharing double/twin room)	
PRICE RANGE	CATEGORY	PRICE RANGE	CATEGORY
Under £25	S£	**Under £25**	D£
£26-£35	S££	**£26-£35**	D££
£36-£45	S£££	**£36-£45**	D£££
Over £45	S££££	**Over £45**	D££££

This is meant as an indication only and does not show prices for Special Breaks, Weekends, etc. Guests are therefore advised to verify all prices on enquiring or booking.

THE NEW INN,
High Street, Clovelly,
Near Bideford,
Devon EX39 5TQ

Tel: 01237 431303 Fax: 01237 431636

8 bedrooms, all with private shower/bath; Real ale;
Historic interest; Children welcome;
Bar and restaurant meals; Barnstaple 19 miles;
S££, D££££.

This unspoilt heritage village is filled with colourful flower-strewn cottages that seem to tumble over one another down the steep and narrow cobbled street which descends towards the tiny harbour. To stay at the New Inn in the heart of the village is to wake up to the sights and sounds of a seafaring way of life that has changed little over the last hundred years. Each of the hotel bedrooms is beautifully decorated. The magic touch of a talented interior designer is to be seen everywhere. The restaurant serves local and regional specialities. This really is a short break paradise. 👑👑👑 *Highly Commended, AA ** 73%, Johansen.*

RIVERSIDE INN
Bovey Tracey,
Devon TQ13 9AF

Tel: 01626 832293
Fax: 01626 833880

10 bedrooms, all with private bathroom; Free House with real ale; Historic interest;
Bar and restaurant meals; Non-smoking areas; Newton Abbot 5 miles; S££.

Beautifully placed only three miles from Dartmoor's rugged slopes and 20 minutes from the South Devon coast, this pleasant inn is the ideal venue for a combined sea and country holiday. New friends will soon be made in the old-world atmosphere of the well-stocked Tracey Bar and relaxing moments may be spent strolling along the leafy banks of the River Bovey on which the inn enjoys fishing rights, whilst Bovey itself is a charming and historic little town. The accommodation is excellent, each one of the en suite bedrooms being appointed with colour television, radio, direct-dial telephone, tea and coffee-making facilities and hair dryer. Diners have the choice of à la carte and table d'hôte menus, plus bar snacks and daily specials. *AA/RAC***

THE PALK ARMS INN,
Hennock, Bovey Tracey,
Devon TQ13 9QS

Tel: 01626 836584

3 bedrooms; Free House with real ale; Historic interest; Children and pets welcome;
Bar meals, restaurant weekends only; Non-smoking areas; Exeter 13 miles, Torquay 8; S£, D££.

The Palk Arms is a traditional country pub with log fires, real ales, darts, bar billiards and other pub games; village shop and post office downstairs. Bar meals are available during the week, and the restaurant (22 covers) is open from Friday night to Sunday night (bookings preferred) and enjoys seven-mile views across the Teign Valley to Exeter Racecourse and Haldon Hill. There are three bedrooms (one with four-poster) and a residents' sitting room, and the inn is ideal for weekend breaks and short stays. The Palk Arms is situated inside Dartmoor National Park (guided tours available) ,with fishing on three 70-acre lakes a mile away and also birdwatching and walks. Fishing licences and equipment are available in the shop. Newton Abbot races three miles, nearest beach at Teignmouth (seven miles). We welcome pets and smokers.

SMUGGLERS HAUNT HOTEL
Church Hill, Brixham
Devon TQ5 8HH

Tel: 01803 853050; Fax: 01803 858738
e-mail: enquiries@smugglershaunt-hotel-devon.co.uk
website: www.smugglershaunt-hotel-devon.co.uk

Bedrooms with private bathroom; Children and pets welcome; Bar and restaurant meals; Torquay 5 miles; S££, D££.

This friendly, 300-year-old private hotel is situated in the centre of old Brixham, just a few hundred yards from the bustling and picturesque harbour. An extensive range of food is available, from excellent quality bar menus to an extensive à la carte selection; there is a good vegetarian choice and a popular children's menu. En suite bedrooms are comfortable and well equipped, with colour television, radio, and tea/coffee facilities. Brittany Ferries Approved. Amex/Barclaycard/Diners/Mastercard ♛♛♛, AA**.

HOOPS INN,
Horns Cross, Near Clovelly, Bideford,
Devon EX39 5DL

Tel: 01237 451222; Fax: 01237 451247
e-mail: hoopsinn@webleicester.co.uk
website: www.hoopsinn.co.uk

12 bedrooms, all with private bathroom; Real ales; Historic interest; Restaurant meals; Non-smoking areas; Bideford 5 miles.

This lovingly cared for picturebook thatched country inn blends 13th century charm with 20th century luxury and extends a warm welcome to its guests. Relax by one of the open log fires to soak up the olde worlde atmosphere while enjoying a real ale or wine before dining on the best of local fish, game or meat, including house favourites: seafood platters, half shoulder of lamb in onion gravy, crackly pork, or traditional steak and kidney pudding. All bedrooms are en suite, individually furnished and well appointed. The superior rooms under the old thatch have romantic antique four-poster beds. The Hoops is a splendid base for a combined sea, country or touring holiday, with opportunities for walking, cycling, fishing, golf, together with historic gardens, houses, and the world-famous fishing village of Clovelly on the doorstep, and Dartmoor and Exmoor within easy reach. ♛♛♛ *Commended, RAC** and Merit Award, Which? Good Pub Guide, CAMRA.*

THE RED LION INN,
Dittisham, Near Dartmouth,
Devon TQ6 0ES

Tel: 01803 722235

6 bedrooms, all with private facilities; Free House with real ale; Children over 12 years welcome; Bar and restaurant meals; Non-smoking areas; Dartmouth 6 miles; ££.

The Red Lion has been offering generous hospitality since 1750 when it was a Coaching House. Log fires and gleaming brass in a friendly old bar, hearty English breakfasts, terraced gardens overlooking the River Dart, and an exceptionally warm welcome all await you. Bedrooms are individually furnished, with comfortable beds, central heating, colour television, tea-making facilities and telephones. An extensive menu includes daily specials and features fresh produce, prime local meats, fresh fish and locally grown vegetables. Picturesque countryside and a mild climate make this a perfect holiday retreat. ♛♛♛ *Commended.*

Please mention
Recommended WAYSIDE & COUNTRY INNS
when seeking refreshment or accommodation
at a Hotel mentioned in these pages.

THE ROYAL OAK INN
Dunsford, Near Exeter,
Devon EX6 7DA

Tel: 01647 252256

*8 bedrooms, 5 with private bathroom; Free House with real ale; Children welcome;
Bar food; Exeter 6 miles, Moretonhampstead 4; £.*

Enjoy a friendly welcome in our traditional Country Pub in the picturesque thatched village of Dunsford. Quiet en suite bedrooms are available in the tastefully converted cob barn. An ideal base for touring Dartmoor, Exeter and the coast, and the beautiful Teign Valley. Real ale and home-made meals are served. Well behaved children and dogs are welcome. Please ring Mark or Judy Harrison for further details. *Tourist Board Listed Approved, CAMRA, Good Pub Guide.*

THE GISSONS ARMS,
Kennford, Exeter,
Devon EX6 7UD

Tel: 01392 832444

*6 bedrooms, all with private bathroom; Free House with real ale; Historic intertest; Children welcome;
Bar and restaurant meals; Non-smoking areas; Exeter 4 miles; S££, D£££.*

Motorists bound for the Torbay resorts, Plymouth or Cornwall can see this handsome, timber-framed house lying a few yards off the thrumming A38 at Kennford as one leaves the environs of Exeter. Nobly performing the age-old traditions of the wayside inn, this is a wonderful place to stop for refreshment or even an overnight break. The range of food, including a carvery, is extensive in the choice of main courses and desserts; en suite guest rooms are luxuriously furnished and have colour television and tea and coffee-making facilities. The inn makes a fine holiday headquarters in its own right with the coast and the Dartmoor National Park within easy reach and terms are most reasonable. *AA QQQQ.*

THE DREWE ARMS,
Drewsteignton, Exeter
Devon EX6 6QN

Tel: 01647 281224

3 bedrooms, all with private bathroom; Whitbread House with real ale; Historic interest;
Children welcome, pets in bar only; Bar meals, restaurant evenings only; Non-smoking areas;
Moretonhamstead 3 miles; D£.

This character inn is a much loved old friend renowned for being the home of Aunt Mabel Mudge who retired a short while ago at the age of 99 after running the pub for all of 75 years. Aunt Mabel's former kitchen has been skilfully and sympathetically transformed in to a notable à la carte restaurant although the original range and furniture still remain in use. The extensive menu features several fresh fish and local game dishes and the delicious sweets are worthy of special mention. Janice and Colin Sparks now preside over the largely unaltered Snug and Tap rooms serving a choice of real ales. Three delightfully furnished rooms with four-poster beds serve overnight visitors. *AA, Good Pub Guide.*

THE OLD THATCH INN,
Cheriton Bishop, Near Exeter,
Devon EX6 6HJ

Tel: 01647 24204
Fax: 01647 24584

2 bedrooms, each with private bathroom; Free House with real ale; Historic interest;
Guide dogs only; Bar meals; Non-smoking areas; Crediton 6 miles; S£££, D££.

Justifiably proud of its reputation for quality, choice and value for money in respect of the substantial home cooked meals served in the bar, lounge and Travellers Nook, this 16th century one-time coaching house stands on the eastern fringe of the Dartmoor National Park. Now a Grade II Listed building with beamed ceilings and an open stone fireplace where a log fire crackles a welcome in winter, the old hostelry retains an ambience seasoned by time and enhanced by high standards of friendly service. For touring the area, comfortable overnight accommodation is available in double bedrooms, all with en suite facilities, colour television, radio/alarm and tea and coffee-makers.

THE GLOBE HOTEL
Fore Street, Topsham, Near Exeter,
Devon EX3 0HR

Tel: 01392 873471
Fax: 01392 873879

17 bedrooms, all with private bathroom; Free House with real ale; Historic interest;
Bar and restaurant meals; Exeter 4 miles; S£££, D££.

Dark oak panelling, comfortable leather settles and period prints all contribute to the traditional character of this sixteenth century coaching inn which stands on the main street of the ancient town of Topsham, on the estuary of the River Exe. Those seeking overnight accommodation will find comfortable bedrooms, all with private bathrooms, colour television, direct-dial telephone, and tea and coffee making facilities. For an extra touch of luxury, rooms are available with four-poster or half-tester beds. The good value range of bar meals includes all the traditional favourites, and in the restaurant a full à la carte menu is served with courtesy and efficiency. *South West Tourist Board* ♨♨♨ *Commended.*

THE FOREST INN,
Hexworthy, Princetown,
Devon PL20 6SD

Tel:01364631211
Fax: 01364 631515

11 bedrooms, 4 with private bathroom; Free House with real ale; Historic interest;
Pets welcome; Bar meals, restaurant evenings only; Ashburton 7 miles; S£, D££.

Set amongst some of the most beautiful walking and trekking country in the south-west, the Forest Inn is full of the Dartmoor tradition – good food, good ale and the warmest of welcomes. Close to the famous beauty spot of Dartmeet, the inn is a splendid place in which to stay, with superb opportunities for walking, riding and fishing in the immediate vicinity. A wide range of good-value accommodation is available, from comfortable en suite bedrooms to a bunkhouse with showers and a kitchenette. Home-cooked meals and an extensive range of snacks cater for appetites sharpened by clean fresh air. Short Breaks available. *ETC* ◆◆◆ *, Good Beer Guide.*

MONKTON COURT,
Monkton, Near Honiton,
Devon EX14 9QH

Tel: 01404 42309
Fax: 01404 46861

8 bedrooms, 6 with bathrooms; Free House with real ale; Children welcome;
Bar meals, restaurant evenings only; Non-smoking areas; Honiton 2 miles; S£££, D££.

Between the beautiful Otter Valley and the rolling Blackdown Hills, this fine old country house is believed to date from the 17th century. It is a familiar sight on the A30 a short distance from Honiton and is a recommended port of call for sampling excellent à la carte fare served in the candlelit restaurant, whilst the oak-beamed lounge bar with its central log-burning fireplace bids one tarry longer. Why not? There are spacious and well-furnished bedrooms available, all with colour television, direct dial telephone, and private facilities. For touring Dorset and East Devon there can be few better places to use as a base. ✿✿✿ *Commended, AA **.*

THE KINGS ARMS INN,
Stockland, Near Honiton,
Devon EX14 9BS

Tel: 01404 881361; Fax: 01404 881732
e-mail: paul@kingsarms.net
website: www.kingsarms.net

3 bedrooms, all with private bathroom; Free House with real ale; Historic interest;
Children and pets welcome; Bar lunches, restaurant meals; Axminster 5 miles; S££, D£££.

The delights of rural East Devon, a friendly and intimate atmosphere. excellent home cooking and easy access to the coast and many places of interest represent four-square reasons for singling out this recommended hostelry for a visit. The mouth-watering menu is displayed on the blackboard in the Cotley Restaurant Bar and the style of cooking is an appetising blend of the classic, nouvelle and modern. all combining to produce hearty and memorable meals. An attractive place in which to stay, the inn has first-rate accommodation, comprising one twin and two double rooms, each with bathroom en suite, television, telephone and tea and coffee makers. *CAMRA, Egon Ronay, Which? Good Food Guide 'Devon Dining Pub of the Year' 1999.*

OLD SAWMILL INN,
Watermouth, Ilfracombe,
Devon EX34 9SX
Tel: 01271 882259

4 bedrooms, all with private bathroom; Free Hous with real ale; Hisoric interest; Children welcome; Bar meals; Non-smoking areas (summer); Barnstaple 9 miles; D£.

Beautifully placed on the rugged North Devon coast, this interesting inn was originally a water-driven sawmill. It still retains an "olde worlde" atmosphere with its original beams, open fire, stone fireplace and original saw blades on display. Food is served every lunchtime and evening and the bar also offers a selection of real ales as well as traditional pub activities such as pool, darts and skittles. Excellent en suite accommodation has been introduced above a recent extension: all rooms are furnished in pine and have colour television, hairdryer and tea and coffee making facilities. Terms for Bed and Breakfast are extremely reasonable.

DOLPHIN INN,
Kingston, Near Bigbury,
Devon TQ7 4QE
Tel & Fax.01548 810314
website: www.dolphininn.freeserve.co.uk

3 bedrooms, all with private bathroom; Ushers House with real ale; Historic interest; Children welcome; Bar meals; Non-smoking areas; Modbury 3 miles; S£££, D££££.

Hidden away amidst the leafy lanes and high hedges of the South Hams with the thatched cottages of a tranquil village as near neighbours, this is a gem of a retreat far removed from the hustle and bustle of urban life. Tubs and hanging baskets of colourful blooms greet the visitor's entrance into an ambience of time-honoured hospitality. Sit in the inglenook with a glass of one's fancy and enjoy excellent home-cooked food served seven days a week. Why not stay for a few days? Hosts, Neil and Annie Williams, will welcome and care for you. Pretty Wonwell Beach is nearby and there are lovely walks by the River Erme. Three en suite bedrooms are available offering full Bed and Breakfast with colour television and coffee-making facilities. *AA, Good Food Guide, Good Pub & Hotel Guide.*

RISING SUN HOTEL,
Harbourside, Lynmouth,
Devon EX35 6EQ

Tel: 01598 753223
Fax: 01598 753480

16 bedrooms, all with en suite shower/bathroom; Free House; Historic interest;
Bar and restaurant meals; Non-smoking areas; Barnstaple 20 miles, Minehead 17; S££££, D££££.

This fourteenth century smugglers' inn overlooking the harbour and river is steeped in history, with oak panelling, crooked ceilings, thick walls, and uneven oak floors. All the bedrooms have recently been refurbished to a very high standard. The excellent restaurant specialises in local game and seafood. It is claimed that R.D. Blackmore wrote part of his novel *Lorna Doone* whilst staying at The Rising Sun. The poet Shelley spent his honeymoon in 1812 in a cottage, now named after him, which is part of the hotel. It has a four-poster bed and a comfortable sitting room, and is ideal for a special holiday occasion. Guests can relax in the beautifully landscaped garden and free fishing is available on the hotel's private stretch of salmon river. *AA** and Two Rosettes for Food, RAC** and Merit Awards, Johansens "Inn of the Year 1991", Egon Ronay, Les Routiers Casserole Award, Good Hotel Guide Recommended, Good Pub Guide.*

EXMOOR SANDPIPER INN,
Countisbury, Near Lynmouth,
Devon EX35 6NE

Tel: 01598 741263
Fax: 01598 741358
e-mail: exmoorsandpiper@demon.co.uk

16 bedrooms, all with private bathroom; Free House with real ale; Historic interest;
Children and pets welcome; Bar and restaurant meals; Non-smoking areas; Lynton 2 miles; ££££.

This fine old coaching inn, reputedly dating in part from the 13th and 15th centuries, lies in a beautiful setting amidst rolling moors, high above Lynmouth on the coastal road with the dramatic backdrop of Exmoor. Bedrooms are designed for your every comfort, with tea-making, colour television and bathroom en suite. After a traditional English breakfast, discover the magic of Exmoor by car or on foot, along Doone Valley following the river to the majestic Watersmeet, or further to the Valley of Rocks and beyond to the Devon/Somerset borders. Delicious five-course dinners include smoked salmon, seafood platters with lobster, steaks and a delicious selection of sweets. Brochure on request. ♛♛♛ *Commended, RAC**.*

THE THREE HORSESHOES
Branscombe, Seaton,
Devon EX12 3BR

Tel: 01297 680251

Accommodation; Real ale; Historic interest; Sidmouth 5 miles; £.

A lovely 16th century coaching house with log fires and brasses, set in an area of outstanding natural beauty. Central for sea or country; footpaths lead through woodland and cliff walks. Wonderful wildlife in the area. Honiton, which has many antique shops and is noted for lace making, is nearby, as is historic Exeter; Sidmouth is just ten minutes away. All bedrooms are centrally heated and have tea/coffee making facilities. There is "trad" jazz every Saturday night in the function room, and there is a lounge bar for those who want a quiet drink. Jan and John Moore will give you the warmest of welcomes and help you plan your outings if you wish.

GEORGE HOTEL,
Broad Street, South Molton,
Devon EX36 3AB

Tel and Fax: 01769 572514
e-mail: george@s-molton.freeserve.co.uk
website: www.s-molton.freeserve.co.uk

8 bedrooms, all with private bathroom; Real ale; Historic interest; Children welcome,
pets allowed in bar only; Bar meals, restaurant Tues-Sat evenings only; Barnstaple 11 miles; S££, D££.

A family-run 17th century posting inn offering a warm welcome to visitors, home cooking, and traditional ales, the George Hotel has overlooked the centre of South Molton for centuries. Recorded in 1692 as an old and established Inn, the brick facade added in 1730 conceals a much older building, the origins of which have been lost in the mists of time. Today's visitors will find personal, friendly service, and comfortable accommodation in en suite and standard bedrooms, all with colour television and hot drinks facilities. Fine local produce features on the weekly changing menus which are supplemented by daily specials. ♛♛♛ *Commended, AA, CAMRA.*

STAG INN
Rackenford, Near Tiverton
Devon EX16 8DT
Tel: 01884 881369

3 bedrooms, one en suite; Free House with real ale; Historic interest; Children and pets welcome; Bar meals, restaurant evenings only; Witheridge 4 miles; £.

Quietly slumbering in deepest Devon, the thatched Stag is a long-established acquaintance. It is one of the oldest hostelries in the country, having been built in 1232 and one of its interesting features is an old tunnel, said to have been used by the notorious highwayman, Tom King. Enter the cosy bar with its low beams and Jacobean panelling and relax, if it be winter, before a blazing log fire in the inglenook. The intrepid challenger at the dart board or skittle alley will be accommodated by the locals with a knowing but appreciative smile. Home-cooked meals are served in the bar or Well Room Restaurant; children have their own special menu. This is a superb place in which to stay with Exmoor, Dartmoor and both coasts within easy reach.

THE DURANT ARMS,
Ashprington, Totnes,
Tel: 01803 732240/732471
Devon TQ9 7UP
Fax: 01803 732471

3 bedrooms, all with private bathroom; Free House with real ale; Historic interest; Children and pets welcome; Bar lunches, restaurant evenings only; Non-smoking areas; Totnes 3 miles; S££, D££.

Nestling amidst the verdant beauty of the Dart Valley in a picturesque and well-preserved South Hams village, this attractive inn has all the virtues of a traditional English country inn with the comforts of the contemporary holiday-maker in mind. With many footpaths and bridleways nearby leading to the leafy shores of the River Dart, this neat and tidy hostelry will repay a casual or even longer visit. The cuisine is worthy of special mention with a wide range of main courses catering for all tastes plus an interesting selection of imaginative desserts. Just three miles past the Elizabethan town of Totnes, this is a fine overnight stop and several beautifully appointed bedrooms suit the purpose admirably. *AA* ◆◆◆◆ *and Rosette.*

CHURCH HOUSE INN,
Harberton, Near Totnes,
Devon TQ9 7SF
Tel: 01803 863707

3 bedrooms; Free House with real ale; Historic interest; Children and pets welcome; Bar and restaurant meals; Non-smoking areas; Totnes 2 miles; S£, D£.

Just off the A381 Totnes to Kingsbridge road, this picturesque old inn is a heart-warming sight. It stands, appropriately, in the shadow of the village church and is believed to date from about 1100 when it served masons working on the church, later becoming a Chantry House for monks. Renovations in 1950 revealed massive beams of fluted oak and a fine, medieval oak screen, one of the oldest in the country; a Tudor window frame with its original hand-made glass may still be seen. This is a lovely place, full of atmosphere, in which to enjoy good ale and a painless history lesson whilst savouring one's choice from a wide range of appetising meals.

THE CRIDFORD INN,
Trusham, Newton Abbot,
Devon TQ13 0NR

Tel and Fax: 01626 853694
e-mail: cridford@eclipse.co.uk
website: www.uk-explorer.co.uk/cridford

6 bedrooms, all with private bathroom; Free House with real ale; Children and pets welcome; Bar and restaurant meals; Non-smoking areas; Chudleigh 2 miles; S£££, D££.

Many inns and hostelries claim to be steeped in history, but few can match the proud boast of the ancient Cridford Inn, which is mentioned in the Domesday Book and retains many fascinating medieval features. Everywhere there is evidence of the loving care and attention to detail lavished on it by the proud owners. Traditional beers, wines and a full range of refreshments will satisfy a thirst worked up in the clean Devon air, while hearty appetites are amply catered for by the tempting selection of food on offer in the informal surroundings of the bar, or amidst the gleaming silver, sparkling crystal and candlelight of the elegant dining room. Six comfortable en suite bedrooms provide cosy accommodation for those tempted to linger in this peaceful spot. *CAMRA*

DIPLOMA WINNERS 1999

Each year we award a small number of diplomas to holiday proprietors whose services have been specially commended by our readers. The following were our FHG Diploma Winners for 1999.

ENGLAND

Mr & Mrs Haskell, Borwick Lodge, Outgate, Hawkshead, Cumbria LA22 0PU (015394 36332)

Mrs Val Sunter, Higher House Farm, Oxenholme Lane, Natland, Kendal, Cumbria LA9 7QH (015395 61177)

Mrs Ellis, Efford Cottage Guest House, Milford Road, Everton, Lymington, Hampshire SO41 0JD (015906 42315)

Mrs Melanie Smith, Capernwray House, Capernwray, Via Carnforth, Lancashire LA6 1AE (01524 732363)

Mrs D. Cole, Hillcrest House, Barrasford, Hexham, Northumberland NE48 4BY (01434 681426)

Mrs J. Hartsilver, Perhams Farm, Templecombe, Somerset BA8 0NE (01963 371123)

SCOTLAND

Mr Ewan, Glen Lyon Lodge, Nairn, Nairnshire IV12 4RH (01667 452780)

Mr Sutton, Linnhe Caravan and Camping Park, Corpach, Fort William, Inverness-shire PH33 7NL (01397 772376)

WALES

Mrs Hazel Davies, Caebetran Farm, Felinfach, Brecon, Powys LD3 0UL (01874 754460)

Mrs Bronwen Prosser, Upper Genffordd Guest House, Talgarth, Brecon, Powys LD3 0EN (01874 711360)

SEA TROUT INN,
Staverton, Near Totnes,
Devon TQ9 6PA

Tel: 01803 762274

Fax: 01803 762506

10 bedrooms, all with private bathroom; Free House wih real ale; Children and pets welcome; Bar and restaurant meals; Totnes 2 miles; £££.

Over the years, this old friend, so conveniently placed for Dartmoor and the pleasures of Torbay and the South Devon coast, has served countless happy holidaymakers. Hidden away in the tranquil Dart Valley, the inn dates back to to the 15th century, and until thirty or so years ago was known as the Church House, an inn name that abounds in the county. Visually the archetypal traditional English inn, the Sea Trout has two attractive bars with oak beams, log fires, brasses and prize specimens of fish in showcases. With an excellent selection of bar meals, cask-conditioned ales and a wide range of wines, spirits and especially, malt whiskies, relaxation is easy, and the friendly locals in the adjoining Village Bar will be happy to accept challenges at pool and darts. The spruce restaurant is an elegant place in which to enjoy an imaginative and intriguing choice from the à la carte and set dinner menus in the evenings, with vegetarian dishes always available. Delightful bedrooms in cottage style await the overnight guest; all are delectably furnished and appointed with private bathroom, individually controlled central heating, colour television, and direct-dial telephone. Permits for trout, sea trout and salmon fishing are available from the Inn, the unofficial headquarters of the Dart Angling Association. For a real taste of rural Devon, the Sea Trout has it all! ✿✿✿ *Commended, Good Pub Guide, Egon Ronay.*

Dorset

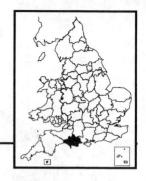

ANVIL HOTEL & INN,
Salisbury Road, Pimperne, Blandford, Dorset DT11 8UQ

Tel: 01258 453431
Tel and Fax: 01258 480182

11 bedrooms, all with private bathroom; Free House; Historic interest; Children and pets welcome; Bar and restaurant meals; Non-smoking areas; Bournemouth 26 miles, Salisbury 24, Poole 16; D£££.

A long, low thatched building set in a tiny village deep in the Dorset countryside two miles from Blandford – what could be more English? And that is exactly what visitors to the Anvil will find – a typical old English hostelry dating from the sixteenth century, set in an English country garden and offering good old-fashioned English hospitality. A mouthwatering menu with delicious desserts is available in the charming beamed restaurant and a wide selection of bar meals in the attractive, fully licensed bar. All bedrooms have private facilities. Ample parking. 👑👑👑 *Commended, Good Food Pub Guide, Les Routiers.*

ACORN INN,
Evershot, Dorchester, Dorset DT2 OJW

Tel: 01935 83228; Fax: 01935 83707
e-mail: stay@acorn-inn.co.uk
website: www.acorn-inn.co.uk

9 bedrooms, all with private bathroom; Free House with real ale; Historic interest; Children and pets welcome; Bar and restaurant meals; Non-smoking areas; Yeovil 9 miles; S£££, D£££.

This splendid 16th century village inn has remained true to its origins and although now blessed with the finest modern practicalities, the atmosphere and charm of its beamed bars remain to beguile guests to this idyllic Dorset village. Evershot is in fact "Evershead" in Hardy's Tess of the D'Urbervilles and the individually decorated and exceptionally well equipped bedrooms take their names from the novel. Dining by candlelight, having chosen from an imaginative and reasonably-priced à la carte menu and an extensive wine list, is a special pleasure. There is a well equipped games room for the young and young-in-heart, and a choice of cosy lounge and bar areas. *ETC* ◆◆◆, *Johansens.*

THE POACHERS INN,
Piddletrenthide, Dorchester,
Dorset DT2 7QX

Tel: 01300 348358
Fax: 01300 348153

18 bedrooms, all with private bathroom; Pets and children welcome; Dorchester 6 miles; ££.

This delightful Country Inn is set in the heart of the lovely Piddle Valley, within easy reach of all Dorset's attractions. All rooms are en suite and have colour television, tea/coffee making facilities and telephone. For relaxation there is a swimming pool and a riverside garden. Half board guests choose from our à la carte menu at no extra cost. Brochure with full details on request. *ETC/AA* ◆◆◆.
See also Colour Advertisement on page 4.

KING'S ARMS INN,
East Stour Common, Near Gillingham,
Dorset SP8 5NB

Tel: 01747 838325

3 bedrooms, all with private bathroom; Free House with real ale; Children welcome, pets allowed in bar; Bar lunches and restaurant meals; Gillingham 2 miles; S£,D£.

This lovely old inn nestling in the lush beauty of the Blackmore Vale is of direct appeal to country lovers seeking rest and relaxation. Its situation just west of Shaftesbury (Hardy's "Shaston") is near perfect and the welcome from the Langton family heartwarming. There are fine views all around and one may explore a pastoral landscape on foot or horseback amidst a maze of small roads, footpaths and bridleways; fishing and clay pigeon shooting may also be enjoyed locally. An excellent centre from which to visit the Dorset coast, Longleat, Cheddar, Stonehenge and numerous other places of interest, the 'Kings Arms' offers splendid en suite accommodation with everything one needs for a rejuvenating break. *ETC* ◆◆◆, *AA*

THE SCOTT ARMS,
Kingston, Corfe Castle,
Dorset BH20 5LW

Tel: 01929 480270
Fax: 01929 481570

2 bedrooms, both with private bathroom; Scottish & Newcastle House with real ale; Historic interest; Children welcome; Bar and restaurant meals; Non-smoking areas; Swanage 5 miles; S££££, D££££.

Situated on the Isle of Purbeck, close to the Dorset Coastal Path, the Scott Arms is a traditional 18th century inn with a character all of its own. With exposed oak beams, open fireplaces, friendly atmosphere and a truly breathtaking view of Corfe Castle from our beer garden, it is easy to see why this inn has been popular for many years. We offer a superb menu every lunchtime and evening featuring our extensive specials board. To complement the food we have a selection of well-kept traditional ales, lagers, fine wines and spirits. Country inn accommodation is available at reasonable rates, with all the amenities you would expect, including en suite facilities, tea/coffee making, hairdryer, colour television, and, of course, our full English breakfast. For that added hint of luxury, our bedrooms have four-poster beds.

Please mention
Recommended WAYSIDE & COUNTRY INNS
when seeking refreshment or accommodation
at a Hotel mentioned in these pages.

MARINERS HOTEL,
Silver Street, Lyme Regis,
Dorset DT7 3HS

Tel: 01297 442753

Fax: 01297 442431

12 bedrooms, all with private bathroom; Free House; Historic interest; Pets by arrangement; Bar meals, restaurant evenings only; Non-smoking areas; Yeovil 20 miles; S£££, D£££.

Retaining all the character of its 17th century origins, this lovely old hostelry is the perfect complement to the charm of historic Lyme Regis. Half-a-mile from the beach and harbour, it enjoys wonderful views to Lyme Bay, especially from the spacious, secluded garden, where soaking up the sun, drink in hand, is a special pleasure. Delightfully decorated, the 'Mariners' combines the fascination of the past with comforts of the present day. Guest rooms have en suite facilities, colour television, direct-dial telephone and tea and coffee-makers. Just as impressive is the well-balanced à la carte and table d'hôte cuisine with fresh local fish figuring prominently. A charismatic holiday venue. *ETC ★★, AA**.*

MILL HOUSE HOTEL,
Lulworth Cove, West Lulworth,
Dorset BH20 5RQ

Tel: 01929 400404

Fax: 01929 400508

e-mail: dukepayne@aol.com

9 bedrooms, all with private bathroom; Children welcome; Wareham 10 miles.

The Mill House Hotel is situated within the heart of Lulworth Cove overlooking the Mill Pond and only a short walk from the sea. It provides a convenient location for guests to explore this part of Dorset which is a designated Area of Outstanding Natural Beauty. There are nine en suite bedrooms (double, twin and family), all tastefully furnished in country house style, with direct-dial telephone, radio, colour television and hospitality tray. The residents' lounge offers magnificent sea views over Lulworth Cove and the surrounding countryside, while the Mill House Bar has a cosy atmosphere and a door leading into the garden. Jenny Hen's Tearoom provides a full range of meals and snacks during the day. Local attractions include Corfe Castle, Bovington Army Tank Museum and the resorts of Poole, Swanage and Weymouth.

ANTELOPE HOTEL,
Greenhill, Sherborne,
Dorset DT9 4EP

Tel: 01935 812077
Fax: 01935 816473

19 bedrooms, all with private bathroom; Free House with real ale; Historic interest; Children welcome; Bar and restaurant meals; Non-smoking areas; Yeovil 4 miles; S£££, D££.

No need to go out of your way to find somewhere for a welcome rest en route to or from the West Country, for this pretty, Georgian-fronted inn is perfectly situated on the main A30 trunk road Those in a hurry will perhaps prefer one of the appetising bar lunches, while visitors with more time on their hands can make their choice from the excellent à la carte menu and perhaps stay overnight in one of the comfortable, well-appointed en suite bedrooms, which include two four-poster rooms and one on the ground floor. Whatever your needs you can safely leave them in the capable hands of the friendly proprietors and their efficient staff. ♛♛♛♛, *AA ****.

SWAN INN,
Market Place, Sturminster Newton,
Dorset DT10 1AR

Tel: 01258 472208
Fax: 01258 473767

5 bedrooms, all with private bathroom; Hall & Woodhouse House with real ale; Historic interest; Children welcome; Bar and restaurant meals; Non-smoking areas; Blandford Forum 8 miles; S£££, D£.

Modern improvements blend unobtrusively with the charm and character of this 18th century inn's origins. A popular town centre hostelry, it commands attention by reason of its good real ale and bar snacks, and the excellent food served in its restaurant, the extensive menu including several traditional Dorset specialities. Sturminster Newton is a vibrant little country town in the midst of a lovely rural landscape of quiet byways and sleepy villages. Those in need of getting away from it all may find sprucely furnished accommodation here, each room having a bathroom en suite, colour television, telephone, hairdryer and tea and coffee maker. *ETC* ★★

THE BANKES ARMS COUNTRY INN,
Studland, Near Swanage,
Dorset BH19 3AU

Tel: 01929 450225
Fax: 01929 450307

10 bedrooms, 8 with private bathroom; Free House with real ale; Historic interest; Children over 5 years and pets welcome; Bar and restaurant meals; Non-smoking areas; Swanage 3 miles; S£££, D££££.

This friendly little stone-built hotel gazes seawards from the pretty village of Studland, which is situated on the Dorset coast in a designated Area of Outstanding Natural Beauty. Guest rooms are furnished to a most pleasing standard, and most have private bathrooms in addition to the colour television and tea and coffee facilities which are provided in all. A good selection of meals and snacks is offered daily in the bar, and also in the evening, when residents may eat in the cosy private dining room. Safe bathing can be enjoyed nearby, and watersports are also available. ♛♛♛, *CAMRA.*

SMUGGLERS INN,
Osmington Mills, Near Weymouth,
Dorset DT3 6HF

Tel: 01305 833125
Fax: 01305 832219

4 bedrooms, all with private bathroom; Woodhouse Inns House with real ale; Historic interest; Children welcome; Bar meals, restaurant evenings only; Non-smoking areas; Dorchester 6 miles; D££££.

Those with a taste for romance – or lobsters – will be drawn to this lovely 13th century inn once they have discovered its almost secret whereabouts. An ideal landing place for contraband, The Smugglers is hidden away in a cleft in the coastal path with a tinkling stream running by. The famous Pierre Latour (or French Peter) once sought refuge at the hostelry. Today, seekers of sanctuary come here to enjoy a variety of pleasures. There is a patio and gardens; families are very welcome and children have a safe play area to occupy them. The inn dispenses first-class à la carte food, including vegetarian dishes. Excellent overnight accommodation is available. *Good Pub Guide.*

Durham

THE DEVONPORT,
Middleton One Row, Darlington,
Durham DL2 1AS

Tel: 01325 332255
Fax: 01325 333242

15 bedrooms, all with private bathroom; Free House with real ale; Historic interest; Children welcome; Bar meals, restaurant evenings only; Non-smoking areas; Darlington 4 miles; S££, D££££.

This beautiful country inn dates back some 300 years and has retained all the values of a traditional hostelry of character. Set high above the River Tees it has fabulous views towards the Cleveland Hills. Recent refurbishment has provided superb hotel facilities, the accommodation consisting of handsomely-appointed en suite bedrooms all with remote-control colour television, radio, direct-dial telephone, hair dryer and tea/coffee making facilities. Fresh local produce features prominently on the imaginative menus served in both the bar and the stylish restaurant, where first-class service and relaxed surroundings make dining out a real pleasure. *AA **.*

Essex

YE OLDE WHITE HART HOTEL,
The Quay, Burnham-on-Crouch,
Essex CM0 8AS
Tel and Fax: 01621 782106

19 bedrooms, 11 with private bathroom; Free House with real ale; Historic interest; Children and pets welcome; Bar and restaurant meals; Non-smoking areas; Maldon 9 miles; S£/£££, D£/££.

Known to generations of yachting enthusiasts who find this fine old inn a popular rendezvous, the Olde White Hart has its own jetty on the River Crouch and even landlubbers will appreciate the estuary views from the comfortable window seats in the bar. The hotel was built in the 17th century and many of the original beams and fireplaces are now exposed. Traditional furnishings, panelling and old maritime pictures contribute greatly to its character. The bar menu offers à la carte and table d'hôte menus at lunchtime and in the evening. Excellent overnight accommodation is available, the majority of rooms having private facilities, television and radio. *ETC/RAC ★.*

The **£** symbol when appearing at the end of the italic section of an entry shows the anticipated price, during 2000, for full Bed and Breakfast.

Normal Bed & Breakfast rate per person (in single room)		*Normal Bed & Breakfast rate per person (sharing double/twin room)*	
PRICE RANGE	CATEGORY	PRICE RANGE	CATEGORY
Under £25	S£	**Under £25**	D£
£26-£35	S££	**£26-£35**	D££
£36-£45	S£££	**£36-£45**	D£££
Over £45	S££££	**Over £45**	D££££

This is meant as an indication only and does not show prices for Special Breaks, Weekends, etc. Guests are therefore advised to verify all prices on enquiring or booking.

THE CRICKETERS,
Clavering, Near Saffron Walden,
Essex CB11 4QT

Tel: 01799 550442; Fax: 01799 550882
e- mail: cricketers@lineone.net
website: www.wilkinson.ndirect.co.uk/the_cricketers/

8 bedrooms, all with private bathroom; Free House with real ale; Historic interest; Children welcome; Bar meals, restaurant evenings only, plus Sun. lunch; Non-smoking areas; Saffron Walden 8 miles; S£££££, D£££.

Welcome to the heart of rural Essex and this lovely, traditional English country inn with its beamed ceilings, roaring log fires, cask ales and friendly, relaxed atmosphere. Here, the cuisine is a revelation, talented chefs producing a splendid bill of 'flair' in the restaurant, each superb dish cooked to order. Less formal but no less worthy sustenance is obtainable from the buffet bar, from a snack to a three-course meal. In addition, there are always the daily 'blackboard specials'. Fish dishes, a roast carvery and delicate and delicious sweets are specialities of the house and there is an extensive wine list. So come and be spoilt. You can stay here too, in beautifully furnished en suite rooms. 👑👑👑 *Highly Commended, Egon Ronay, AA, Good Pub Guide, Which? recommended.*

RED LION HOTEL,
High Street, Colchester,
Essex CO1 1DJ

Tel: 01206 577986
Fax: 01206 578207
website: www.brook-hotels.co.uk

22 bedrooms, all with private bathroom; Free House; Historic interest; Children and pets welcome; Bar and restaurant meals; Non-smoking areas; London 51 miles; S£££, D££££.

Steeped in history dating back to Roman times when it was the first capital of Roman Britain, Colchester has infinite character portrayed, in particular, at this fine old inn. The 'Red Lion' (c.1465) is one of the oldest inns of East Anglia and certainly one of the most attractive with the magnificent Parliament Restaurant situated in the beamed Tudor banqueting hall. For its brasserie-style meals it enjoys an excellent reputation; the atmosphere is relaxed and informal and is a most popular meeting place at lunchtimes and for morning coffee and afternoon tea. Specially themed weekends are organised as well, including murder mysteries, none of which seems to have discomforted the resident ghost! Ideal for business or pleasure purposes, the accommodation offers the choice of antique-style luxury bedrooms in the Tudor building where original features include exposed wattle and daub walls, leaded windows and antique furniture or those of contemporary mode in a purpose-built extension. All have fine en suite facilities, colour television, radio, direct-dial telephone and tea and coffee-makers. The Tudor Room can cater for up to 45 conference delegates and provides up-to-date visual equipment. Service in all aspects is friendly and efficient. *ETC* ★★★

Please mention *Recommended Wayside & Country Inns*

when enquiring about accommodation featured in these pages.

Gloucestershire

THE OLD NEW INN,
Bourton-on-the-Water,
Gloucestershire GL54 2AF

Tel: 01451 820467
Fax: 01451 810236
e-mail: old_new_inn@compuserve.com

12 bedrooms, 9 with private bathroom; Bass House with real ale; Historic interest; Children welcome; Bar and restaurant meals; Non-smoking areas; Stow-on-the-Wold 4 miles; S£££, D£££.

Dating from the early 18th century, this traditional country inn is situated in the heart of the Cotswolds and is an ideal centre for a country holiday – golf, fly or coarse fishing, and horse riding can all be arranged nearby. Most rooms are en suite, and all have television and tea/coffee making facilities. There is also a comfortable residents' lounge, and three bars where guests can enjoy a drink and a chat. A comprehensive table d'hôte menu is served each evening and light lunches and bar meals are available daily; packed lunches can be provided if required. An interesting feature is the model village at the rear of the inn, a one-ninth size replica of the actual village, built by local men in 1937. ♛♛♛ *Commended, AA**.*

BROCKWEIR COUNTRY INN,
Brockweir, Near Chepstow,
Gloucestershire NP16 7NG

Tel: 01291 689548

3 bedrooms; Free House with real ale; Historic interest; Children welcome, dogs on lead only; Bar meals; Chepstow 5 miles; £.

Popular with the many walkers who enjoy rambles up the steep pastures to Offa's Dyke and the Devil's Pulpit, this friendly 17th century inn on the banks of the River Wye offers hospitality to all. Real ales and farm ciders are supplemented by regularly changing guest brews, and good wholesome bar food can be enjoyed in the snug main bar, where in winter a log fire blazes a welcome to all. In fine weather, refreshments can be enjoyed outside in the sheltered garden. Those inclined to try local pastimes such as salmon fishing, canoeing or horse riding can be comfortably accommodated in cosy bedrooms, one of which has a four-poster bed and is reputed to be haunted.

FOSSEBRIDGE INN,
Fossebridge, Near Cheltenham, Gloucestershire GL54 3JS

Freephone: 0800-074-1387
Fax: 01285 720793

11 bedrooms, all with private bathroom; Free House with real ale; Historic interest;
Children and pets welcome; Bar and restaurant meals; Cheltenham 12 miles; S££££, D£££.

Diners here are spoiled for choice by the variety of delicious home-cooked fare offered. The Bridge Restaurant and Bar both present imaginative menus based on the finest local produce, and a comprehensive bar snack menu with daily changing specials caters for lighter appetites or diners with limited time to spare. With origins as a coaching inn in Tudor times, the Fossebridge is most delightfully situated, with beautiful lawned gardens leading down to the River Coln. If the charm of the Cotswolds prove irresistible, individually styled bedrooms, some with lake and garden views, provide comfortable overnight accommodation. 👑👑👑, *AA ** and Rosette.*

THE MASONS ARMS,
28 The High Street, Meysey Hampton, Near Cirencester, Gloucestershire GL7 5JT

Tel and Fax: 01285 850164

e-mail: jane@themasonsarms.freeserve.co.uk

8 bedrooms, all with shower and toilet; Free House with traditional ale;
Bar and restaurant meals (not Sun. evening); Non-smoking areas; Fairford 2 miles; S£££, D££.

Set beside the village green, the Masons Arms dates from the 17th century and lies on the southern fringe of the Cotswolds. Apart from the many Cotswold beauty spots, Oxford, Bath, Cheltenham and Stratford-upon-Avon are within easy reach. Here is an opportunity to enjoy excellent food and drink in delightful surroundings. The menu is an intriguing blend of imaginative starters and home-cooked traditional fare, whilst the daily 'specials' make interesting reading. For the discerning, this is a gem of a place in which to stay. Comfortable, individually decorated rooms all have en suite facilities, heating, remote-control colour television and tea and coffee tray. 👑👑 *Commended, AA QQQ.*

WILD DUCK INN,
Drakes Island, Ewen, Near Cirencester, Gloucestershire GL7 6BY

Tel: 01285 770310
e-mail: wduckinn@aol.com

10 double bedrooms, all with private bathroom; Historic interest; Free House with real ale;
Bar and restaurant meals; Chippenham 18 miles, Cheltenham 16, Swindon 16, Tetbury 9,
Cirencester 3, Kemble Station 1; D£££.

Nestling in delightful, unspoilt Gloucestershire countryside, this is an old inn of outstanding character, with original beams and inglenook open fires giving a traditional atmosphere of warmth and friendliness. Food is of the highest quality, with an extensive menu operating at lunchtime and in the evenings. Bar lunches are also available. Three bedrooms have four-posters and overlook the delightful, award-winning garden. All ten rooms have private bath en suite, colour television, tea/coffee making facilities and telephone, making this a desirable overnight or weekly holiday base, in addition to being an enchanting place to quench one's thirst. Access, Visa, Amex accepted. 👑👑👑, *RAC***, AA Rosette, Les Routiers Inn of the Year 1994, Ashley Courtenay, Egon Ronay.* **See also Inside Back Cover.**

THE ELIOT ARMS HOTEL,
Clarks Hay, South Cerney, Cirencester, Gloucestershire GL7 5UA

Tel: 01285 860215
Fax: 01285 861121

12 bedrooms, all with private bathroom; Free House with real ale; Historic interest;
Bar and restaurant meals; Non-smoking areas; Cirencester 4 miles; S£££, D££.

An excellent varied menu serving meals of quality represents only one of many reasons for visiting this charming 16th century inn in the heart of the Cotswold Water Park where excellent coarse and trout fishing may be found. There are 100 beautiful lakes to choose from and facilities for sailboarding, water-skiing, sailing and sub-aqua sport. Delightfully decorated, beamed bars exude a warm welcome with a log fire adding its cheer in winter. The old hostelry stands in an attractive garden within minutes of the fascinating Roman town of Cirencester. With the amenities of a first class country hotel, the Eliot Arms has splendidly-appointed rooms, all with en suite bath or shower, colour television, direct-dial telephone and tea and coffee-makers. 🏵🏵🏵 *Commended, AA QQQQ Selected.*

WHEATSHEAF HOTEL,
West End, Northleach, Gloucestershire GL54 3EZ

Tel: 01451 860244
Fax: 01451 861037

9 bedrooms, all with private bathroom; Free House with real ale; Historic interest;
Bar and restaurant meals; Non-smoking areas; Cirencester 10 miles; S£££, D£££.

This creeper-clad period coaching inn in the heart of the Cotswolds is a feast for the eyes – and for the rest of the system too, for it has a high reputation for the imaginative home-cooked food served in the elegant restaurant. There are two spruce bars and an attractive dining room whilst, upstairs, a number of individually furnished double bedrooms have bathrooms or showers en suite, king-size beds, colour television, direct-dial telephone and tea-making facilities; ideal accommodation for guests touring the Cotswolds or visiting Cheltenham racecourse. *ETB Listed, Egon Ronay.*

FALCON INN,
Painswick, Gloucestershire GL6 6UN

Tel: 01452 814222
Fax: 01452 813377
e-mail: blennins@clara.net

12 bedrooms, all with private bathroom; Free House with real ale; Historic interest;
Children and pets welcome; Bar and restaurant meals; Non-smoking areas; Stroud 3 miles; S£££, D££.

Being situated right on the popular Cotswold Way, this fine 16th century coaching inn and posting house is a particular favourite with walkers and touring parties who appreciate the ambience of the bars with their stone floors, wood panelling and log fires; there is even a special drying room for ramblers should the weather disappoint. The inn has a fascinating history, having, in its time, served as a courthouse, the venue for cockfights and as an important coaching inn with stage coaches leaving regularly for destinations throughout the country. It also claims the world's oldest bowling green in the grounds. Excellent accommodation awaits guests, facilities being on a par with those offered by the restaurant which is renowned for its superb fare. *ETC ★★, CAMRA, AA, Good Pub Guide.*

PLEASE MENTION THIS GUIDE WHEN YOU WRITE

OR PHONE TO ENQUIRE ABOUT ACCOMMODATION.

IF YOU ARE WRITING, A STAMPED,

ADDRESSED ENVELOPE IS ALWAYS APPRECIATED.

YE OLDE MALT SHOVEL INN,
Ruardean,
Gloucestershire GL17 9TW

Tel: 01594 543028
e-mail: mark@maltshovel.u-net.com
website: www.maltshovel.u-net.com

6 bedrooms, all with private bathroom; Free House with real ale; Historic interest; Children and pets welcome; Bar and restaurant meals; Non-smoking areas; Cinderford 3 miles; S££, D£.

In spring, there is a breathtaking display of bluebells and foxgloves, in autumn, the spectacular red and gold of the trees; such are the visual attractions surrounding this mellow 12th century inn so happily placed between the Royal Forest of Dean and the Wye Valley. One of the oldest hostelries in Britain, the 'Malt Shovel' has recently been restored to a very high standard using traditional oak and Forest stone with which modern amenities blend to perfection. En suite bedrooms, furnished with antiques, have the convenience of colour television, direct-dial telephone and tea and coffee-making facilities. The dining room is supported by a 24ft oak tree and bordered by mahogany doors and windows from such places as 10 Downing Street!

ROSE AND CROWN INN,
Nympsfield, Stonehouse,
Gloucestershire GL10 3TU

Tel: 01453 860240
Fax: 01453 860900

4 bedrooms, all with private bathroom; Free House with real ale; Historic interest; Children welcome; Bar and restaurant meals; Nailsworth 3 miles; S££, D££.

With the ancient Cotswold Way footpath nearby inviting excursions into a landscape of outstanding scenic beauty, this old coaching inn is a recommended retreat at lunchtime or after a day's sightseeing. With its origins in the 16th century, the inn has attractive, beamed bars which, although modernised, still retain their time-honoured ambience. Its reputation for providing the best of home-made food is well deserved; the dining room, candlelit in the evenings, presents a wide choice of dishes; something for all ages and tastes, including vegetarian dishes. There is a large garden and a safe play area for children. First-class accommodation comprises twin and double-bedded rooms with a high standard of amenities. 👑👑👑 *Commended, AA, RAC, CAMRA, The Circle, Les Routiers.*

AMBERLEY INN,
Culver Hill, Near Stroud,
Gloucestershire GL5 5AF

Tel: 01453 872565
Fax: 01453 872738
website: www.oldenglish.co.uk

15 bedrooms, all with private bathroom; Free House with real ale; Historic interest; Children and pets welcome; Bar and restaurant meals; Non-smoking areas; Gloucester 8 miles; S££, D££.

Combining all the amenities of a first-class country hotel with the ambience of a true English wayside inn, the 'Amberley' lies amidst ideal walking and riding country. An excellent base for touring the Cotswolds, the inn has tastefully furnished bedrooms awaiting the overnight guest, all rooms being equipped with en suite facilities, colour television, radio, telephone, beverage-makers and each enjoying views of either the colourful gardens or the rolling Woodchester Valley. Real ales and bar meals are offered daily in the Country Bar and oak-panelled lounge, both warmed during winter months by heartening log fires. The restaurant boasts an outstanding fixed price menu and a full à la carte. *ETC* ★★, *AA**.*

FHG PUBLICATIONS

publish a large range of well-known accommodation guides. We will be happy to send you details or you can use the order form at the back of this book.

OLD STOCKS HOTEL
The Square, Stow-on-the-Wold, Gloucestershire GL54 1AF

Tel: 01451 830666
Fax: 01451 870014

18 bedrooms, all with private bathroom; Free House; Historic interest; Bar and restaurant meals; Non-smoking areas; London 84 miles, Stratford-upon-Avon 21, Cheltenham 18; S£££, D£££.

The charming old town of Stow-on-the-Wold lies in the heart of the Cotswolds and is an ideal base for touring this beautiful area. Those seeking accommodation here could do no better than the Old Stocks Hotel, whose tasteful guest rooms are in keeping with the hotel's old world character. Cotswold stone walls and oak beams contrast magnificently with modern amenities of colour television, tea/coffee facilities, radio, hairdryer, direct-dial telephone and en suite bathroom. Five superior rooms are also available, providing an even greater range of comforts. Although the hotel concentrates on providing excellent value for money, no corners are cut in providing mouth-watering menus offering a wide range of choices. Special bargain breaks are also available and the resident proprietors, Alan and Julie Rose, or indeed any of the caring staff will be happy to provide advice on exploring this enchanting area. 👑👑👑👑, *AA***, *Les Routiers.*

RAGGED COT INN,
Hyde, Chalford, Near Stroud, Gloucestershire GL6 8PE

Tel: 01453 884643/731333
Fax: 01453 731166

10 bedrooms, all en suite; Free House with real ale; Children welcome; Non-smoking restaurant; Bath 35 miles, Cheltenham 15, Cirencester 8.

Set beside 400 acres of National Trust common land, this historic owner-run freehouse combines the charm of a traditional inn with modern comfort. The warm and welcoming bars, with a selection of real ales, ciders and 75 malt whiskies, and superb range of home-made meals make the Ragged Cott an ideal place to unwind or explore the Cotswolds. The ten bedrooms are beautifully appointed, set apart from the main building in converted stables. Recommended in the Good Beer Guide, the Good Pub Guide and commended by the English Tourism Council, the Ragged Cott offers excellent value for money.

PLEASE MENTION THIS GUIDE WHEN YOU WRITE

OR PHONE TO ENQUIRE ABOUT ACCOMMODATION.

IF YOU ARE WRITING, A STAMPED,

ADDRESSED ENVELOPE IS ALWAYS APPRECIATED.

Hampshire

AMPORT INN,
Amport, Near Andover,
Hampshire SP11 8AE

Tel: 01264 710371

Fax: 01264 710112

9 bedrooms, all with private bathroom; Free House with real ale; Historic interest; Children welcome; Bar meals, restaurant evenings only; Andover 4 miles; £££.

A winsome village pub with the facilities of a modern hotel, this little gem of a retreat has a situation to warm the cockles of any romantic's heart. Amport is the epitome of the village of fond recollection with its own green, cricket pitch and riding school. Nearby is Thruxton motor racing circuit, whilst Stonehenge, Salisbury and Winchester may be reached in 30 minutes. The joys of discovering this haven, just off the A303, are not confined to the aesthetic for there is a plethora of attractions: indoor-heated swimming pool and superb accommodation comprising a suite and bedrooms with double or twin beds, all of which have television, telephone, video and tea and coffee-makers. 🛇 🛇 🛇

JACK RUSSELL INN,
Faccombe,
Hampshire SP11 0DS

Tel: 01264 737315

3 bedrooms, all with private bathroom; Free House with real ale; Children in restaurant only, pets welcome; Bar and restaurant meals; Non-smoking areas; Newbury 8 miles; S£££, D££££.

In the tranquil heart of the verdant Hampshire countryside, a great area for walkers. this little pub faces the village pond, representing the very essence of English rural life. Visitors may be sure of a good pint of real ale and first-rate wholesome food. It is well worth venturing the three miles off the A343 to call in at this friendly little inn, and for those seeking temporary respite from the demands of urban life, there are three comfortable bedrooms, all en suite, with colour television and tea/coffee making facilities. Children are welcome in the conservatory, and there is a large beer garden and play equipment.

FHG PUBLICATIONS

publish a large range of well-known accommodation guides.

We will be happy to send you details or you can use the

order form at the back of this book.

THE JOLLY MILLER,
North Warnborough, Hook,
Hampshire RG29 1ET

Tel: 01256 702085
Fax: 01256 704030

12 bedrooms, all with private bathroom; Free House with real ale; Children and pets welcome; Bar and restaurant meals; Non-smoking areas; Basingstoke 5 miles; S£££, D££.

Delicious home-made food and the warmest of welcomes: you'll be glad you stopped at this attractive hostelry. Menus present an imaginative range of choice in addition to the daily 'specials'. So eat drink and be merry and, in summer, why not stay for a barbecue held in the spacious garden? Better still, why not stay overnight? Comfortable, single, double, twin and family rooms are available; most have en suite facilities and all have colour television, direct-dial telephone and tea and coffee-makers. For superb food and hospitality and, maybe, a friendly game of skittles, a night spent at the 'Jolly Miller' is a pleasurable experience, with a hearty English breakfast in the morning. *RAC* ◆◆◆

WELLINGTON ARMS HOTEL,
Stratfield Turgis, Hook,
Hampshire RG27 0AS

Tel: 01256 882214
Fax: 01256 882934

35 bedrooms, all with private bathroom; Hall & Woodhouse House with real ale; Historic interest; Children and pets welcome; Bar and restaurant meals; Basingstoke 6 miles; S££££, D£££.

This lovely old establishment has graduated from 17th century farmhouse to a superb Grade II listed hotel. Charming and with a captivating air of serenity, this is just the place to escape the trammels of the workaday world. Retaining many of the characteristics of a traditional English inn, especially with regard to the fine home-cooked food, the hotel has a delightful restaurant whilst good bar food is also available. The Wellington Arms boasts excellent accommodation, all bedrooms in the main building and garden wing having en suite facilities, remote-control colour television, radio, direct-dial telephone, tea and coffee tray as well as a welcome pack. *ETC* ★★★, *AA*.

THE WHITE HART HOTEL,
London Road, Hook,
Hampshire RG27 9DZ

Tel: 01256 762462
Fax: 01256 768351

21 bedrooms, all with private bathroom; Allied/Carlsberg Tetley House with real ale; Historic interest; Children and pets welcome; Bar and restaurant meals; Non-smoking areas; Basingstoke 6 miles.

Original beams, natural brickwork and open fires complement the atmosphere of the bar in this lovely 16th century coaching inn where an extensive range of real ales and good home-cooked meals may be enjoyed. Children are catered for and the hotel has a large garden with play equipment. All guest rooms are en suite and offer such amenities as colour satellite television, trouser press, hairdryer, direct-dial telephone and tea/coffee making facilities. The hotel is situated within walking distance of Hook Railway Station and is under a mile away from the M3.

STRING OF HORSES COUNTRY HOUSE HOTEL,
Mead End Road, Sway, Near Lymington,
Hampshire SO41 6EH

Tel: 01590 682631

e-mail: relax@stringof horses.co.uk   website: www.stringofhorses.co.uk

8 bedrooms, all with private bathroom; Free House; Bar and restaurant meals; Non-smoking areas; Brockenhurst 3 miles; S£££f, D££££.

Unique, secluded hotel set in two acres in the heart of the New Forest. Friendly, relaxed atmosphere with service, cuisine and accommodation of the highest standard. Eight luxurious double bedrooms each with its own en-suite jacuzzi and shower plus full facilities including remote-controlled television, telephone and hospitality tray. Four-poster bed and mini bars are a special feature in several rooms. Romantic dining 'francais' in the oak beamed award-winning 'Carriages Restaurant'. Heated swimming pool in tranquil gardens. Close to yachting resorts, golf, riding stables and cycle hire. Smoke-free common areas. Regrettably no children or pets. *ETC/AA* ★★★, *AA Rosette* **See also Colour Advertisement on page 5.**

YE OLDE GEORGE INN,
Church Street, East Meon, Near Petersfield
Hampshire GU32 1NH

Tel: 01730 823481
Fax: 01730 823759

5 bedrooms, all with private bathroom; Hall & Woodhouse House with real ale; Historic interest; Children and pets welcome; Bar and restaurant meals; Non-smoking areas; Petersfield 5 miles; S££, D£.

This lovely character hostelry consists partly of a pair of converted 15th century cottages complete with original inglenook fireplaces, exposed brickwork and beams. The George complements the historic village with its famous church in every way. The bar welcomes you with its old pine tables, open fires, horse brasses and a selection of excellent ales and wines, and quality selection of home-cooked dishes on blackboard menus. Night time sees the Inn at its best, with polished tables and horse brasses reflecting the warm glow of candles and firelight. The desire may arise to linger longer in this charming place. *ETC* ◆◆◆

WHITE HART HOTEL
The Square, Whitchurch,
Hampshire RG28 7DN

Tel: 01256 892900
Fax: 01256 896628

20 bedrooms, 12 with private bathroom; Free House with real ale; Historic interest;
Bar and restaurant meals; Non-smoking areas; Andover 6 miles; ££.

Steeped in period atmosphere, this traditional coaching inn has been welcoming travellers since 1461. The hospitality and personal service is no less warm and welcoming today. The hotel is widely known for its first-class food, whether it be a tasty home-cooked bar snack, a delicious cream tea or an à la carte dish in the charming Lord Denning Restaurant with its genuine Queen Anne ceiling. Judge for yourself! Catering for the modern businessman and casual traveller alike, the White Hart has a variety of period rooms, mostly of Georgian design. The majority have en suite facilities and all have colour television and tea/coffee makers. Prices, in all respects, are extremely competitive. 👑👑👑, *RAC **, Les Routiers.*

THE WOODFALLS INN,
The Ridge, Woodfalls
Hampshire SP5 2LN

Tel: 01725 513222; Fax: 01725 513220
e-mail: woodfalls@aol.com
website: www.trad-inns.co.uk/woodfalls

10 bedrooms, all with private bathroom; Free House with real ale;
Children welcome; Bar and restaurant meals; Non-smoking areas;
Bournemouth 20 miles, Southampton 15, Salisbury 7; S£££, D££££.

Nestling on the northern edge of the New Forest, on an old route to the cathedral city of Salisbury, this award-winning inn has provided hospitality to travellers since 1870. Ideal for visiting the New Forest, Stonehenge, Romsey and Winchester. After recent refurbishment, all bedrooms are tastefully and individually decorated, with en suite facilities (some with four-poster beds). There is an award-winning restaurant and a bar serving food and real ales. *ETC* ◆◆◆◆ *and Silver Award, AA QQQQQ Premier Selected, Johansens, Ashley Courtenay.* **See also Colour Advertisement on page 4**.

PLEASE MENTION THIS GUIDE WHEN YOU WRITE

OR PHONE TO ENQUIRE ABOUT ACCOMMODATION.

IF YOU ARE WRITING, A STAMPED,

ADDRESSED ENVELOPE IS ALWAYS APPRECIATED.

Herefordshire

THE GREEN MAN,
Fownhope,
Herefordshire HR1 4PE

Tel: 01432 860243
Fax: 01432 860207

19 bedrooms, all with private bathroom; Free House with real ale; Historic interest;
Children welcome; Bar food, restaurant evenings only; Non-smoking areas;
Gloucester 24 miles, Monmouth 22, Ross-on-Wye 9, Hereford 7; S£££, D££.

This ancient black and white timbered inn provides an ideal base for exploring the beautiful surrounding countryside and nearby places of interest. There are two bars, an oak-beamed restaurant, a buttery for bar snacks and a large attractive garden. The resident proprietors place great emphasis upon the quality of food and an informal and friendly atmosphere. An extensive bar food menu is available mornings and evenings; afternoon teas and dinners à la carte are served in the restaurant. Bedrooms all have colour television/satellite, radio alarm, direct-dial telephone, tea/coffee making equipment, central heating and many extras. Indoor swimming pool, sauna, steam room, jacuzzi, gym, squash court. ♛♛♛ *Commended, AA**, RAC**, Egon Ronay.* **See also Outside Back Cover.**

RHYDSPENCE INN,
Whitney-on-Wye, Near Hay-on-Wye,
Herefordshire HR3 6EU

Tel: 01497 831262
Fax: 01497 831751

7 bedrooms, all with private bathroom; Free House with real ale; Historic interest;
Bar and restaurant meals; Non-smoking areas; Hay-on-Wye 4 miles; S£££, D£££.

This picturesque black-and-white timbered inn can claim to be both the first and last in England, standing as it does on the border between Herefordshire and Powys. Indeed it can trace its intriguing history back to the time when it offered food and sustenance to Welsh cattle drovers on their way to the English markets. Today it is popular with both locals and visitors, providing an excellent selection of traditional and more unusual bar and restaurant meals, accompanied by an extensive choice of wines, beers and spirits. Those fortunate enough to be able to linger awhile in this captivating spot will find immaculate en suite bedrooms, tastefully furnished and decorated in traditional style. ♛♛♛ *Highly Commended, AA QQQQQ Premier Select.*

RIVERSIDE INN & RESTAURANT,
Aymestrey, Near Leominster,
Herefordshire HR6 9ST

Tel: 01568 708440
Fax: 01568 709058

7 bedrooms, 5 with private bathroom; Free House with real ale; Historic interest; Children and pets welcome; Bar and restaurant meals; Non-smoking areas; Leominster 6 miles; S££, D££££.

In an idyllic situation on the banks of the dreamy River Lugg, this beautiful, half-timbered building dates from 1580 and became a coaching inn in 1740. It is only about a mile from the scene of one of England's bloodiest battles at Mortimer's Cross in 1461, during the Wars of the Roses. Peace reigns supreme today here on the Welsh borders and there are some wonderful walks to be had in the vicinity, especially for the stout-hearted and booted, the 25-mile Mortimer Trail between Ludlow and Kington. Proprietors, Val and Steve Bowen, can arrange transportation to any point along the trail. With a wealth of original features, the 'Riverside' is renowned for its superlative cuisine and tastefully decorated en suite accommodation. *CAMRA, Good Beer Guide, Good Food Guide, Which? Guide.*

THE NEW INN,
Market Square, Pembridge, Leominster,
Herefordshire HR6 9DZ

Tel: 01544 388427

6 bedrooms; Free House with real ale; Historic interest; Children welcome, pets in bedrooms only; Bar meals, restaurant evenings only; Non-smoking areas; Kington 6 miles; S£, D£.

The last battle of the Wars of the Roses was fought just a few miles from here at Mortimers Cross, and the treaty which gave England's crown to the Yorkist leader is believed to have been signed in the courtroom of this fourteenth century inn. Two ghosts are said to haunt the Inn: one a girl who appears only to women; the other a red-coated soldier armed with a sword. Comfortable accommodation is available, and a good breakfast is included in the rate for a nicely furnished, spick and span bedroom. A varied and interesting menu is offered at most reasonable prices in the bar, which has a log fire to warm it on chillier days, and the attractive lounge area is a popular venue for cosy evening dinners.

MILL RACE INN AND RESTAURANT,
Walford, Ross-on-Wye,
Herefordshire HR9 5QS

Tel: 01989 562891
Fax: 01989 768876

No accommodation; Free House; Children welcome; Bar and restaurant meals; Ross-on-Wye 3 miles.

When John and Anne Lewis bought this attractive hostelry in 1990, they set about restoring features that had long since been deemed unsightly or un-modern. An old fireplace, stone walls and oak beams reappeared, to which various artifacts such as old settles and even a church door were added. Today, the inn is a 'Mecca' for visitors who appreciate excellent cask ales and good food at reasonable prices with an ample choice of dishes in both bar and restaurant. We were intrigued by the appearance on the Sunday Lunch menu of 'Kiss the Blarney' Gateau and wondered whether one has to be suspended backwards to enjoy it! Apparently not! This justly popular rendezvous has a large garden where children may play safely.

THE NEW INN,
St Owen's Cross, Near Ross-on-Wye,
Herefordshire HR2 8LQ

Tel: 01989 730274

2 bedrooms, both with private bathroom; Free House with real ale; Historic interest; Children and pets welcome; Bar and restaurant meals; Non-smoking areas; Ross-on-Wye 5 miles; S£££, D£££.

With its black and white timbered facade decorated with colourful hanging baskets, this one-time coaching inn dates from around 1540 and its time-hallowed character is epitomised by its many beams and huge inglenook fireplaces. Owners, Nigel and Jane Donovan, have been at the New Inn for ten years and have a fine reputation for supplying outstanding food and drink; the majority of the dishes on the extensive menu being home-made and prepared from fresh local produce. On fine days, there are few better places in which to relax with a glass of one's fancy than in the spacious beer garden with views stretching across undulating countryside towards the Black Mountains. For a revivifying break away from so-called civilization, the inn has two well-appointed four-poster bedrooms.

Isle of Wight

NEW INN,
Mill Road, Shalfleet,
Isle of Wight PO30 4NS

Tel: 01983 531314
Fax: 01983 741283
e-mail: martin.bullock@virgin.net

No accommodation; Real ale; Historic interest; Children and pets welcome; Bar and restaurant meals; Non-smoking areas; Yarmouth 4 miles.

A charming little inn close by Shalfleet Creek and the National Trust protected Newtown estuary, the New Inn is full of traditional, old-world charm epitomised by snug bars with real fires burning in the inglenooks, just the place in which to relax with a glass of one's fancy on cool days, whilst on sunny days the garden beckons. However, come rain or shine, visitors are recommended to study a menu featuring mouth-watering dishes which are available at lunchtime and in the evening, fish dishes being a speciality of the house. A small inn with a big heart.

The **£** symbol when appearing at the end of the italic section of an entry shows the anticipated price, during 2000, for full Bed and Breakfast.

Normal Bed & Breakfast rate per person (in single room)		*Normal Bed & Breakfast rate per person (sharing double/twin room)*	
PRICE RANGE	CATEGORY	PRICE RANGE	CATEGORY
Under £25	S£	**Under £25**	D£
£26-£35	S££	**£26-£35**	D££
£36-£45	S£££	**£36-£45**	D£££
Over £45	S££££	**Over £45**	D££££

This is meant as an indication only and does not show prices for Special Breaks, Weekends, etc. Guests are therefore advised to verify all prices on enquiring or booking.

CLARENDON HOTEL AND WIGHT MOUSE INN,
Chale,
Isle of Wight PO38 2HA
Tel and Fax: 01983 730431

14 bedrooms, 3 family suites, all with private bathroom or shower;
Free House with 6 real ales and 365 whiskies; Historic interest; Children most welcome;
Bar and restaurant meals; Non-smoking areas; Newport 9 miles, Ventnor 7; ££.

Our Hotel, The Clarendon, is a 17th century Coaching Inn of immense charm and character enjoying an enviable reputation for excellent food, wine, comfort and hospitality. Standing in its own lovely grounds, it overlooks the magnificent West Wight coastline and is surrounded by beautiful National Trust countryside. Children are very welcome, at reduced rates, and we are a few minutes from Blackgang Chine and several beautiful beaches. We have absolutely everything for your comfort, including our first class restaurant and cocktail bar. We are also included in the Egon Ronay guide "AND BABY COMES TOO", and have a yellow duck award for our baby/child care expertise. All rooms are en suite and have colour television, direct-dial telephones and tea and coffee making facilities, and all bathrooms have hairdryers.

Our Pub, The Wight Mouse Inn, which is attached to the hotel, has great atmosphere, open fires, six real ales, 365 different whiskies, excellent meals and live entertainment nightly all year round, and is open all day every day for meals and drinks. Our beautiful gardens have swings, slides, climbing frames, pets' corner, plus ballpond, bouncy castle, trikes and Shetland pony rides with Arthur, plus "Mouse World", our spectacular new indoor children's play area in the garden. Golf, Shooting, Fishing, Horse Riding, Hang Gliding and Car Hire can easily be arranged.

Chale Bay Farm and Seagulls Restaurant, our farm adjacent to the Clarendon has 10 luxury en suite bedrooms with beautiful views of the sea and sunset. AA QQQQQ, the highest grade, unique on the island. For a brochure and full details please write to John and Jean Bradshaw.

ETB 👑👑👑 *Highly Commended, 5 times UK National Family Pub of the Year, UK Whisky Pub of the Year 1994, Les Routiers, Ashley Courtenay, AA**, RAC** and Merit Awards for Hospitality, Comfort and Service, CAMRA Recommended.*

SPYGLASS INN,
The Esplanade, Ventnor,
Isle of Wight PO38 1JX

Tel: 01983 855338

3 suites; Free House with real ale; Historic interest; Children welcome; Bar and restaurant meals; Non-smoking areas; Shanklin 3 miles; D£££.

Yo, ho, ho and a bottle of what you fancy – to go with your choice of freshly prepared fare from the extensive menu and served in a nautical environment. This fine seafront hostelry is renowned for its magnificent cuisine with seafood, naturally, a speciality of the house. One of the most famous inns on the delectable island, the Spyglass is a happy, friendly place to visit with entertainments and special events held regularly. Conviviality reigns in the bar, a mood to which a glass or two of the fine real ales contributes not a little. Bed and breakfast accommodation is provided in three self-contained suites comprising a double bedroom with bathroom en suite and a lounge and patio with wide sea views. Your hosts are Neil, Stephanie and Rosie Gibbs. *Egon Ronay Recommended.*

BUGLE HOTEL,
The Square, Yarmouth,
Isle of Wight PO41 0NS

Tel: 01983 760272
Fax: 01983 760883

10 bedrooms, 8 with private bathroom; Whitbread House with real ale; Historic interest; Children and pets welcome; Bar and restaurant meals;Non-smoking areas; Newport 9 miles; S£££, D££.

A mere stone's throw from the yacht harbour, this delectable, 17th century listed Inn-cum-hotel is one of the most interesting in the idyllic Isle. Immersed in maritime history, it has innate character expressed in the oak-panelled walls, beams and blazing log fires of the Poachers Lounge Bar, whilst keeping pace with modern trends, the Galleon Bar has a large television screen showing leading sporting events, and live entertainment is held here several times a week. Both bars provide excellent food and real ales and the restaurant is renowned for its appetising cuisine, courtesy of course, of the spectral female figure which is reputed to haunt the kitchens. A splendid place in which to stay, the 'Bugle' provides first-rate en suite accommodation. *ETC* ★★

FHG PUBLICATIONS

publish a large range of well-known accommodation guides. We will be happy to send you details or you can use the order form at the back of this book.

Kent

CHEQUERS INN,
Smarden, Ashford,
Kent TN27 8QA

Tel: 01233 770217
Fax: 01233 770623

5 bedrooms, 3 with private bathroom; Free House with real ale; Historic interest;
Children and pets welcome; Bar and restaurant meals; Charing 7 miles; S££, D££££.

With its wealth of oak beams and open fires, the Chequers will gladden the hearts of confirmed and convinced traditionalists for there is no music and not a single fruit machine to sully the ambience of a hostelry hallowed by time. The Chequers first opened its doors on to a vastly different world in 1387, since when centuries and customers have come and gone and little is known of the majority of the intervening years. Suffice to say that it requires little effort to ascertain that the refreshment offered to today's traveller into deepest Kent is of the highest calibre and that the proverbial room at the inn is sumptuously comfortable and blessed with fine modern appointments. *ETC* ◆◆◆

THE ROYAL OAK INN,
High Street, Charing, Near Ashford
Kent TN27 0HU

Tel: 01233 712612
Fax: 01233 713355

8 bedrooms, all with private bathroom; Free House with real ale; Historic interest; Children welcome;
Bar and restaurant meals; Non-smoking areas; Ashford 6 miles; S£££, D££££.

The ancient village of Charing nestles in the lee of the North Downs, midway between the cathedral cities of Rochester and Canterbury, with the Channel Tunnel less than 20 minutes away. Pilgrims, archbishops and, possibly, kings have supped ale in the village through the ages. Today. the welcoming Royal Oak carries on the same tradition with distinction. Built round a courtyard, it has a snug bar and a restaurant with a wealth of exposed beams where generous portions of home-cooked food more than satisfy popular demand. Bar meals, 'blackboard specials' or main courses, the choice is extensive and prices reasonable. This is also a most congenial place in which to stay and rooms are appointed to the highest standard. 👑👑👑 *Commended.*

THE BULL HOTEL,
Wrotham, Near Sevenoaks,
Kent TN15 7RF

Tel: 01732 789800/789819

Fax: 01732 886288

10 bedrooms, 7 with private bathroom; Free House with real ale; Historic interest; Children welcome; Bar meals, restaurant evenings only; Non-smoking areas; Tonbridge 8 miles; S£££, D££.

Once a stopping-off point for pilgrims on their way to Canterbury, the Bull Hotel is a family-run fourteenth century Coaching Inn of great charm and character in the historic village of Wrotham. It specialises in comfortable accommodation and superb cooking at reasonable prices, with an à la carte restaurant, set menus and home-made bar snacks. All rooms have colour television, telephone and tea-making facilities. Ideal as a base for visiting London and places of local interest, it lies just off the M20/M26, 40 minutes by train from London and near the Channel ports and Gatwick.

THE ST CRISPIN INN,
The Street, Worth,
Kent CT14 0DF

Tel: 01304 612081

Fax: 01304 614838

6 bedrooms with private bathroom; Real ales; Children welcome; Restaurant meals; Sandwich 1 mile.

Traditional Kentish country pub set in an area of outstanding natural beauty. Large garden and covered patio. 28-seater restaurant with a fine selection of wines and real cask ales and open log fire. Six rooms en suite. Families always welcome. Plenty of parking space. Many golf clubs in the locality. *Twice winner of Kent Country Pub of the Year, Egon Ronay recommended.*

Please mention *Recommended Wayside & Country Inns*

when enquiring about accommodation featured in these pages.

Lancashire

OWD NELL'S CANALSIDE TAVERN,
Guy's Thatched Hamlet, St Michael's Road,
Bilsborrow, Lancashire PR3 0RS

Tel: 01995 640010
Fax: 01995 640141

53 bedrooms, all en suite; Free House with real ale; Children welcome; Bar and restaurant meals; Non-smoking areas; M6/M55 3 miles, Garstang 3; S£££, D£.

Here's one for collectors of the unusual and the idyllic – a thatched oldtime refreshment house tucked away by the side of the Lancaster Canal. Open all day dispensing the best of home made country tavern fayre, Owd Nell's is renowned for its range of tempting bar dishes designed to serve all palates and pockets, as well as its great selection of cask-conditioned ales. This gem is just one unit in the complex that is Guy's Thatched Hamlet, where guests can step back in time and enjoy the good things in life in a relaxed and unfussy atmosphere. Superb overnight accommodation with the highest modern standards is provided in Guy's Lodgings, comprising en suite rooms with colour television, telephone and tea and coffee making facilities. For dining "par excellence", guests just have to follow their noses to the adjacent Guy's Eating Establishment, where the emphasis is on tasteful informality, the variety of dishes ranging from freshly made pizza to a succulent sirloin steak. Without venturing beyond this quaint and attractive complex one may confirm the time warp illusion by strolling through the old world elegance of Spout Lane and School House Square to visit the craft shops. Our own cricket ground with thatched pavilion can be hired, and there is crown green bowling. Other amenities include conference rooms and a licensed pavilion. Golf (two miles) can be arranged. Short breaks are available – ring for further information.

THE BLUE ANCHOR,
68 Main Street, Bolton-le-Sands, Carnforth,
Lancashire LA5 8DN

Tel: 01524 823241
Fax: 01524 824745

4 bedrooms, all with private bathroom; Mitchells House with real ale; Historic interest; Children and pets welcome; Bar and restaurant meals; Non-smoking areas; Lancaster 4 miles; S£, D£££.

This sturdy stone-built inn makes an ideal base for those wishing to explore both the Lake District and the seaside attractions of Morecambe and the North West coast, situated as it is in the picturesque village of Bolton-le-Sands, with easy access from the M6 motorway. The cosy, freshly decorated bedrooms all have private facilities, colour television, tea/coffee makers and hairdryers, making a stay here, however long or short, a real pleasure. Those seeking refreshment will find their needs amply met by the extensive bar menu available each lunchtime and evening, with a good value table d'hôte menu providing additional choice. 🍺🍺🍺

When making enquiries or bookings,
a stamped addressed envelope is always appreciated.

MOORCOCK INN,
Waddington, Near Clitheroe,
Lancashire BB7 3AA

Tel: 01200 422333
Fax: 01200 429184

*11 bedrooms, all with private bathroom; Free House with real ale; Historic interest;
Children welcome, no pets in public rooms; Bar meals, restaurant Sat./Sun. only;
Non-smoking areas; Clitheroe 2 miles; S£££, D££.*

The imposing facade of this distinguished inn with its panoramic views of the Ribble Valley, hides many attributes, from its welcoming atmosphere reflected in gleaming copper, oak beams and fresh flowers to its wide range of uncomplicated, freshly-prepared dishes, all of which are competitively priced. Being near to the famed Trough of Bowland, the inn is justly popular with walkers of fell and forest, both activities which generate keen appetites. There can be no higher recommendation. To cater for discerning guests to this scenic and historic area, this fine hostelry has eleven splendid double/twin rooms with private facilities, television and tea and coffee-makers. *ETC* ★★ *Hotel.*

THE STRAWBURY DUCK HOTEL,
Overshores Road, Entwistle, Near Bolton,
Lancashire BL7 0LU

Tel: 01204 852013

*4 bedrooms, all with private bathroom; Free House with real ale; Historic interest; Children welcome;
Excellent food (closed Monday lunchtime except Bank Holidays and peak summer period);
Non-smoking areas; Manchester 10 miles; S££, D£.*

Small and cosy and bursting with old-fashioned charm, this welcoming free house sits comfortably by the Manchester/Blackburn railway line and offers four nicely furnished guest bedrooms to the weary traveller, three with four-poster bed and all with full en suite facilities and tea/coffee making. Bar fare ranges from sandwiches to genuine Aberdeen Angus steaks served on a hot sizzle plate. Also a choice of vegetarian dishes and a wide range of authentic Indian and Balti cuisine. Pub renowned for fine selection of hand-drawn real ales (weekly guest beers). **See also Colour Advertisement on p 5.**

SCALE HALL FARMHOUSE TAVERN,
Morecambe Road, Lancaster,
Lancashire LA1 5JB

Tel: 01524 69255

*5 bedrooms, all with private bathroom; Free House with real ale; Historic interest;
Children and pets welcome; Bar meals; Non-smoking areas; Morecambe 1 mile; S£££, D£.*

Built as a farmhouse some three-and-a-half centuries ago, Scale Hall has a fascinating history involving all the trials and tribulations of the Civil War that can be traced through its oak panelling, antique furniture and artifacts. There is a hidden hiding place dating from the reformation and legend also claims the existence of a secret tunnel leading to Lancaster Castle. The Farmhouse Tavern with its well-stocked bars and individual furnishings, has several unusual features with much of the woodwork culled from a German luxury liner decommissioned around the turn of the century. Splendid farmhouse-style English cooking dominates the comprehensive menu and there is a newly refurbished bedroom wing to serve overnight guests. ♛♛♛, *RAC.*

CARTFORD COUNTRY INN AND HOTEL,
Cartford Lane, Little Eccleston, Preston,
Lancashire PR3 0YP

Tel: 01995 670166
Fax: 01995 671785

6 bedrooms, all with private bathroom; Free House with real ale; Historic interest;
Children and pets welcome; Bar meals; Non-smoking areas; Blackpool 9 miles; ££.

This sturdy, white-painted inn stands guard by the toll bridge over the River Wyre, and offers a warm welcome and the opportunity to indulge in traditional country pursuits. Those in search of bright lights need only travel 15 minutes to find Blackpool's golden sands, while the lovely Lake District can be reached in less than one hour. Cosy en suite bedrooms with colour television and tea making facilities offer overnight accommodation to those wishing to take advantage of this convenient location. A good bar menu offers all the traditional favourites, plus blackboard specials and a range of curries and pizzas. The inn now hosts the Hart Brewery, the only brewery on the Fylde. ♛♛♛ *Approved, CAMRA.*

Leicestershire
including Rutland

THE BRANT INN,
The Brantings, Near Groby,
Leicestershire LE6 0DU

Tel: 0116 287 2703
Fax: 0116 287 5292
e-mail: hotel@brantinn.co.uk

8 bedrooms; Everards House; Children welcome; Bar and restaurant meals;
Non-smoking areas; Leicester 5 miles; S£/£££, D££/££££.

A traditional country inn and hotel in an idyllic rural setting, the stylish Brant Inn has three congenial bars, all of different character, where good meals are served at lunchtimes and in the evenings. The attractive restaurant features a wide variery of dishes to suit all tastes, as does a comprehensive à la carte selection. A special children's menu is also available. The inn is conveniently placed just four miles south of Junction 22 of the M1 and on the A50 only minutes away from the centre of Leicester. Fully en suite bedrooms await overnight guests, all with colour television, direct-dial telephone, alarm-call facilities, tea-makers and hairdryers.

THE OLD BARN INN,
St Andrew's Lane, Glooston, Market Harborough,
Leicestershire LE16 7ST

Tel and Fax: 01858 545215

2 bedrooms, both with private bathroom; Free House with real ale; Historic interest; Children
welcome; Bar and restaurant meals; Non-smoking areas; Market Harborough 6 miles; S£££, D££££.

Where better to escape the cares and cacophony of the urban world than this rural 16th century inn? In tranquil countryside close to Rutland Water, an area steeped in history, this visually attractive retreat specialises in good, quality food, freshly cooked, whether in the (non-smoking) restaurant or the oak-beamed bar where a log fire burns in winter. Real ales are served and one may savour one's choice without the intrusion of piped music or passing traffic. Comfortable overnight accommodation is available, rooms having a shower en suite, wc, colour television, hairdryer, trouser press and tea and coffee-making facilities. ♛♛ *Commended, Which? Good Pub Guide.*

THE GEORGE AT GREAT OXENDON,
Great Oxendon, Market Harborough,
Leicestershire LE16 8NA

Tel and Fax: 01858 465205

*3 bedrooms, all with private bathroom; Free House with real ale; Historic interest;
Children and pets welcome; Bar and restaurant meals (not Sun. evenings); Non-smoking areas;
Leicester 20 miles, Northampton 18; S££££, D££££.*

Attracting first by its lovely setting and then by its traditional ambience and first-rate facilities, this true and typical English wayside inn is a real find. Colourful gardens cosset this part-16th century hostelry and, on entering, visual delight will soon give way to delight of a practical nature as one relaxes with a pint of real ale or seeks more substantial fare in the cosy, candlelit restaurant, meals being cooked to order, including vegetarian dishes. The surrounding green Leicestershire countryside holds many relatively undiscovered pleasures, so why not stay awhile? Superb en suite accommodation is available in a new purpose-built wing. ♛♛♛ *Commended.*

THE NEVILL ARMS,
12 Waterfall Way, Medbourne,
Leicestershire LE16 8EE

Tel: 01858 565288
Fax: 01858 565509

*8 bedrooms, all with private bathroom; Free House with real ale; Children welcome; Bar meals;
Non-smoking areas; Market Harborough 6 miles; S£££, D££££.*

This attractive little house, off the beaten track in one of Leicestershire's most picturesque villages, has a charm all its own. It stands in the peaceful Welland Valley alongside a tinkling stream, in summer the habitat of ducks, doves and (no doubt!) tiddlers. The heavily-beamed bar with its great inglenook fireplace in which log fires blaze a welcome in winter months, is sheer delight and there is always a range of tempting bar snacks and real ales available. For those wishing to linger awhile in this delightful spot, full en suite accommodation is offered in a comfortable and pretty cottage wing, all rooms having colour television, radio and tea and coffee tray. An understated wayside gem.

THE EXETER ARMS,
Wakerley, Oakham,
Rutland LE15 8PA

Tel: 01572 747817
Fax: 01572 747100

*5 bedrooms, all with private bathroom; Free House with real ale; Historic interest;
Children and pets welcome; Bar meals (not Mon.); Stamford 7 miles; S££, D£.*

Welcome back Rutland (although we know you never went away!) and welcome also to this homely inn set in the picturesque Welland Valley with Rockingham Forest harbouring a host of interesting walks. Burghley House and Rockingham Castle are nearby as is Rutland Water, Europe's largest man-made lake which offers-excellent fishing, sailing and bird watching. Good wholesome fare is available at prices that represent real value for money. A newly-renovated annexe provides attractive accommodation with all rooms having en suite facilities, colour television, tea/coffee-makers and central heating. This is a quiet and well-run hostelry ideal for a break that is just that little bit different. *CAMRA.*

FHG PUBLICATIONS

publish a large range of well-known accommodation guides. We will be happy to send you details or you can use the order form at the back of this book.

KING'S ARMS INN,
Top Street, Wing,
Rutland LE15 8SE

Tel: 01572 737634; Fax: 01572 737255
e-mail: enquiries@thekingsarms-wing.co.uk
website: www.thekingsarms-wing.co.uk

8 bedrooms, all with private bathroom; Free House with real ale; Historic interest; Children welcome;
Bar and restaurant meals; Non-smoking areas; Oakham 4 miles; S££, D££.

A pride of England's smallest county now properly restored to the fold (although residents insist it never went away!), this homely, 350-year-old inn run by Neil and Karen Hornsby, lies just two miles from man-made Rutland Water and within 8 miles of the historic towns of Oakham, Uppingham and Stamford. Recognised for the high quality of its food, service and accommodation, the hostelry has considerable old-world appeal in its beamed bar and hidey-hole nooks and crannies and where a log fire thwarts winter chill. Locally brewed real ales prove justly popular and one may eat informally in the bar or, in more regal state, in the restaurant having chosen from the list of appetising and reasonably priced 'blackboard specials'. As a palate prompter, just consider Smoked Salmon, Ricotta Cheese and Prawn Coronets, served with a Marie Rose Dressing as a starter, followed by Roast Guinea Fowl on cidered Spinach with a Dijon Cream Dressing and one of a selection of delicious home-made desserts – all for under £20. Magnificent value! Accommodation in the inn itself or in the recently acquired Old Bakehouse opposite is delightfully furnished in rich fabrics and appointed with en suite baths and showers, colour television, radio alarm clock, telephone, hair dryer and tea and coffee hospitality tray. AA ◆◆◆

Lincolnshire

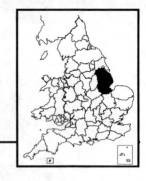

THE CHEQUERS,
Woolsthorpe-by-Belvoir, Grantham, Lincolnshire NG32 1LU

Tel: 01476 870701
Fax: 01476 870085

4 bedrooms, all with private bathroom; Free House with real ale; Historic interest; Pets welcome; Bar meals, restaurant evenings only (not Sun); Non-smoking areas; Grantham 5 miles; S£££, D££.

On the borders of Lincolnshire and Leicestershire and only a mile or so from Belvoir (pronounced 'Beever') Castle, this popular pub with a notable restaurant, is surrounded by open countryside. Summer barbecues and a variety of games may be enjoyed in a large garden and adjoining cricket field. The varied à la carte menu, based on French and old-English recipes, changes with the seasons and bar snacks are always available. Regular jazz nights held twice a month are a new and popular feature at this delightful country hostelry run by Nick and Yoanna Potter. A stable block has been converted to provide four well-appointed letting rooms with en suite facilities and there are plans afoot to build more accommodation overlooking the cricket field.

GEORGE HOTEL,
Leadenham, Lincolnshire LN5 0PN

Tel: 01400 272251
Fax: 01400 272091

7 bedrooms, 4 with private bathroom; Free House with real ale; Historic interest; Children and pets welcome; Bar and restaurant meals; Sleaford 8 miles; S£, D£.

A homely atmosphere and reputation for fine food served in the Tudor Restaurant makes this worthy little country hotel a haven for tourist and holidaymaker alike. It is situated on the A17 midway between Newark and Sleaford, just 8 miles from the A1. Appetising bar food awaits at lunchtime and evening daily, and the aptly named Scotch Lounge features around 500 different whiskies from all over the world as well as numerous draught beers. Accommodation for overnight guests is housed in a quiet cottage behind the inn and the reasonable charge for a comfortably furnished room with television and tea-maker includes a substantial English breakfast. Some rooms with en suite facilities are available. ♕♕♕, *Les Routiers.*

THE MARQUIS OF GRANBY,
High Street, Wellingore, Lincoln, Lincolnshire LN5 0HW

Tel: 01522 810442
Fax: 01522 810740

7 bedrooms, all with private bathroom; Free House with real ale; Historic interest; Children and pets welcome; Bar and restaurant meals; Lincoln 9 miles; S£, D£

Equidistant from Lincoln, Sleaford, Newark and Grantham, this friendly and go-ahead hostelry attracts a healthy business clientele as well as discerning tourists. In fact, this is a great place to stay; all rooms have private facilities, colour television and tea and coffee-makers and the reasonable terms include a full English breakfast. Also offering excellent value for money are the dishes featured on an expansive menu with daily 'specials' also available. Friday is very much 'fish day' with an appetising range of fresh produce on offer at lunchtime and in the evening. Traditional roasts served each Sunday lunchtime prove extremely popular.

LEA GATE INN,
Lea Gate Road, Coningsby,
Lincolnshire LN4 4RS

Tel: 01526 342370; Fax: 01526 345468
e-mail: markdennison4@virgin.net
website: www.leagateinn.co.uk

8 bedrooms, all with private bathroom; Free House with real ale; Historic interest; Children welcome; Bar meals, restaurant evenings only; Non-smoking areas; Woodhall Spa 4 miles; S£££, D££.

Dating from 1542 and with its ancient timbers, open fireplaces and secret recesses exuding an atmosphere absorbed through centuries of care and comfort for the weary traveller of the fens, this fine old inn is traditional personified. The treacherous bogs and marshes have been tamed and the gallows that used to cast its grim shadow at the front of the inn has not been employed for years. It is said that the 'Last Supper' engraving over the fireplace in the main lounge was where last rites were given to condemned souls; this same fireplace featuring a priests' hole where Roman Catholic priests hid from Cromwell and his Roundhead soldiers. But cast gloom aside, for today this historically fascinating hostelry extends the most cheerful of welcomes from hosts, Mark and Sharon Dennison, and a new hotel extension is planned for early 2000. One may still enjoy honest ale from the cask and the most appetising fare, including imaginative vegetarian dishes, which are served in a comfortable restaurant transformed some time ago from an old barn. Meals are served all week at lunchtimes and in the evenings and families are catered for. The inn stands in lovely gardens where children may play safely whilst their parents relax. A recommended wayside inn of great charm

SKIPWORTH ARMS,
Station Road, Moortown, Market Rasen,
Lincolnshire LN7 6HZ
Tel & Fax: 01472 851770

3 bedrooms; Free House with real ale; Children and pets welcome; Bar and restaurant meals;
Non-smoking areas; Market Rasen 8 miles; S£, D£.

An unpretentious pub and restaurant on the winding B1205 a few miles north of Market Rasen, the Skipworth Arms, nevertheless, has all the qualities of a highly regarded wayside inn. One may call in for a light snack or a full three-course meal at the most reasonable prices and seek diversion playing darts or pool in the games room. Dyed-in-the-wool anglers are also drawn to this little hostelry for there is a ¾-acre lake stocked with carp, tench, rudd and bream at the rear of the property, with day tickets available. Bed and Breakfast terms also offer excellent value. The inn also operates an adjacent 4½ acre caravan site.

FINCH HATTON ARMS HOTEL,
43 Main Street, Ewerby, Sleaford,
Lincolnshire NG34 9PH
Tel: 01529 460363
Fax: 01529 461703

8 bedrooms, all with private bathroom; Free House with real ale; Historic interest; Children welcome;
pets by arrangement; Bar and restaurant meals; Non-smoking areas; Sleaford 4 miles; S£££, D££

This is something of a surprise – a fully equipped small hotel of some distinction in a picturesque little village, if not in the middle of nowhere, then precious near to it! Its success is due, in no small part, to its attractive Tudor-style bar and restaurant where traditional ales and an imaginative menu draw custom from nearby Sleaford and even Newark, Grantham, Boston and Lincoln to prove the proposition that value for money is a sure winner. The hotel wing provides first-class overnight accommodation, each room having a bath/shower en suite, remote-control colour television, direct-dial telephone and tea and coffee-making facilities and there is the promise of a hearty English breakfast in the morning. *Tourist Board Listed.*

THE OLDE FARMHOUSE HOTEL,
Immingham Road, Stallingborough,
Lincolnshire DN41 8PB
Tel and Fax: 01469 560159

7 bedrooms, all with private bathroom; Free House with real ale; Children and pets welcome;
Bar meals, restaurant evenings only; Grimsby 5 miles; S££, D££££.

This large and attractively decorated wayside hostelry with its associated Schofield's Restaurant, provides all the requisites and more for a refreshing break with the assurance of splendid, freshly-prepared food and superb en suite accommodation, ideal for those seeking a quiet holiday away from urban strife. Warmed in cool weather by open-hearth coal fires, spacious and convivial bars offer a wide selection of drinks, 'blackboard special' meals and snacks. For serious dining, the neat and tidy Schofield's Restaurant supplies appetising à la carte fare, including vegetarian dishes and Sunday lunches. Within easy distance of both Immingham and Grimsby, the hotel is popular with business folk for whom meeting facilities are available.

Norfolk

SPREAD EAGLE COUNTRY INN,
Church Road, Barton Bendish, King's Lynn,
Norfolk PE33 9DP

Tel: 01366 347295
Fax: 01366 347995
mobile: 07808 906201

e-mail: seagle.barton@virgin.net website: http//:freespace.virgin.net/seagle.barton/

3 bedrooms; Real ales; Well-behaved children and pets by arrangement; Bar and restaurant meals; Non-smoking areas; Swaffham 5 miles; S£, D£.

This true country inn, run personally by the Gransden family for the past six years, stands in the centre of a quiet, picturesque, old village, in a large, well-stocked garden with customer seating. Barton Bendish lies south of RAF Marham off the A1122, with Swaffham and Downham just six miles away. There is a mainline station at Downham, with Cambridge half-an-hour by train. King's Lynn and beyond, Sandringham and the unspoilt Norfolk coast are a 30 minute drive away. Bedrooms (double en suite and twins with bathroom close by) are well-furnished with television, tea-making facilities, etc. The two restaurants, one non-smoking, serve excellent home-cooked food; real ales and other drinks are available in the bar, which has a log fire. Open all year.

FEATHERS HOTEL,
Manor Road, Dersingham, King's Lynn,
Norfolk PE31 6LN

Tel & Fax: 01485 540207

5 bedrooms, all with private bathroom; Punch Taverns House with real ale; Historic interest; Children and pets welcome; Bar and restaurant meals (evenings only); Hunstanton 7 miles; S££, D££.

In the gently undulating countryside of north-west Norfolk, this solid and welcoming stone-built inn stands on the fringe of Sandringham Estate, one of the Queen's favourite country homes. While not claiming to compete with that offered to Her Majesty, the Feathers provides comfortable and reasonably priced en suite accommodation with bedrooms simply furnished in the modern style and each having colour television. Real ale is served in the two popular bars, the Saddle Room and the Sandringham, and a right royal cuisine is provided with both à la carte and table d'hôte menus available. Well-tended gardens make a most pleasant setting for this attractive hostelry. *CAMRA*

THE HALF MOON INN,
Rushall, Near Diss,
Norfolk IP21 4QD

Tel & Fax: 01379 740793

10 bedrooms, 8 with private bathroom; Free House with real ale; Historic interest; Children welcome; Bar and restaurant meals; Non-smoking areas; Harleston 3 miles; S£, D££££.

This 16th century coaching inn offers a warm welcome to business guests and holidaymakers alike. Seven bedrooms are in modern chalet-style accommodation, and the remainder are in the inn which has a wealth of exposed beams. Bedrooms have colour television and tea and coffee making facilities. An excellent selection of home-cooked meals are available and reservations may be made in the conservatory dining area. The bar offers a range of real ales and a good value wine list is available. The friendly atmosphere, reasonably priced accommodation and delightful rural location combine to make this an excellent base for visiting East Anglia. *South Norfolk Council Gold Award Winner 98/99.*

THE BOAR INN,
Great Ryburgh, Fakenham,
Norfolk NR21 0DX

Tel: 01328 829212

5 bedrooms, all with private bathroom; Free House with real ale; Children welcome; Bar and restaurant meals; Non-smoking areas; Fakenham 3 miles; S££, D£.

The Boar is a 300-year-old village inn and restaurant in a small village in the heart of Norfolk, convenient for the coast, Norwich and the Broads. 1998 has seen the completion of improvement at The Boar to ETB Two Crowns standard, with all guest bedrooms now having full en suite facilities, as well as television, tea/coffee making etc. With a choice of meals from our extensive bar and restaurant menu, a new games room and friendly bar, you need never leave The Boar at all (but we suggest you do, to discover the delights of Norfolk and its glorious coastline).

THE JOHN H. STRACEY,
West End, Briston, Melton Constable,
Norfolk NR24 2JA

Tel: 01263 860891

3 bedrooms, 1 with private bathroom; Free House with real ale; Historic interest; Children welcome; Bar and restaurant meals; Holt 4 miles; £.

Named after a local lad who found fame in the boxing ring a few years ago, this fine old inn, in fact, dates from the 16th century when it was a staging post on the Wells to Norwich road. We were captivated by the time-honoured ambience exuded by its low ceilings, oak beams and copper knick-knacks reflecting the glow of a welcoming log fire. The old hostelry used to be called the Three Horseshoes and synonymous with the change of name, the stables were converted into a splendid, well-patronised restaurant known for its wholesome, home-cooked fare. This is a place of infinite character in tranquil, rural Norfolk with the coast within easy reach. *Les Routiers.*

THE PLOUGH INN,
Norwich Road, Marsham,
Norfolk NR10 5PN

Tel: 01263 735000

10 bedrooms, all with private bathroom; Free House with real ale; Historic interest; Children welcome, pets by arrangement; Bar and restaurant meals; Non-smoking areas; Aylsham 2 miles; S££, D£.

Within easy reach of the Broads and the resorts of Cromer and Sheringham, the well-appointed Plough Inn will appeal to the lover of outdoor pursuits and the tranquil way of life. This is good terrain for unexacting country walks and for the fishing enthusiast there are several lakes and rivers offering excellent sport. A ride on the Bure Valley Narrow Gauge Railway through the peaceful Norfolk countryside is another attraction. For a place to stay, one need look no further than this first-class coaching inn, free house and restaurant where resident owners, Stephen and Carole Yates, extend the warmest of welcomes to guests. The cuisine is of the highest calibre and accommodation comprises handsomely equipped en suite guest rooms.

CROWN HOTEL,
Crown Road, Mundford, Thetford,
Norfolk IP26 5HQ

Tel: 01842 878233
Fax: 01842 878982

22 bedrooms, 16 with private bathroom; Free House with real ale; Historic interest; Children and pets welcome; Bar and restaurant meals; Thetford 8 miles; S££, D££.

This is a traditional Norfolk inn dating back to 1652 that has performed many roles over the years, having been, in turn, a renowned hunting inn and magistrates court whilst, until recently, the restaurant was used as a doctor's waiting room. Revered on account of its good, old-fashioned hospitality, the Crown has many facets that demand attention. Sustenance comes in a variety of forms; wholesome pub fare served in the congenial Squire's and Village Bars, daily 'blackboard specials' and a regularly changed à la carte menu in the characterful Old Court Restaurant. For a quiet country holiday or even a brief visit, the hostelry has much to recommend it with comfortable accommodation of a high standard available.

MARSHAM ARMS FREEHOUSE & INN,
Holt Road, Hevingham, Norwich,
Norfolk NR10 5NP

Tel: 01603 754268
Fax: 01603 754839

8 bedrooms, all with private bathroom; Free House with real ale; Historic interest; Children welcome; Bar and restaurant meals; Non-smoking areas; Norwich 8 miles; £££.

For the taste of traditional English home-cooking in the heart of the East Anglian countryside, this well-loved Victorian hostelry has a peerless reputation. Dishes are cooked to order and prices reflect good value. A popular feature is the Salad Bar where diners may choose from no less than 16 chill-fresh salads from Tabbouleh to Oriental Mushroom. A spacious bar with beams and a large open fireplace has infinite character and there a variety of snacks and an interesting selection of beers may be enjoyed. Delightfully decorated rooms await the overnight guest, with private bath and shower, television, radio, direct-dial telephone, intercom and tea-making facilities. Recently introduced is a specially equipped conference suite. ♚♚♚ *Commended.*

THE SWAN,
Branden Road, Hilborough, Thetford,
Norfolk IP26 5BW

Tel: 01760 756380

2 bedrooms; Free House with real ale; Children welcome; Bar and restaurant meals; Swaffham 6 miles; £.

Here in rural Norfolk, unspoilt, peaceful and a real tonic for the city dweller, this unpretentious 18th Century Coaching Inn on the A1065 between Swaffham and Mundford, is well worth a visit to re-establish values frequently forgotten. Traditional ales, log fires, delicious home cooked food and a warm welcome from Licensee, Eddie Ball, will soon set the world to rights. There are plenty of diversions of a pastoral nature in the pretty Breckland area, so why not stay for a night or two. Excellent, if limited, accommodation is obtainable at very moderate cost with evening meals available in the bar or restaurant.

THE THREE HORSESHOES INN,
Main Road, Titchwell, Near Brancaster,
Norfolk PE31 8BB

Tel: 01485 210202

6 bedrooms, all with private bathroom; Free House with real ale; Children over 5 years and pets welcome; Bar and restaurant meals; Non-smoking areas; Hunstanton 5 miles; S££, D£.

On the A149 coast road between Hunstanton and Wells, this traditional inn will appeal to walkers, cyclists and all those interested in the quieter side of life; in particular it attracts birdwatchers for it overlooks the RSPB Titchwell Marsh Bird Reserve, probably the premier reserve in the UK. Background classical music is played; a log fire adds cheer in winter and there is a pleasant garden and paddock area overlooking the sea. An excellent selection of home-cooked food is served in a non-smoking dining room or either of the bars. Several en suite rooms are fully equipped with king size beds, colour television, radio alarm, tea and coffee making facilities and hairdryers. Some bedrooms have sea views. This is an area of outstanding natural beauty, ideal for birdwatching, walking, sailing or golf. *ETC* ♦♦♦.

Northamptonshire

THE FALCON HOTEL,
Castle Ashby,
Northamptonshire NN7 1LF

Tel: 01604 696200
Fax: 01604 696673

16 bedrooms; Historic interest; Wellingborough 6 miles; S££££, D££££.

The Falcon Hotel is on the estate of the Marquess of Northampton who lets it to resident proprietors Michael and Jennifer Eastwick on some kind of feudal arrangement known only to marquesses. The Falcon is a magnificent inn and is four hundred years old, though as Michael points out there's no-one around to disprove it. It started life as a farm, then got mixed up in religious pop festivals and now has the Silverstone motor racing circuit within handy distance. If this sounds pretty mixed up, don't wait up at night to see Arthur the ghost. Michael invented him. Michael and Jennifer organise painting weekends, though this is not believed to be a way of getting guests to decorate their own bedrooms. **See also Colour Advertisement on page 5.**

THE WHITE SWAN,
Seaton Road, Harringworth, Corby,
Northamptonshire NN17 3AF

Tel: 01572 747543
Fax: 01572 747323

6 bedrooms, all with private bathroom; Free House with real ale; Historic interest; Children welcome; Bar and restaurant meals; Non-smoking areas; Corby 6 miles; S£££, D££.

Harringworth is one of the prettiest villages in the Rockingham Forest area and contributing to the scene, this 15th century coaching inn will certainly repay a visit for a break in a relatively unexplored part of rural England. Rutland Water is just 6 miles away and there are numerous stately homes and picturesque market towns within easy reach. An oak, hand-carved bar offering a range of real ales is decorated with interesting memorabilia, and excellent meals are served in an attractive dining room. The inn has country-style bedrooms, all en suite and with colour television, radio alarm, hairdryer and tea and coffee making facilities. All are centrally heated. ♛♛♛ *Commended, The Circle.*

THE RED LION HOTEL,
East Haddon,
Northamptonshire NN6 8BU

Tel: 01604 770223
Fax: 01604 770767

5 bedrooms; Traditional House with real ale; Historic interest; Children welcome; Bar and restaurant meals; Northampton 8 miles; S££££, D£££.

This traditional, stone-built inn sits snugly in the charming village of East Haddon, just seven miles from Junction 18 on the M1 and eight miles from Northampton. Leisure facilities in the area are excellent – golf, fishing, squash, swimming and snooker are all available locally. Those wishing to make the most of a relaxing weekend break will find comfortable, spick-and-span bedrooms with full en suite facilities, television, etc. Good English cooking is the basis of the carefully balanced à la carte menu and a comprehensive range of gourmet bar food is available at lunchtime and in the evening. Lighter appetites are well catered for in the brass and copper bedecked bars, with a tasty range of gourmet bar food, accompanied by one's choice from the well-kept ales, beers, wines and other refreshments. *Egon Ronay, Good Food Guide.* **See also Colour Advertisement on page 5.**

THE BENEFIELD WHEATSHEAF HOTEL,
Upper Benefield, Oundle,
Northamptonshire PE8 5AN

Tel: 01832 205254
Fax: 01832 205245

9 bedrooms, all with private bathroom; Free House with real ale, Historic interest; Children welcome;
Bar lunches, restaurant meals; Peterborough 12 miles; ££££.

Amidst rolling countryside, this hospitable house is just the place to stop for excellent refreshment. On the A427 between Corby and Oundle, it is hardly in a tourist-infested area but it is all the better for it, promoting that wonderful feeling of discovery that we, ourselves, felt. What is perhaps surprising is the range and quality of the food served in the obviously popular Garden Bistro and Regency Dining Rooms and the wide selection of wines and real ales. The time will come to move on—reluctantly. But why not stay? There is first-rate accommodation available, all rooms having en suite facilities and the amenities of a vaunted country hotel. No wonder businessmen from Stamford and Peterborough find this well-run hostelry so attractive.

THE GLOBE HOTEL
High Street, Weedon, Northampton,
Northamptonshire NN7 4QD

Tel: 01327 340336
Fax: 01327 349058

18 bedrooms, all with private bathroom; Free House; Historic interest;
Bar and restaurant meals; Non-smoking areas; Daventry 4 miles; ££.

Weedon Village, at the very heart of England, was for many years a cavalry training centre, particularly during the Napoleonic Wars. The Globe itself dates from that time and has been totally refurbished by Peter and Penny Walton to a most comfortable standard, whilst still retaining its historic character. All 18 rooms are fully equipped and are en suite. We offer a Weekend Giveaway Break Bed and Breakfast rate of only £22.50 per person per night (double). Situated on the crossroads of the A5/A45, three miles west of Junction 16 of the M1, within easy touring distance of Warwick Castle, Leamington Spa, Stratford-upon-Avon, Naseby Battlefield, Althorp House (Princess Diana's ancestral home), Stoke Bruerne Waterways Centre and Museum, and Silverstone Grand Prix Circuit. Our comprehensive food operation OPEN ALL DAY features a home fayre bar meals menu, pies (our speciality) and a value-for-money à la carte menu. Send for our free tour and information pack. ✿✿✿✿ *Commended, RAC**.*

The £ symbol when appearing at the end of the italic section of an entry shows the anticipated price, during 2000, for full Bed and Breakfast.

Normal Bed & Breakfast rate per person
(in single room)

Normal Bed & Breakfast rate per person
(sharing double/twin room)

PRICE RANGE	CATEGORY	PRICE RANGE	CATEGORY
Under £25	S£	**Under £25**	D£
£26-£35	S££	**£26-£35**	D££
£36-£45	S£££	**£36-£45**	D£££
Over £45	S££££	**Over £45**	D££££

This is meant as an indication only and does not show prices for Special Breaks, Weekends, etc. Guests are therefore advised to verify all prices on enquiring or booking.

Northumberland

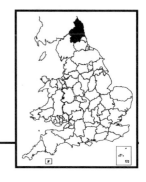

THE COTTAGE INN,
Dunstan Village, Craster, Alnwick,
Northumberland NE66 3SZ

Tel: 01665 576658
Fax: 01665 576788

10 bedrooms, all with private bathroom; Free House with real ale; Children welcome; Bar meals, restaurant evenings only plus Sun. lunch; Non-smoking areas; Alnwick 4 miles; S££, D££.

Unspoiled Northumberland has something for everyone, whether your idea of a good holiday is strolling along an uncrowded sandy beach, visiting historic castles, or enjoying a wide range of leisure activities such as golf, watersports, fishing or even parachute jumping. And if your idea of relaxation is to do absolutely nothing, then this is the ideal place to do it! Just a few minutes from the coast, the Cottage Inn offers a friendly welcome and comfortable accommodation, all bedrooms having bath and shower, television, tea and coffee tray, and telephone. The fully licensed Harry Hotspur Restaurant provides first-rate food in a most delightful setting, with meals also available in the beamed bar and in the airy conservatory. *ETB* ◆◆◆, *AA, Les Routiers.*

THE VICTORIA HOTEL,
Front Street, Bamburgh,
Northumberland NE69 7BP

Tel: 01668 214431
Fax: 01668 214404

30 bedrooms, all with private bathroom; Free House with real ale; Historic interest; Children and pets welcome; Bar meals, restaurant evenings only, plus Sun. lunch' Non-smoking areas; Belford 5 miles; S£££, D££.

The Victoria Hotel overlooks the village green in the heart of historic Bamburgh, resting place of heroine, Grace Darling. Dominated by its magnificent castle and miles of sandy beach, with Holy Island and the Farnes seen from its ramparts. This fine stone building has been sympathetically renovated and upgraded by its new owners. All 30 bedrooms are individually named and are en suite, with co-ordinating fabrics and furniture. Our stylish brasserie offers innovative cuisine using fresh local produce. Open all year. You are assured of a welcome that is both personal and genuine in this refreshingly different environment. *AA** and Rosette, Consort/Best Western Hotel.*

BATTLESTEADS HOTEL,
Wark, Near Hexham,
Northumberland NE48 3LS

Tel: 01434 230209; Fax: 01434 230730
e-mail: info@battlesteads-hotel.co.uk
website: www.battlesteads-hotel.co.uk

10 bedrooms; Free House with real ale; Historic interest; Children and pets welcome; Bar and restaurant meals; Non-smoking areas; Bellingham 4 miles; S££, D£

Well-placed for those wishing to visit unspoilt Northumberland is this comfortable little hotel offering service which is both friendly and efficient. This is a perfect place to enjoy a glass of good beer and a tasty meal in the restaurant or friendly bar, with a pleasant garden and views of the surrounding countryside. The en suite bedrooms are well appointed and spick and span, all having colour television and hairdryers. The hotel offers an excellent base for those wishing to visit Hadrian's Wall, the Kielder Reservoir and forest, historic houses and castles, and the nearby beauty spots and places of interest. ♛♛♛ *Commended.*

COOK AND BARKER INN,
Newton-on-the-Moor, Felton, Morpeth,
Northumberland NE65 9JY

Tel: 01665 575234

5 bedrooms, all with private bathroom; Free House with real ale; Historic interest; Children welcome; Bar meals, restaurant evenings only; Non-smoking areas; Alnwick 5 miles; A£££, D££.

Two families with historic associations with the village of Newton-on-the-Moor have given their names to this sturdily-built stone inn which lies just off the A1, offering a peaceful haven for business travellers and holidaymakers alike. With an excellent reputation locally – and indeed, farther afield (good news travels!), the creative kitchen brigade use only the best and freshest of ingredients to produce tempting à la carte menus; bar lunches are also available, and in finer weather can be enjoyed in the attractive beer garden. Accommodation is of an equally high standard, all the cosy bedrooms having en suite facilities, colour television, tea/coffee maker and trouser press as standard. Add to these virtues a friendly welcome and efficient service, and you have all the ingredients for a relaxing break. ♕♕♕ *Highly Commended.*

Nottinghamshire

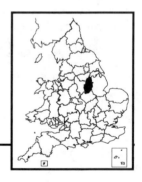

THE HOLE IN THE WALL
Main Road, Underwood,
Nottinghamshire NG16 5GQ

Tel: 01773 713936

12 bedrooms, all with private bathroom; Whitbread House with real ale; Historic interest; Children welcome; Restaurant meals; Non-smoking areas; Nottingham 11 miles; S££, D£££.

To find this sturdy roadside inn turn off the M1 at Junction 27 onto the A608 and then the B600 – well worth the detour if you are bored by motorway food (and horrified by the prices charged!). The original building, parts of which still stand, dates from the time of the English Civil War, and the name is thought to refer to damage inflicted then. Present-day travellers will find good food and good ale dispensed with cheerful efficiency. All the traditional favourites such as steak and kidney pie, fish and steaks find a place on the very reasonably priced menu, and are supplemented by daily specials. Those seeking overnight accommodation will find comfortable en suite single, double and twin rooms.

Oxfordshire

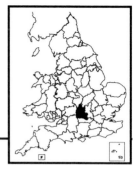

THE DOG HOUSE HOTEL,
Frilford Heath, Abingdon,
Oxfordshire OX13 6QJ

Tel: 01865 390830
Fax: 01865 390860
e-mail: doghouse@morland.co.uk

20 bedrooms, all with private bathroom; Morland House with real ale; Historic interest;
Children welcome; Bar and restaurant meals; Non-smoking areas; Oxford 6 miles; S£££££, D£££££.

It is seldom that one would claim to be delighted to be 'in the dog house', but when the establishment in question is this sturdy stone-built inn, a stay here is a privilege, not a punishment! The attractively furnished bedrooms, all en suite, offer a full range of facilities, and special Friday and Saturday rates make a weekend break a particularly attractive proposition. The Hotel Restaurant offers an extensive choice of menu with the emphasis very firmly on quality and professional service; meals can be enjoyed in the light and airy conservatory or in the bar, where a range of blackboard specials prove excellent value for money. The golfing enthusiast will be delighted to find two 18-hole golf courses almost next door.

THE INN FOR ALL SEASONS,
The Barringtons, Burford,
Oxfordshire OX18 4TN

Tel: 01451 84432; Fax: 01451 844375
e-mail: sharp@innforallseasons.com
website: www.innforallseasons.com

10 bedrooms, all with private bathroom; Free House with real ale; Historic interest; Children and pets
welcome; Bar and restaurant meals; Non-smoking areas; Witney 7 miles; S£££/££££, D£££.

If a visit to the beautiful Cotswolds area is among your plans, then this delightfully named establishment is sure to meet your every requirement, whether for accommodation on a longer stay, or for food and refreshment on a "day out". Thoughtful planning and an eye for detail have ensured that the modern facilities expected by today's traveller blend seamlessly with the original stone walls, sturdy beams and traditional furnishings of this former coaching inn. Private bathrooms, telephone and colour television come as standard in the elegant bedrooms, each of which enjoys views over the rolling countryside. A la carte and table d'hôte menus presented in the restaurant feature the finest local ingredients, and lighter appetites are well catered for in the friendly bar. 👑👑👑👑, *AA* and Rosette.*

THE ROMANY INN,
Bridge Street, Bampton,
Oxfordshire OX18 2HA

Tel: 01993 850237
Fax: 01993 852133

10 bedrooms, all with private bathroom; Free House with real ale; Historic interest;
Children and pets welcome; Bar and restaurant meals; Non-smoking areas; Witney 5 miles; S££, D£.

An attractive village known for its time-honoured Morris dancing, Bampton is a fine centre from which to explore the rural charms of the Cotswolds and this 17th century hostelry has all the qualities of a typical English wayside inn. As such, it makes a wonderful touring base with extensive menus providing solid sustenance and traditional beers pumped up from the Saxon cellars below. It is a cheerful place at all times of year: summer sees popular use made of the large secluded garden whilst, in winter, logs burn merrily in the open fireplace. Excellent en suite accommodation awaits overnight guests. *ETC/AA* ★★, *Good Beer Guide, Good Pub Guide.*

THE WHITE HART,
High Street, Dorchester-on-Thames,
Oxfordshire OX10 7HN

Tel: 01865 340074
Fax: 01865 341082

19 bedrooms, all with private bathroom; Free house with real ale; Children and pets welcome;
Bar and restaurant meals; Wallingford 4 miles; S££££, D£££.

A warm welcome awaits you at the White Hart, which is perfectly situated for exploring the South Oxfordshire countryside, yet only a short drive from Oxford, Henley, Marlow and Windsor. As one would expect from an ancient coaching inn, the hotel is rich in character with 19 individually styled rooms, some with four-posters and original beams, all with modern day amenities. A paradise for lovers of antiques, there is an abundance of choice close by and the area offers some of the finest riverside walks on this lovely stretch of the Thames. Our award-winning restaurant, "Hartes", offers an extensive menu and a diverse range of fine wines at very competitive prices. Comfort, warmth and good old-fashioned hospitality guaranteed all year round. *AA ** and Two Rosettes, RAC ***.*

SHEPHERDS HALL INN,
Witney Road, Freeland,
Oxfordshire OX8 8HQ

Tel: 01993 881256
Fax: 01993 883455

5 bedrooms, all with private bath or shower and toilet; Free House with real ale; Children welcome;
Bar food; Oxford 12 miles, Witney 4, Woodstock 4; S£, D£.

One of the finest houses for miles, the welcoming Shepherds Hall stands on the A4095 Woodstock to Witney road, in an area famed for its sheep rearing, hence its name. Rooms are now modernised, with colour television, direct-dial telephones and tea/coffee making facilities, yet retain the atmosphere of a true country inn, and proprietors Liz and David Fyson present a comprehensive selection of appetising meals and snacks in the bar every day. This is a good place to bring the family (perhaps after visiting Woodstock and Blenheim Palace) for there is an attractive beer garden and children's play area. Wholesome accommodation is available at reasonable rates and this includes a full English breakfast. 👑👑 *Commended*

THE WHITE HORSE,
Woolstone, Near Faringdon,
Oxfordshire SN7 7QL

Tel: 01367 820726
Fax: 01367 820566

6 bedrooms, all with private bathroom; Free House with real ale; Historic interest; Children welcome, pets by arrangement; Bar and restaurant meals; Non-smoking areas; Wantage 7 miles; S££££, D££.

The famous Uffington White Horse (Ancient Monument) has a good view of this quaint old hostelry which dates from the 16th century. Thomas Hughes, author of *Tom Brown's School Days* is said to have written his works here. The oak-beamed bar with its log fires and relaxed ambience is a convivial place in which to enjoy a glass of one's favourite tipple, maybe one of the 50-or so malt whiskies on offer or a pint of real ale. There is an extensive bar menu and for more formal dining there is an intimate à la carte restaurant. The verdant Vale of the White Horse holds many pleasures and treasures for the tourist and the inn has exceptionally well-appointed en suite accommodation available. *Tourist Board Listed Commended, AA ◆◆◆◆, RAC Highly Acclaimed.*

THE KING'S HEAD INN AND RESTAURANT,
Bledington, Near Kingham,
Oxfordshire OX7 6XQ

Tel: 01608 658365; Fax: 01608 658902
e-mail: kingshead@btinternet.com

12 bedrooms, all with private bathroom; Free House with real ale; Historic interest; Children welcome; Bar food, restaurant evenings only; Non-smoking areas; Stow-on-the-Wold 4 miles; S££££, D££.

Facing Bledington's village green with its brook and ducks stands the 15th century King's Head Inn, an establishment which has echoed with the sounds of convivial hospitality for over four centuries. Bledington nestles in the heart of the Cotswolds and is within easy reach of all top tourist attractions. The charming accommodation is in keeping with the atmosphere, all bedrooms (en suite) having television, telephone and hot drinks facilities. High quality and inventive bar fare is served, with full à la carte and table d'hôte menus in the award-winning restaurant in the evenings. A selection of real ales and interesting whiskies is served in the bar which has original old beams and an inglenook fireplace. ♛♛♛ *Commended, Egon Ronay *, AA QQQQ Selected, Good Pub Guide Dining County Pub of the Year, Logis.*

THE TOLLGATE INN AND RESTAURANT,
Church Street, Kingham,
Oxfordshire OX7 6YA

Tel: 01608 658389
Fax: 01608 659467

10 bedrooms, all with private bathroom; Free House; Historic interest; Children and pets welcome; Bar and restaurant meals; Non-smoking areas; Chipping Norton 4 miles; S£££/££££, D££££.

Originally a Georgian farmhouse built about 1750, this delightful little hotel has recently undergone complete refurbishment to provide two splendid inter-communicating bars and an attractive restaurant on the ground floor whilst, upstairs, new en suite bedrooms, remarkable for their tasteful furnishings and fabrics, present a harmony of colour: each room has colour television and direct-dial telephone. Dining in informal style is a special pleasure, the dishes featuring fresh seasonal ingredients and being well supported by an interesting wine list. With cool weather thwarted by the cheerful crackle of log fires, the bars also sport a tasty snack menu. Kingham is a picturesque Cotswold village and the inn makes a fine touring base. *AA Two Rosettes, Johansens.*

CRAZY BEAR HOTEL,
Bear Lane, Stadhampton,
Oxfordshire OX44 7UR

Tel: 01865 890714
Fax: 01865 400481

7 bedrooms and two private cottages, all with private bathroom; Free House with real ale; Historic interest; Children welcome; Bar and restaurant meals; Non-smoking areas; Wallingford 6 miles; S££££, D££££.

Built in the early part of the 16th century, this remarkable hotel and restaurant was completely refurbished between 1993 and 1996 and now comprises a most attractive bar, restaurant, a brasserie, and a number of superbly-appointed en suite bedrooms. An exciting and romantic weekend location, this delightfully decorated pleasure complex is only 45 minutes from London and 10 minutes from the dreaming spires of Oxford. The bar is a meeting place of inspired moods from the flamboyant to the snugly intimate; attractive colours predominate, the à la carte restaurant offering an unrivalled selection of classic and creative dishes supported by an exhilarating wine list. An imaginatively designed and innovative brochure will be sent on request. *AA* ◆◆◆◆ *and Two Rosettes.*

BLOWING STONE INN,
Kingston Lisle, Wantage,
Oxfordshire OX12 9QL

Tel & Fax: 01367 820288
website: www.wellysweb.freeserve.co.uk

4 bedrooms, all with private bathroom; Free House with real ale; Children and pets welcome; Bar and restaurant meals; Non-smoking areas; Wantage 5 miles; £££ (per room).

Popular with the horse-racing fraternity, this neat and tidy hostelry, run by resident proprietors, Geoffrey and Amanda Snelson, has all the benefits of modern times which blend harmoniously with old-fashioned warmth and hospitality. Set in attractive gardens amongst the beautiful Berkshire Downs, the inn has two convivial bars with log fires where snacks are served daily (except during the traditional Sunday carvery lunch) along with fine draught beers. The Conservatory Restaurant is a popular meeting place, imaginative home cooking being a speciality of the house, particularly the fish and game dishes. En suite accommodation is available by prior booking.

FHG PUBLICATIONS

publish a large range of well-known accommodation guides. We will be happy to send you details or you can use the order form at the back of this book.

ROSE REVIVED INN,
Newbridge, Near Witney,
Oxfordshire OX8 6QD

Tel: 01865 300221
Fax: 01865 300115
e-mail: andy@therose.demon.co.uk

7 bedrooms, 3 with private bathroom; Morlands House with real ale; Historic interest;
Children and pets welcome; Bar and restaurant meals; Non-smoking areas; Witney 7 miles; S£££, D££.

A beautiful inn dating from the 14th century, the Rose Revived is set idyllically on the banks of the River Thames at Newbridge, oddly enough one of the oldest crossing points on the river. All the traditional virtues are here at this haunting spot; wholesome sustenance in bar or restaurant, good cheer and companionship – an ideal place in which to relax and unwind. Such ambience breeds popularity and a desire to extend one's stay. To cater for this highly likely eventuality, the inn has a number of attractively furnished bedrooms, all with colour television, direct-dial telephone and tea and coffee-making facilities – but book in advance if possible to avoid disappointment.

KILLINGWORTH CASTLE INN,
Glympton Road, Wootton, Woodstock,
Oxfordshire OX20 1EJ

Tel & Fax: 01993 811401
e-mail: kil.cast@btinternet.com
website: www.oxlink.co.uk/woodstock/kilcastle

4 bedrooms, all with private bathroom; Morland House with real ale; Historic interest;
Children welcome; Bar and restaurant meals; Non-smoking areas; Woodstock 2 miles; S£££, D££.

Built in 1637, this one-time coaching halt on the Worcester to London run stands on the edge of a picturesque village just outside Woodstock. Now run by Paul and Maureen Barrow, the inn retains much of its original character. Acknowledged for the quality of its cask-conditioned ales, the inn is also known for its extensive à la carte meal selection available seven days a week in the bar area. A small separate dining area caters for non-smokers and family parties. Adjoining is a games room, and a pleasant lawned garden, safe for children, includes 'Aunt Sally', the traditional Oxfordshire game. Close to Blenheim Palace and the Cotswolds, this fine hostelry offers spacious, tastefully decorated, en suite accommodation. *Cask Marque.*

The £ symbol when appearing at the end of the italic section of an entry shows the anticipated price, during 2000, for full Bed and Breakfast.

Normal Bed & Breakfast rate per person
(in single room)

Normal Bed & Breakfast rate per person
(sharing double/twin room)

PRICE RANGE	CATEGORY	PRICE RANGE	CATEGORY
Under £25	S£	**Under £25**	D£
£26-£35	S££	**£26-£35**	D££
£36-£45	S£££	**£36-£45**	D£££
Over £45	S££££	**Over £45**	D££££

This is meant as an indication only and does not show prices for Special Breaks, Weekends, etc. Guests are therefore advised to verify all prices on enquiring or booking.

Shropshire

THE BULLS HEAD INN,
Chelmarsh, Bridgnorth,
Shropshire WV16 6BA

Tel: 01746 861469
Fax: 01746 862646

10 bedrooms, all en suite; Free House with real ale; Bar and restaurant meals;
Non-smoking areas; Bridgnorth 4 miles; S££, D£.

Excellent accommodation and a traditional welcome in the heart of Shropshire. Relax and enjoy your break in the warm, friendly atmosphere of a traditional country inn. Set amidst Shropshire's rolling hills, The Bulls Head Inn is a splendid base for exploring Wenlock Edge, Ironbridge Gorge and the glorious Severn valley. All bedrooms (one with four-poster bed) are luxuriously appointed with en suite bathrooms, full central heating, colour television and tea/coffee making facilities. There are ground level rooms with access and facilities for people with disabilities. Fishermen's storage facilities available. Choose from our comprehensive menus, served in our bar or one of our dining rooms. Self-catering accommodation also available (4 Keys Commended). Mastercard and Visa accepted. 👑👑👑 *Commended, AA QQQ Recommended.*

FALCON HOTEL,
St. John Street, Lowtown, Bridgnorth,
Shropshire WV15 6AG

Tel: 01746 763134
Fax: 01746 765401

14 bedrooms, all with private bathroom; Free House with real ale; Historic interest;
Children and pets welcome; Bar and restaurant meals; Non-Smoking areas;
Shrewsbury 20 miles; S£££, D£.

Built on two levels, Bridgnorth is a fascinating town characterised by its well-preserved Tudor, Georgian and Victorian buildings. Notable amongst them is this fine 17th century coaching inn by the River Severn. Full of character, the oak-beamed bar/restaurant with its open fires and unusual curios exudes an air of warm hospitality honed over the years. The menu features fresh, wholesome food, such as char-grilled steaks, game pie and fish dishes plus daily 'specials' and some interesting vegetarian dishes. Shropshire and the Severn Valley have much to offer the tourist and this well-run hotel boasts first rate accommodation, each bedroom having a private bathroom, television, direct-dial telephone and beverage-makers. 👑👑👑, AA, RAC.

THE KING'S ARMS HOTEL,
Church Street, Cleobury Mortimer,
Shropshire DY14 8BS

Tel: 01299 270252
e-mail: bernie@aol.com

6 bedrooms, all with private bathroom; Bass House with real ale; Historic interest; Children welcome; Bar and restaurant meals; Ludlow 10 miles; S££, D£££.

This 15th century coaching inn is situated in the centre of a beautiful village and is an excellent touring centre, convenient for Ludlow, Worcester, Long Mynd, Shrewsbury, Bridgnorth and Ironbridge; close by are golf courses, fishing, Severn Valley Railway, Safari Park and many National Trust properties. This is a busy, friendly, family-run pub famous for superb home-cooked food, real ales and exceptional accommodation. Three of the bedrooms have en suite facilities, and all have television, washbasins, central heating, tea/coffee-making equipment, shaver points and hairdryers. Snacks, full meals and a vegetarian choice are available in the oak-beamed bars which have an inglenook fireplace. *CAMRA.*

STOKESAY CASTLE COACHING INN,
School Road, Craven Arms,
Shropshire SY7 9PE

Tel and Fax: 01588 672304

12 bedrooms, all with private bathroom; Free House with real ale; Historic interest; Children welcome; Bar and restaurant meals; Non-smoking areas; Ludlow 7 miles; S££, D££.

Shropshire has a special magic which, once experienced, casts a lasting spell. Rich in undulating farmland and dotted with quiet market towns, the county has, in the past, taken a leading role in often violent struggles across its border with Wales typified by Stokesay Castle, a perfectly preserved 13th century fortified manor house from which this little gem of an hotel takes its name. The present owners lost no time in enhancing the inn's reputation for excellent, well presented food with a positive flair for traditional home cooking by bringing in first class, well-trained staff with a special gift of making visitors feel welcome. To discover the secret allure of the area, acquaintance with this friendly retreat is strongly recommended. First-rate accommodation is available in rooms with en suite facilities, satellite television and tea and coffee-makers.

THE MALTHOUSE,
The Wharfage, Ironbridge,
Shropshire TF8 7NH

Tel: 01952 433712
Fax: 01952 433298

6 bedrooms, all with private bathroom; Restaurant meals; Children welcome; Bridgnorth 9 miles; D££.

The Malthouse is a country pub restaurant and bar with rooms. Accommodation is available in double and twin bedrooms, all en suite. Guests are assured of a warm welcome, a great restaurant with friendly prices, and live entertainment in the Jazz Bar. Set in the heart of the famous Ironbridge Gorge, this is an ideal spot for a short break. French spoken.

THE CHURCH INN,
Buttercross, Ludlow,
Shropshire SY8 1AW

Tel: 01584 872174
Fax: 01584 877146

9 bedrooms, all with private bathrooms; Free House with real ale; Historic interest; Children welcome; Bar lunches, restaurant evenings only; Non-smoking areas; Shrewsbury 24 miles; S££, D£.

This historic inn has undergone several changes of name over the centuries – it was originally called the "Cross Keys" – but retains the fine old-fashioned traditions of good ale and good food which have ensured its lasting popularity through the ages. Nine cosy en suite bedrooms provide first-rate overnight accommodation, and a full range of catering, from freshly cut sandwiches to succulent steaks, ensures that appetites large and small will be amply satisfied. Regularly changing guest beers supplement the already extensive range of wines, spirits and ales on offer. The ancient town of Ludlow is an ideal base for exploring the Border counties and the Welsh Marches, and is conveniently located for road and rail links to the Midlands. *ETC/AA/RAC ◆◆◆, CAMRA, Egon Ronay.*

BEAR HOTEL & COUNTRY INN,
Hodnet, Near Market Drayton,
Shropshire TF9 3NH

Tel: 01630 685214

Fax: 01630 685787

8 bedrooms, all with private bathroom; Free House with real ale; Historic interest; Children welcome; Bar and restaurant meals; Non-smoking areas; Market Drayton 5 miles; S£££, D££.

Opposite the magnificent 60-acre Hodnet Hall Gardens and close to four fine golf courses, including Hawkstone Park, the Bear has developed from a 16th century coaching inn and now offers the facilities of a noteworthy country hotel. Nevertheless, the ambience of a bygone age has been carefully preserved. Oak beams and open fires create a warm and inviting atmosphere and Jasper, the friendly ghost, still wanders the cellar garden. The restaurant menu is designed to suit all tastes with vegetarian dishes always available. Medieval banquets are held regularly, just one of the popular functions organised. Accommodation is of a high standard, all bedrooms having en suite facilities, colour television, telephone, tea and coffee-makers and central heating. Some four-posters are available. ♛♛♛ *Commended, AA/RAC***.*

LONGVILLE ARMS,
Longville-in-the-Dale, Much Wenlock,
Shropshire TF13 6TD

Tel: 01694 771206

Fax: 01694 771742

5 bedrooms, all with private bathroom; Free House with real ale; Historic interest; Children and pets welcome; Bar and restaurant meals; Non-smoking areas; Church Stretton 6 miles; S£/££, D£.

From the very doorstep of this homely inn one may walk directly on to Wenlock Edge, the notable hill ridge and viewpoint, following paths laid out by the National Trust. On all sides are visual delights – to the north, the medieval county town of Shrewsbury; to the south, historic Ludlow with its imposing Norman castle; to the east, Bridgnorth beyond which lies the great Midland urban conurbation and, to the west, the peaceful Shropshire Hills. A fine place to stay to enjoy all these historic and pastoral bounties, the Longville Arms provides good food every lunchtime and in the evening until 9.30 pm, and excellent family, double and twin-bedded rooms of character have en suite facilities, colour television and tea and coffee-makers.

All the information in this book is given in good faith in the belief that it is correct. However, the publishers cannot guarantee the facts given in these pages, neither are they responsible for changes in policy, ownership or terms that may take place after the date of going to press. Readers should always satisfy themselves that the facilities they require are available and that the terms, if quoted, still apply.

GASKELL ARMS HOTEL,
Much Wenlock,
Shropshire TF13 6AQ

Tel: 01952 727212
Fax: 01952 728505

11 bedrooms, 6 with private bathroom; Free House with real ale; Historic interest; Children welcome; Bar and restaurant meals; Non-smoking areas; S£££, D££.

A fascinating little town in the beautiful Shropshire countryside, Much Wenlock is steeped in history with many of its buildings dating back to the 15th century. The mellow Gaskell Arms did not take its place until the 17th century but it is now one of the features of the town. Warm, traditional hospitality is the order of the day at this typically English wayside inn. An interesting and varied selection of hot and cold food is always available in the cosy lounge with a full à la carte menu on offer in the oak-beamed restaurant. Overnight accommodation is provided in delightfully decorated guest rooms appointed with television, telephone and tea and coffee-making facilities. Additional superior Coach House Suite, sleeps four. *ETC/AA* ◆◆◆

The **£** symbol when appearing at the end of the italic section of an entry shows the anticipated price, during 2000, for full Bed and Breakfast.

Normal Bed & Breakfast rate per person (in single room)		*Normal Bed & Breakfast rate per person (sharing double/twin room)*	
PRICE RANGE	CATEGORY	PRICE RANGE	CATEGORY
Under £25	*S£*	**Under £25**	*D£*
£26-£35	*S££*	**£26-£35**	*D££*
£36-£45	*S£££*	**£36-£45**	*D£££*
Over £45	*S££££*	**Over £45**	*D££££*

This is meant as an indication only and does not show prices for Special Breaks, Weekends, etc. Guests are therefore advised to verify all prices on enquiring or booking.

FHG PUBLICATIONS

publish a large range of well-known accommodation guides. We will be happy to send you details or you can use the order form at the back of this book.

Somerset

THE WHEATSHEAF,
Combe Hay, Bath,
Somerset BA2 7EG

Tel and Fax: 01225 833504

3 bedrooms. all with private bathroom; Free House with real ale; Historic interest; Children welcome. pets allowed (on leads); Bar and restaurant meals; Non-smoking areas; Bath 3 miles; S£££, D££££.

Hidden away down the leafy lanes of 'Smiling Somerset', Combe Hay is an attractive and historic village and it is hard to believe that the Roman and Georgian glories of Bath are only three miles away. Once a refuelling stop for bargemen on the now defunct Somerset Coal Canal, the 'Wheatsheaf' is a wide-fronted, traditional country pub known for its delicious home-made food, cask-conditioned ales and old-fashioned hospitality. Set in terraced gardens with panoramic views of the lovely surrounding countryside, this 18th century hostelry with its wooden beams and log fires emanated from an original building constructed in 1576. Three delightfully furnished and spacious bedrooms in a separate refurbished stable block serve overnight guests. *Tourist Board Listed Commended*, AA ◆◆◆◆

THE KINGS ARMS,
Litton, Near Bath,
Somerset BA3 4PW

Tel: 01761 241301

No accommodation; Free House with real ale; Children and pets welcome; Bar meals; Wells 6 miles.

It was a glorious sunny day and the popularity of this charming hostelry was easy to see for the lovely garden was crowded with visitors enjoying an appetising selection of hot and cold dishes as well as well-kept ales tapped from the cask. Thought to have been converted from two cottages, the inn dates from the 15th century and is as pretty as a picture, with its pantiled roof and windows topped by gently curved oak beams. Children are welcome here and the swings and slides in the garden will amuse them whilst parents relax. Tucked away down the B3114 between West Harptree and Chewton Mendip, this little gem is a real find.

THE MALT SHOVEL INN,
Blackmoor Lane, Cannington, Bridgwater,
Somerset TA5 2NE

Tel: 01278 653432

2 bedrooms, both with private bathroom; Free House with real ale; Historic interest; Children welcome; Bar meals; Taunton 9 miles; ££.

Those who follow the Malt Shovel signpost near Cannington on the A39 west of Bridgwater will be amply rewarded. In addition to well-kept real ale and a most cheering welcome from licensees, Phillip & Sally Monger, they will find a tempting array of reasonably priced bar food, ranging from a freshly cut sandwich to more substantial homemade pies, and succulent fillet and sirloin steaks. There are daily specials and vegetarian dishes. Comfortable bed and breakfast accommodation is available, and residents who would dine in style are recommended to the very good restaurant which attracts both local and passing trade. Children are welcomed.

BLACK SMOCK INN,
Stathe, Near Burrowbridge,
Somerset TA7 0JN

Tel: 01823 698352
e-mail: blacksmock@aol.co.uk
website: www.blacksmock.co.uk

4 bedrooms, 2 with private bathroom; Free House with real ale; Historic interest;
Children welcome; Bar and restaurant meals; Langport 3 miles; S£, D£.

By the banks of the River Parrett and just north of Sedgemoor, site of the last battle to be fought on English soil in 1685, this well-regarded moorland inn offers a warm welcome. The surrounding Somerset Levels hold many beauty spots and are ideal for walking, cycling and fishing. The inn has a skittle alley and pool table and the beer patio/garden has far-reaching views. The wholesome fare on offer includes Aberdeen Angus steaks grilled to customers' requirements, and delicious home-made dishes are a speciality. To experience the true heartbeat of English rural life, a sojourn here is to be recommended and good overnight accommodation is available in well-appointed bedrooms, some en suite. *ETC* ◆◆◆

LION HOTEL,
Bank Square, Dulverton,
Somerset TA22 9BU

Tel: 01398 323444
Fax: 01398 323980

13 bedrooms, all with private bathroom; Free House with real ale; Historic interest; Children and
pets welcome; Bar and restaurant meals; Non-smoking areas; Tiverton 10 miles; S££, D££.

The perfect headquarters for exploring the magic land of heather-clad moors, leafy lanes, nature trails, red deer and wild ponies of Exmoor, the attractive and comfortable Lion Hotel is set in the heart of the delightful little town of Dulverton, on Exmoor's southern fringe. Warm and friendly, the hotel takes great pride in the delicious home-cooked cuisine on offer in the charming restaurant. Alternatively, there is an extensive selection of meals available in the lounge bar. Full of character, guest rooms are fully en suite and have colour television, direct-dial telephone and beverage makers. Sporting activities available locally include riding, river and reservoir fishing, and golf. 👑👑👑, *AA***

THE FULL MOON AT RUDGE,
Near Frome,
Somerset BA11 2QF

Tel: 01373 830936; Fax: 01373 831366
e-mail: fullmoon@lineone.net
website: thefullmooninn.bath.co.uk

5 bedrooms, all with private bathroom; Free House with real ale; Historic interest; Children and pets
welcome; Bar and restaurant meals; Non-smoking areas; Frome 3 miles; S£££, D££££.

This snug rural hostelry is what this book is all about – the retreat of our dreams; unassuming, maybe, but offering traditional standards of refreshment and hospitality in the time-honoured way, thanks to owners, Patrick and Christine Gifford, who have worked wonders with this 17th century house. When they took over in 1990, there were no inside toilets and there was no food available, not even a packet of crisps! Today, visitors may be sure of sustenance either at the bar, in company with cask-conditioned ales, or choose from a chef-inspired à la carte menu at lunchtime and in the evening seven days a week. This is a difficult place to leave and excellent en suite accommodation serves those charmed into staying overnight. *CAMRA.*

THE EXMOOR WHITE HORSE INN,
Exford,
Somerset TA24 7PY

Tel: 01643 831229
Fax: 01643 831246
e-mail: exmoorwhitehorse.demon.co.uk

Bedrooms with private bathroom; Children and pets welcome; Bar and restaurant meals; Dunster 9 miles.

Situated in the delightful Exmoor village of Exford, overlooking the River Exe and surrounded by high moorland on almost every side, this family-run 16th century Inn is an ideal spot for that well-earned break. The public rooms are full of character with beams, log fires (October-April) and Exmoor stone throughout. All bedrooms have en suite facilities, colour television, tea-making and central heating, and are furnished in keeping with the character of the Inn. A variety of dishes to excite the palate is served in the restaurant, including lobster, seafood platters, local venison and fish, whilst the bar has an extensive snack menu, with home made pies, local dishes and is renowned for its carvery. The menus change regularly with daily specials available. This is excellent walking country with a selection of circular walks from the Inn, plus many other local walks available. The village is also noted for its excellent riding facilities.

THE HOOD ARMS,
Kilve,
Somerset TA5 1EA

Tel: 01278 741210
Fax: 01278 741477

5 bedrooms, all with private bathroom; Free House with real ale; Historic interest; Children and pets welcome; Bar meals, restaurant Fri/Sat; Non-smoking areas; Williton 5 miles; S£££, D££.

The Hood Arms nestles in the heart of the Quantocks in an area which is totally unspoilt. A traditional black and white 17th century coaching inn owned by Barry and Vanessa Eason, it is set in landscaped lawns, with a spacious walled garden. The comfortable bars have distinct character created by old beams, large fireplaces with roaring log fires in season, and candlelight for evening dining. The extensive and varied menus will satisfy the heartiest of appetites, with a comprehensive wine list to complement your meal. The five double bedrooms are fully en suite, with television, trouser press, hairdryer and hospitality tray. Two cottages adjacent to the Inn are available for weekend or longer breaks and are ideal for families. Resident managers Matthew Haggett and Brian Pook look forward to welcoming you. *AA QQQQQ.* **See also Colour Advertisement on page 6**.

THE DRAGON HOUSE HOTEL & RESTAURANT,
Bilbrook, Near Minehead,
Somerset TA24 6HQ

Tel: 01984 640215; ax: 01984 641340
e-mail: info@dragonhouse.co.uk

9 bedrooms, all with private bathroom; Free House; Historic interest; Bar and restaurant meals; Non-smoking areas; Dunster 3 miles; S£££, D££.

This charming, family-run 1700's country house is located in three acres of natural beauty between Exmoor and the Somerset coast, an ideal base to explore many renowned beauty spots. All bedrooms encompass the requirements of the modern traveller, with telephone, television and en suite facilities, each room retaining its individuality. The oak-panelled restaurant is the perfect setting to enjoy an evening of fine classical and West Country cuisine, accompanied by an impressive wine list. Simpler light meals, bar snacks, drinks and refreshments are available throughout the day in the comfortable bar, conservatory, colonnaded courtyard or underneath the largest Black Poplar in England.

OLD POUND INN,
Aller, Langport,
Somerset TA10 0RA

Tel and Fax: 01458 250469

6 bedrooms; Free House with real ale; Historic interest; Children and pets welcome;
Bar and restaurant meals; Non-smoking areas; Langport 2 miles; S££, D£.

With all the credentials of a classic wayside inn, the 'Old Pound' changed its name from the 'White Lion' as recently as 1980 as it stands on the site of the old village pound. Starting life as a cider house in 1571, it has pursued its purpose of providing sustenance to the inhabitants of an idyllic Somerset village ever since, quite unmoved by the ravages of the Civil War which raged nearby. Peace reigns today with standards of refreshment and accommodation upgraded to a level somewhat higher than the surrounding fen-like countryside – a rich land of imposing sunsets. Two resident chefs hold sway over a splendid à la carte restaurant and the excellent accommodation comprises rooms with en suite facilities, colour television and tea and coffee-makers. *ETC* ◆◆◆, *Winner of JPC National Award for Best Pub of the Year 1999.*

MANOR ARMS,
North Perrott,
Somerset TA18 7SG

Tel: 01460 72901

8 bedrooms, all with private bathroom; Free House with real ale; Historic interest;
Children welcome; Bar and restaurant meals; Non-smoking areas; Crewkerne 2 miles; S£££, D£.

A focal point in a village of lovely hamstone cottages, this handsome 16th century Grade II Listed building displays abundant character through its exposed stonework, inglenook fireplace and original oak beams, the bar warmed by a log fire in cool weather. Lovingly restored and having acquired a reputation for its superb (and reasonably-priced) English fare, this typical wayside inn overlooks the green. This is a tranquil area of picture-book villages and verdant, undulating countryside with the Dorset coast within 20 minutes' drive and a number of historic houses close at hand. Bed and breakfast accommodation is available in both the Inn and in the Coach House situated in the gardens in a quiet setting behind the inn. All guest rooms have en suite shower rooms and are comfortably furnished, the ideal venue for a quiet and rewarding break. *ETC/AA* ◆◆◆.

THE CARPENTERS ARMS,
Stanton Wick, Near Pensford,
Somerset BS39 4BX

Tel: 01761 490202

Fax: 01761 490763

12 bedrooms, all with private bathroom; Free House with real ale; Historic interest; Children welcome; Bar lunches, restaurant evenings only; Non-smoking areas; Bath 10 miles; S£££££, D£££.

A very civilised establishment, where standards of service and cuisine will satisfy the most discerning, yet where genuine friendliness and courtesy are as natural and refreshing as the clean country air. Converted from a row of old miners' cottages, this is everyone's picture of a real country inn. The beamed restaurant is a stylish and relaxing setting for the enjoyment of imaginative, freshly prepared food, including daily delivered seafood; alternatively, light meals and snacks as well as traditional pub favourites can be taken in the Coopers Parlour. Good wines are something of a speciality here (in particular some fine clarets). If in need of overnight accommodation, 12 delightful en suite bedrooms may provide the solution, especially if you can take advantage of the special weekend break rates.

THE CASTLE HOTEL,
Porlock,
Somerset TA24 8PY

Tel: 01643 862504

Fax: 01643 862504

13 bedrooms, all with private bathroom; Real ale; Children and pets welcome; Bar and restaurant meals; Minehead 5 miles.

The Castle Hotel is a small, fully licensed family-run hotel in the centre of the lovely Exmoor village of Porlock. It is an ideal holiday location for those who wish to enjoy the grandeur of Exmoor on foot or by car. The beautiful villages of Selsworthy and Dunster with its castle are only a short distance away. There are 13 en suite bedrooms, all fully heated, with colour television and tea/coffee making facilities. The Castle Hotel has a well-stocked bar with real ale, draught Guinness and cider. A full range of bar meals are available at lunchtimes and evenings or dine in our restaurant. Children and pets are most welcome. Family room available, cots available on request. Short breaks available **See also Colour Advertisement on page 6**.

THE BULL TERRIER,
Croscombe, Wells,
Somerset BA5 3QJ

Tel: 01749 343658

2 bedrooms, both with private bathroom; Free House with real ale; Historic interest; Bar and restaurant meals; Non-smoking areas; Wells 3 miles; £/££.

Good food and plenty of choice – that is very much the order of the day at this friendly country inn where menus range from freshly cut sandwiches to generous helpings of home-made traditional dishes – and don't forget to leave space for one of the wickedly tempting desserts! A choice of vegetarian meals is available. The three cosy bars serve a good range of refreshments including well-kept real ales, lager and cider. Should overnight accommodation be required, there are two prettily decorated en suite double bedrooms, comfortably furnished and complete with colour television and tea/coffee making facilities. There are many lovely walks in the area and the village itself has a fine church with Jacobean carvings.

HALF MOON INN,
Horsington, Templecombe,
Somerset BA8 0EF

Tel: 01963 370140
e-mail: halfmoon@horsington.com

4 bedrooms, all with private bathroom; Free House with real ale; Historic interest; Children and pets welcome; Bar and restaurant meals; Non-smoking areas; Wincanton 3 miles; S£, D£.

The Half Moon Inn is an 18th century stone-built Inn set in a quiet village within easy reach of the A30 and A303. Its features include log fires and an oak floor. There is ample car parking and large gardens. The pub offers a bar menu plus a changing daily specials board, and caters for vegetarian diets. Our real ales are well-kept, with a choice of four or five brews on offer. The accommodation is located to the rear in converted stables, and all rooms are en suite with tea/coffee making facilities and colour television. *ETC* ◆◆

SPARKFORD INN,
Sparkford, Yeovil,
Somerset BA22 7JN

Tel: 01963 440218
Fax: 01963 440358

6 bedrooms, all with private bathroom; Free House with real ale; Historic interest; Children welcome, dogs allowed in bar on leads; Bar and restaurant meals; Castle Cary 4 miles; £.

This old inn, one of our favourites, has spacious bars with interesting alcoves and is full of character. In the evening, a full à la carte menu is on offer in the candlelit restaurant. Now a free house run by Nigel and Suzanne Tucker, the inn has vitality and a twinkle in its eye in catering for the whole family. Entertainments are held regularly and children will be in their element here (which means that so will their parents!) with a Snakes and Ladders playroom complete with bouncy castle, trampoline, slide, and see-saw. Outside is a fully enclosed garden and a separate adventure trail. This, as visitors will discover, is a difficult place to leave, so why not stay overnight? Excellent bed and breakfast accommodation is available, all rooms having en suite facilities, television, radio and tea/coffee makers.

WHITE HORSE INN,
10 St Michael's Avenue, Yeovil,
Somerset BA21 4LB

Tel: 01935 476471; Mobile: 0771 2824305

3 bedrooms, all with private bathroom; Enterprise Inns House with real ale; Children welcome; Bar meals; Taunton 21 miles; S££, D£££.

This popular local inn has newly refurbished en suite rooms. It is situated within easy walking distance of the town centre and local amenities. Guests are assured of home-cooked inn food in comfortable surroundings, and the day starts with a full English breakfast. Open all year.

Staffordshire

THREE HORSESHOES INN & RESTAURANT,
Blackshaw Moor, Leek,
Staffordshire ST13 8TW

Tel: 01538 300296
Fax: 01538 300320

6 bedrooms, all with private shower; Free House with real ale; Children welcome; Bar and restaurant meals; Non-smoking areas; Derby 28 miles, Stafford 24, Stoke-on-Trent 11, S££.

This family-run inn is situated on the A53, approximately seven miles from Buxton, with breathtaking views of the Staffordshire Moorlands and the bizarre stone formation of The Roaches. Stone walls, oak beams and log fires give an olde worlde atmosphere. Fine traditional foods are served in the Carvery, while the restaurant offers à la carte and candlelit menus using fresh vegetables and local beef, poultry, game and cheeses, accompanied by a fine wine list. At weekends a well-attended dinner dance offers a fine choice of food, wine, music and dancing into the early hours. Accommodation is available in six cottage-style bedrooms, with showers, telephone, television and tea-making facilities. For relaxation in fine weather there are large gardens with patios, terraces and a children's play area.
♕♕♕ *Commended, Johansens, Logis.*

Suffolk

PEACOCK INN,
37 The Street, Chelsworth, Near Lavenham,
Suffolk IP7 7HU
Tel: 01449 740758

3 bedrooms; Free House with real ale; Historic interest; Children and pets welcome;
Bar and restaurant meals; Non-smoking areas; Hadleigh 4 miles; S££, D£.

Amidst the colour-washed cottages of the idyllic village of Chelsworth, the welcoming 'Peacock' dates from 1870 and is full of character. Only a few miles from the picturesque wool town of Lavenham with its Tudor and timber and plaster houses, this is a recommended port of call with genuine oak beams, an impressive inglenook fireplace and a beer garden for warmer weather. Cask-conditioned ales and excellent wines make the perfect complement for the fine food served every lunchtime and evening. A most rewarding place in which to stay, the inn has three comfortable bedrooms full of beams, nooks and crannies. In fact, there is not a level floor or straight wall in the pub! *AA.*

THE FOUR HORSESHOES,
Wickham Road, Thornham Magna, Near Eye,
Suffolk IP23 8HD
Tel: 01379 678777
Fax: 01379 678134

8 bedrooms, all with private bathrooms; Old English Inns House with real ale; Historic interest;
Children and pets welcome; Bar and restaurant meals; Non-smoking areas; Eye 3 miles; S£££, D££.

Offering one of the largest selection of bar meals in Suffolk, the thatched, 12th century 'Shoes' nestles in the depths of the countryside although it is but 400 yards off the A140 Norwich/Ipswich road. Ten minutes' walk from Thornham Country Park, this lovely hostelry dates from 1150. Constructed of oak timbers with walls of mud and daub, the 'Shoes' offers surprisingly sophisticated overnight accommodation, all the sprucely furnished rooms having a private bathroom, colour television, direct-dial telephone and tea and coffee making facilities. The very best of ancient and modern.

The
GOLF
GUIDE
Where to Play
Where to Stay
2000

Available from most bookshops, the 2000 edition of **THE GOLF GUIDE** covers details of every UK golf course – well over 2500 entries – for holiday or business golf. Hundreds of hotel entries offer convenient accommodation, accompanying details of the courses – the 'pro', par score, length etc.

In association with 'Golf Monthly' and including the Ryder Cup Report as well as Holiday Golf in Ireland, France, Portugal, Spain, The USA and Thailand .

£9.95 from bookshops or £10.50 including postage (UK only) from FHG Publications, Abbey Mill Business Centre, Paisley PAI ITJ

SIBTON WHITE HORSE,
Halesworth Road, Sibton, Near Saxmundham,
Suffolk IP17 2JJ

Tel: 01728 660337

e-mail: pauldy@easynet.co.uk

8 bedrooms, all with private bathroom; Free House with real ale; Historic interest; Children and pets welcome; Bar and restaurant meals; Non-smoking areas; Saxmundham 5 miles; S££, D£.

This quiet, sixteenth-century freehouse is set in three secluded acres on the outskirts of Peasenhall. Reasonably priced and good value meals are offered in the bar, which has a feature raised gallery, and in the cosy beamed restaurant, which has a raised Victorian gallery. Separate modern accommodation comprises double, twin and single rooms, most with private bathroom or shower, colour television, and tea and coffee making facilities. There are two pleasant outdoor seating areas, one with an enclosed children's play area. This is an ideal base for touring Suffolk's Heritage Coast (just 20 minutes' drive away), Lowestoft and Great Yarmouth, and Minsmere, the RSPB's premier site.

BELL INN,
Ferry Road, Walberswick, Southwold,
Suffolk IP18 6TN

Tel:01502 723109

Fax:01502 722728

e-mail: bellinn@btinternet.com

6 bedrooms, all with private bathroom; Adnams House with real ale; Historic interest; Children and pets welcome; Bar meals, restaurant Fri/Sat evenings only; Non-smoking areas; Yoxford 8 miles; S££, D££.

Those who really do want to escape from the 21st century will find the perfect retreat in this delightful little Suffolk village at the mouth of the River Blyth – just miles of peaceful, unspoilt beaches and surrounding countryside, as tranquil and uncluttered as it was centuries ago. A recommended halt in this tiny paradise is the 600-year-old Bell Hotel with its stone floors, oak beams, high wooden settles and crackling log fires creating an atmosphere that lulls one into forgetfulness of modern life and its pressures. Traditional pub fare is on hand and overnight accommodation takes the form of pleasantly furnished bedrooms with views over sea or river. *AA, CAMRA, Which? Recommended.*

ANGEL INN,
Stoke-by-Nayland, Near Colchester,
Suffolk CO6 4SA

Tel: 01206 263245

Fax: 01206 263373

6 bedrooms, all with private bathroom; Free House with real ale; Historic interest; Bar and restaurant meals, lunch and evenings; Non-smoking areas; Colchester 8 miles; S££££, D££.

Advice to make a prior booking shows the local popularity enjoyed by the Angel's restaurant – but if one has omitted to do so and is denied the delights of the à la carte dinner menu, all is not lost. Meals on offer in the homely bar prove a worthy alternative and are exceedingly good value as well as being wholesome, satisfying and well presented. Those seeking accommodation in Constable country will be well pleased with what is on offer at this sixteenth-century village inn. En suite guest bedrooms are both attractive and comfortable, and colour television, tea and coffee facilities and telephone are provided in all. 👑👑👑 *Highly Commended.*

THE CROWN,
High Street, Southwold,
Suffolk IP18 6DP

Tel: 01502 722275
Fax: 01502 727263

10 bedrooms, all with private bathroom; Adnams House with real ale; Historic interest;
Children welcome; Bar and restaurant meals; Non-smoking areas; Halesworth 8 miles.

Built round a series of delightful greens and backed by protective marshes, Southwold is the epitome of gentility. Its red brick and flint cottages face the North Sea with equanimity. A line of beach huts beneath grass-topped cliffs, the traditional joy of the British holidaymaker, gaze out over a sand and stony beach reminiscent of Dundee cake. This is also the home of Adnams Sole Bay Brewery and the three splendid hotels in their care. The 'Crown', an old posting inn, has undergone many changes (of name as well) over the years and is now an appealing combination of pub, wine bar, restaurant and small hotel. Now restored to its original character, it is renowned for outstanding food and the convivial atmosphere of its bars.

THE OLD BULL HOTEL,
Church Street, Sudbury,
Suffolk CO10 6BL

Tel: 01787 374120
Fax: 01787 379044

10 bedrooms, all with private bathroom or shower; Historic interest; Children welcome;
Cambridge 23 miles, Ipswich 16, Colchester 13; S£££, D££££.

Originally a 16th century beamed coaching inn, now lovingly converted and restored into a guest house and restaurant, the Old Bull Hotel retains that olde worlde charm with a relaxed atmosphere. Each bedroom has a unique character and charm and offers colour television, satellite, telephone and tea and coffee facilities; most are fully en suite. It is situated in the ancient market town of Sudbury, birthplace of Gainsborough, and is surrounded by many places of interest. Ideal centre for touring the area. Most credit cards accepted. 🏆🏆🏆, AA and RAC Listed.

THE COMPASSES INN,
Wenhaston,
Suffolk IP19 9EF

Tel: 01502 478319

3 bedrooms, all with private bath or shower, Free House with real ale;
Pets welcome; Bistro evenings only; Southwold 6, Dunwich 4; S££, D£.

Relax and unwind in this cosy little inn – a true "get away from it all" where breakfast can be taken late and as large as you like. Comfortable rooms have colour television and drinks facilities. Hidden just off the A12, near Suffolk's Heritage Coast and the RSPB's Minsmere Reserve, the many footpaths and commons of this quiet village won "A Pleasure To Walk" award for Suffolk. The Bistro serves local fish, steaks, etc Monday to Saturday evenings (French/Mediterranean/Mexican specials on request). The bar and Bistro are closed Monday to Saturday lunchtimes. Sorry, no children.

THE FROIZE INN,
Chillesford, Woodbridge,
Suffolk IP12 3PU

Tel: 01394 450282

2 bedrooms, both with private bathroom; Free House with real ale; Historic interest;
Children and pets welcome; Bar and restaurant meals; Non-smoking areas; Orford 3 miles; S££, D££.

Quietly situated in a countryside once exploited by smugglers, this fascinating inn dates from the late 15th century when it was constructed on the site of Chillesford Friary. The name probably derives from the fact that the friars are known to have supplied weary travellers with sustenance in the form of a savoury pancake called a 'froize'. In 1976, permission was sought to convert the building into the unlikely combination of 'Public House, Guest House, Tea Rooms and Piggeries'. Now under the creative genius of Alistair and Joy Shaw, the inn offers first-rate food and wine and spacious, well-appointed accommodation. Of great interest is the selection of locally brewed Nun Beers, amongst them the picturesquely named Naughty Novice, Nun-Chaser, Nun-Trembler and Nun's Revenge! *CAMRA, Good Pub Guide.*

Surrey

THE KING'S ARMS INN,
Stane Street, Ockley, Near Dorking,
Surrey RH5 5TP

Tel and Fax: 01306 711224

6 bedrooms, all with private bathroom; Free House with real ale; Historic interest;
Bar and restaurant meals; Horsham 6 miles; £££.

Within the mellow walls of this 400-year-old hostelry dwell all the traditional virtues associated with a favoured village inn. The unhurried atmosphere is at once friendly, relaxing and informal and the refreshment available in the bar, whether it be a glass of real ale or a snack, will induce many a smile and a nod and a feeling of contentment. For something somewhat grander, something less informal, the superb Cavalier Restaurant provides the opportunity to dine expansively in elegant surroundings. Tastefully-furnished guest rooms gaze out over the pretty gardens at the rear, each room equipped to a high standard with bathroom en suite and colour television amongst its practical appointments. *ETC* ◆◆◆◆

CHASE LODGE HOTEL,
10 Park Road, Hampton Wick,
Kingston-upon-Thames, Surrey KT1 4AS

Tel: 0208 943 1862

Fax: 0208 943 9363

13 bedrooms, all with private bathroom; Free House with real ale; Historic interest; Children and pets welcome; Bar and restaurant meals; Non-smoking areas; London 10 miles; S££££, D£££.

An award-winning hotel with style and elegance set in tranquil surroundings at affordable prices. Quality en suite bedrooms. Full English breakfast and à la carte menu. Licensed bar. Wedding receptions catered for; honeymoon suite available. Easy access to Kingston town centre and all major transport links; 20 minutes from Heathrow Airport. All major credit cards accepted. *London Tourist Board/AA* ★★★, *RAC Highly Acclaimed, Les Routiers.*

Other specialised

FHG PUBLICATIONS

• Recommended COUNTRY HOTELS OF BRITAIN   £4.95

• Recommended WAYSIDE & COUNTRY INNS OF BRITAIN   £4.95

• PETS WELCOME!   £5.25

• BED AND BREAKFAST IN BRITAIN   £3.95

• THE GOLF GUIDE Where to Play / Where to Stay   £9.95

Published annually: Please add 55p postage (UK only)
when ordering from the publishers

FHG PUBLICATIONS LTD
Abbey Mill Business Centre, Seedhill,
Paisley, Renfrewshire PA1 ITJ

West Sussex

WHEATSHEAF INN,
Broad Street, Cuckfield,
West Sussex RH17 5DW

Tel: 01444 454078
Fax: 01444 417265

10 bedrooms, all with private bathroom; Free House with real ale; Historic interest;
Children and pets welcome; Bar meals; Non-smoking areas; Haywards Heath 2 miles; £££/££££.

On the outskirts of the picturesque village of Cuckfield and about a mile from Haywards Heath main line station, the 'Wheatsheaf' is a first-class port of call either for a casual break or as a touring holiday base. The bar with its open fires is split into three distinct areas; the main bar where appetising snacks augment good ale, the quiet and intimate lower lounge and the dining room, famed for its excellent home-cooked meals. The large garden is popular in fair weather and barbecues are organised on warm summer evenings. The accommodation reveals homely comforts and conveniences such as en suite facilities, colour television, direct-dial telephone and tea and coffee makers. 👑👑

PARK HOUSE HOTEL,
Bepton, Midhurst,
West Sussex GU29 0JB

Tel: 01730 812880
Fax: 01730 815643

14 bedrooms, all with private bathroom; Residential licence; Children and pets welcome;
Midhurst 3 miles

Delightfully furnished throughout, this lovely country house favours those with sporting inclinations for its spacious grounds feature two grass tennis courts, putting and croquet lawns, a 9-hole pitch and putt course and a heated swimming pool. Furthermore, it is happily placed only six miles from Goodwood and within easy reach of Cowdray Park (for polo), several golf courses and the Chichester Festival Theatre. In the verdant tranquillity of West Sussex there are numerous beauty spots and the coast is easily accessible. Bedrooms are excellently appointed with bathrooms en suite, colour television, radio and telephone. This delightful establishment is under the personal care of resident proprietors, Michael and Liza O'Brien. 👑👑👑👑, *AA QQQQQ Premier Selected.*

HORSE GUARDS INN,
Tillington, Petworth
West Sussex GU28 9AF

Tel: 01798 342332
Fax: 01798 344351

3 bedrooms, all with private bathroom; Free House with real ale; Historic interest;
Bar and restaurant meals; Non-smoking areas; Petworth 1 mile; D££.

Amidst lovely countryside; open seven days a week for lunch and dinner, this charming 300-year-old inn is renowned for its warm welcome, superb home-cooked food and extensive wine list. Menus are written on two blackboards and are changed twice daily. Seasonal dishes include local game, fresh fish and vegetarian specialities which, with a large selection of home-made puddings, represent excellent value for money. The attractive free house has a pleasant garden where refreshment may be taken in the summer, whilst log fires in the bar will banish winter chill. Comfortable en suite accommodation is available, including a full English breakfast. *AA.*

Warwickshire

HOWARD ARMS,
Lower Green, Ilmington, Near Shipston-on-Stour,
Warwickshire CV36 4LT

Tel and Fax: 01608 682226

e-mail: howard.arms@virgin.net

3 bedrooms, all with private bathrooms; Free House with real ale; Historic interest; Children welcome,
guide dogs only; Bar and restaurant meals; Non-smoking areas; Shipston-on-Stour 4 miles; S££, D£££.

The delightful bar with heavy oak beams, flagstone floor and open fireplaces betrays the 17th century origins of the Howard Arms. On the village green of a pretty Cotswold village of honeystone cottages and within easy reach of Stratford-upon-Avon, the inn is increasingly popular with tourists seeking good food and drink in a tranquil atmosphere. Prices are reasonable and vegetarian fare is available. A 55-seater dining room is provided in addition to accommodation in the form of a twin-bedded room and two king-size bedded rooms, all with full en suite facilities, colour television, hairdryers, and tea and coffee makers. Outside is an attractive garden with tables and chairs where families may refresh themselves in the summer. *ETC* ◆◆

THE OLDE COACH HOUSE INN,
Ashby St Ledgers, Near Rugby,
Warwickshire CV23 8UN

Tel: 01788 890349
Fax: 01788 891922

6 bedrooms, all with private bathroom; Free House with real ale; Historic interest; Children and pets welcome; Bar and restaurant meals; Non-smoking areas; Daventry 4 miles; S££££, D££££.

The Domesday Book records the existence of the tiny village of Ashby St Ledgers and it rose to prominence again in 1605 when the Gunpowder Plot was reputedly hatched in the gatehouse of Ashby Manor. Today, all is tranquillity with thatched houses clustered around the manor and 12th century church. Very much the hub of village life, this sturdy, ivy-clad inn, where hosts, Brian and Phillipa McCabe, hold sway, upholds the traditional virtues of good food, good ale and good cheer. Excellently equipped bedrooms of varying sizes, including a four-poster room, all have en suite facilities, colour television, radio alarm, telephone and tea and coffee-makers and special weekend break terms make a relaxing stopover here a most tempting prospect. The cuisine is worthy of special mention, the extensive menu including additional vegetarian and children's sections. Dishes are well supported by a comprehensive wine list with no less than 12 wines by the glass available. Real ale drinkers are amply catered for, carefully tended regular beers being frequently supplemented by a variety of guest ales. Within minutes of the M1, M6 and A1/M1 link, this award-winning hostelry has a great attraction for family parties and a children's adventure playground in the garden adds to its popularity. This is also a much sought after venue for private functions and board meetings. *CAMRA, Egon Ronay.*

THE HOUNDSHILL,
Banbury Road, Ettington, Stratford-upon-Avon,
Warwickshire CV37 7NS

Tel: 01789 740267
Fax: 01789 740075

8 bedrooms, all with private bathroom; Free House with real ale; Children and pets welcome; Bar and restaurant meals; Stratford-upon-Avon 4 miles; S££, D££.

This handsome white-painted hotel stands on the A422 just four miles from Stratford-upon-Avon and centrally located for the Cotswolds, Oxford and Birmingham, making it an ideal base for visiting the Heart of England on business or pleasure. Light and airy en suite rooms provide comfortable accommodation and are equipped with colour television and tea and coffee making facilities. A full range of meals and refreshments is available, from morning coffee to good value bar snacks and a delicious à la carte restaurant menu. In fine weather the pretty garden is a pleasant setting for the enjoyment of outdoor refreshments. 🏩🏩🏩 *Commended.*

WHITE HORSE INN,
Banbury Road, Ettington, Near Stratford-upon-Avon,
Warwickshire CV37 7SU
Tel: 01789 740641

4 bedrooms, all en-suite; Real ale; Historic interest; Bar and restaurant meals;
Non-smoking areas; Oxford 34 miles, Birmingham 30, Stratford-upon-Avon 6; S££, D££.

What could be more delightful for a holiday or short break in Shakespeare country than a stop-over in this lovely old inn, already conjuring up the atmosphere of days gone by with its furnishings, oak beams and the warmth of its welcome. Guests can enjoy a glass of real ale with their lunch, and for those who choose to stay longer, the Inn's restaurant serves fine fare in the evening. There is a sun patio and beer garden in which to take advantage of warmer weather. The White Horse's accommodation means that tired visitors may take full advantage of its location, six miles from Stratford and close to Warwick Castle and the Cotswolds. Also near to the NEC Birmingham and the Royal Showground at Stoneleigh. All rooms are non-smoking, tastefully furnished and en suite, with colour television, central heating and tea/coffee making facilities. No dogs in rooms, (allowed on Sun Patio). Weekend break reductions from November to April. Credit cards accepted. Proprietors Jane and Steve Barry. ♛♛.

Wiltshire

ROSE AND CROWN HOTEL,
High Street, Ashbury, Swindon, Wiltshire SN6 8NA

Tel: 01793 710222 (01793 710031 24hrs)
Fax: 01793 710029

10 bedrooms, 4 with private bathroom; Arkell's House with real ale; Children welcome;
Bar and restaurant meals; Non-smoking areas; Swindon 7 miles; S£££, D££.

In the centre of a picturesque village, this welcoming inn possesses the facilities of a first-class hotel. Beautifully decorated throughout, it has friendly bars, one with a log fire, where appetising snack meals are served at lunchtime and in the evening, whilst the jewel in the Rose and Crown is undoubtedly its fine restaurant which is well recommended for its excellent à la carte menu, service and surroundings. However this happy retreat has many other attributes: guest rooms represent the best in modern comfort, superb conference facilities exist, and for recreation there is a games room.

NEW INN,
Winterbourne Monkton, Avebury, Wiltshire SN4 9NW

Tel: 01672 539240

5 bedrooms, all with private bathroom; Children welcome; Restaurant meals; Avebury 1 mile; D£.

This small friendly country pub is situated off the A4361, one mile from Avebury ringed village. This is an ideal base for exploring all of Wiltshire. Accommodation is available in two double and three twin bedrooms, all en suite. The inn has an attractive restaurant specialising in traditional fish and chips. The large garden is a very pleasant spot for relaxation in fine weather. Full details from proprietors, Kevin and Doreen Murrin.

THE NEELD ARMS INN,
The Street, Grittleton, Wiltshire SN14 6AP

Tel: 01249 782470
Fax: 01249 782358
e-mail: neeldarms@genie.co.uk

6 bedrooms, all with private bathroom; Free House with real ale; Historic interest;
Children and pets welcome; Bar and restaurant meals (evenings); Chippenham 6 miles; S£££, D££££.

This charming 17th century Cotswold-stone country inn in the unspoiled village of Grittleton offers comfortable accommodation and delicious home-cooked food. There are three twin bedrooms, a family room and two double rooms, one of which has a traditional four-poster bed; all are en suite (bath or shower) with colour television, tea and coffee making facilities, and radio alarm. The rooms are comfortable and cosy, in keeping with the rest of the inn, and each is individually decorated. In the bar, a fine range of wines, spirits and traditional ales are available, which you can enjoy in front of open log fires. The historic town of Bath is nearby, and many places of interest are within easy reach, such as Stonehenge, Avebury, Stow-on-the-Wold and other famous Cotswold towns.

OLD BELL HOTEL,
Abbey Row, Malmesbury,
Wiltshire SN16 0AG

Tel: 01666 822344
Fax: 01666 825145

31 bedrooms, all with private bathroom; Free House with real ale; Historic interest; Children welcome; Bar and restaurant meals; Non-smoking areas; Swindon 14 miles; S££££, D££££.

For hospitality 'par excellence' and many a fascinating history lesson, this lovely, Grade II listed building holds all the qualities associated with a traditional wayside inn of distinction. In the shadow of Malmesbury's imposing Norman abbey, the Old Bell dates from 1220 when it was constructed alongside the cloister to accommodate visitors to the abbey's library. Many of its original features remain to captivate the guest of today and great character is exhibited by its period furnishings. Extended and improved with flair in Edwardian times, this proud hostelry has kept pace nobly with contemporary trends. The bedrooms have two distinctive styles; those in the main house recalling the essence of former days whilst those in the reconstructed coach house portraying a modern oriental theme; all have superb en suite facilities, colour television with satellite channels, direct-dial telephone and radio. As to cuisine, this is in the purely wondrous category and dining here is definitely an experience not to be missed. Families are particularly well catered for here. Some rooms may be brought together to form intercommunicating suites, there is a sophisticated baby-listening system and baby-sitting can be arranged. The hotel stands in delightful gardens which incorporate a play area for children and The Den, a special games room and nursery, is a complimentary service for parents and children with nannies provided on request. *AA****

THE CROWN & ANCHOR,
Ham, Near Marlborough,
Wiltshire SN8 3RB

Tel: 01488 668242

3 bedrooms, all with private bathroom; Free House with real ale; Children welcome; Bar meals; Hungerford 4 miles; S£££, D££.

Janet and Richard would like to welcome you to the Crown and Anchor. The pub is situated just off the green in the beautiful picture-postcard village of Ham, which is ideally located on the Wiltshire/Berkshire/Hampshire border. Many places of interest are within easy reach, including the Wayfarer's Walk, Avebury and Stonehenge Stone Circles, Bilbury Hill, Highclere Castle, Salisbury and Bath. For the less energetic we can offer a range of traditional pub games. At the Crown and Anchor we offer a wide selection of of tasty home-cooked meals, a high standard of accommodation, and a warm and friendly atmosphere. There are one double and two twin bedrooms, all en suite. *ETC* ◆◆◆

THE OLD SHIP HOTEL,
Castle Street, Mere,
Wiltshire BA12 6JE

Tel: 01747 860258
Fax: 01747 860501

20 bedrooms; Hall & Woodhouse House with real ale; Historic interest; Children and pets welcome; Bar lunches, restaurant evenings only; Salisbury 20 miles, Shaftesbury 7; £.

The Old Ship was once the home of 17th century MP Sir John Coventry, whose banishment from Court led to the present day expression "sent to Coventry". However if leaving London meant a return to this fine old building surely he could not have minded too much, for it is indeed a delightful house set in a delightful area of the borders of Wiltshire, Somerset and Dorset. Today there are 20 bedrooms offering guest accommodation, and all have central heating, colour television and tea makers. En suite facilities are available in most rooms. The bar serves an excellent range of meals and snacks as an alternative to the extensive restaurant menu. 🌺🌺🌺 *Approved, Les Routiers, Egon Ronay.*

When making enquiries or bookings,
a stamped addressed envelope is always appreciated.

THE LAMB AT HINDON,
Hindon, Near Salisbury,
Wiltshire SP3 6DP

Tel: 01747 820573

Fax: 01747 820605

13 bedrooms, all with private bathroom; Free House with real ale; Historic interest; Children and pets welcome; Bar and restaurant meals; Bath 28 miles, Salisbury 16; ££.

The fascinating history of this ancient inn is related in its brochure, which reveals among other intriguing facts that it was once the headquarters of a notorious smuggler. No such unlawful goings-on today – just good old-fashioned hospitality in the finest traditions of English inn-keeping. Charmingly furnished single, double and four-poster bedrooms provide overnight guests with cosy country-style accommodation, and the needs of the inner man (or woman!) will be amply satisfied by the varied, good quality meals served in the bar and restaurant. Real ales can be enjoyed in the friendly bar, where crackling log fires bestow charm and atmosphere as well as warmth. 👑👑👑👑, *AA** and Courtesy & Care Award, RAC **.*

THE BECKFORD ARMS,
Fonthill Gifford, Tisbury, Salisbury,
Wiltshire SP3 6PX

Tel: 01747 870385

8 bedrooms, all with private bathroom; Real ale; Historic interest; Bar and restaurant meals; Shaftesbury 7 miles; ££.

This delightful 18th century country inn is highly recommended for its beautiful setting, stylish interiors, gardens, friendly atmosphere and excellent restaurant featuring local produce, imaginatively prepared. Completely refurbished and extended, the Beckford Arms offers a relaxing and comfortable location for walks through an area of outstanding natural beauty or a superb base for many tourist spots including Salisbury, Stonehenge, Bath, New Forest and the South Coast. There are eight tastefully decorated bedrooms, all with colour television and en suite facilities. The Beckford Arms is conveniently situated halfway between London and Plymouth, two miles off the A303 and two miles from Tisbury station. 👑👑👑 *Highly Commended, Egon Ronay Recommended.*

Worcestershire

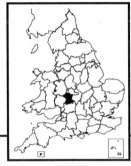

THE CROWN AND TRUMPET INN,
Church Street, Broadway,
Worcestershire WR12 7AE

Tel: 01386 853202
e-mail: ascott@cotswoldholidays.co.uk
website: www.cotswoldholidays.co.uk

4 bedrooms, all with private bathroom; Real ale; Children welcome, pets by arrangement; Bar meals; Evesham 5 miles; S£££, D££.

Built of warm Cotswold stone, this delightful 17th century inn extends a mellow welcome to visitors to picturesque Broadway, known as the 'Gateway to the Cotswolds' and one of the most photographed villages in Britain with its wide main street lined with lovely old cottages and houses. Traditional beers are served in the homely, oak beamed bars and there is an extensive menu of home-cooked and seasonal dishes to tickle the palate. This is an enchanting place in which to stay and a popular touring base: the inn has three centrally heated double rooms and a twin-bedded room, all with en suite facilities, colour television and tea and coffee-makers. Please send for details of seasonal offers. 👑👑👑 *Approved, Which? Good Pub Guide, CAMRA.*

THE BELL INN,
Church Street, Eckington,
Worcestershire WR10 3AN

Tel and Fax: 01386 750205
e-mail: the_bell_uk@hotmail.com
web-site: www.jks.org/bell.html

Bedrooms with private bathroom; Children welcome; Restaurant meals; Pershore 3 miles.

Nestling at the base of historic Bredon Hill between Pershore and Tewkesbury, the Bell Inn is situated in the centre of Eckington village close to the River Avon with plenty of footpaths and bridleways to take in the beautiful scenery. All rooms are individually themed with famous brewery brand names, and all are en suite, with colour television, tea/coffee facilities and hairdryer. Our conservatory restaurant looks onto landscaped garden, offering meals lunchtime and evening. English/foreign fayre, children's menu and Sunday table d'hôte. For your free brochure telephone or write to the above address. *ETC* ◆◆◆.

TALBOT HOTEL,
Knightwick,
Worcestershire WR6 5PH

Tel: 01886 821235
Fax: 01886 821060

*10 bedrooms, 7 with private bathroom; Free House with real ale; Historic interest;
Children welcome, pets by arrangement; Bar and restaurant lunches; Non-smoking areas;
Worcester 9 miles; S££/£££; D£/££.*

Run by two sisters, Annie and Wiz Clift, The Talbot is a traditional country coaching inn which has stood by the ford across the sleepy River Teme for 500 years. Its unique atmosphere remains unspoilt by the 20th century facilities we have provided to improve the comfort and quality of your stay. It is the home of the Teme Valley Brewery, which produces real ale from the Clift family hops. We are well positioned for discovering this little idyll of a backwater, be it the history and culture of the Welsh borders and our surrounding cathedral cities, the oddities and curiosities that abound in our rural area, or simply the wide range of country pursuits that are available. 👑👑👑 *Commended*

MALVERN HILLS HOTEL,
Wynds Point, Malvern,
Worcestershire WR13 6DW

Tel: 01684 540690
Fax: 01684 540327
e-mail: malhilhotl@aol.com

*15 bedrooms, all en suite; Free House with real ale; Historic interest; Children and pets welcome;
Bar and restaurant meals; Non-smoking areas; Great Malvern 4 miles; ££.*

Nestling some 800 feet up the majestic western slopes of the Malverns, a hostelry for travellers has stood here for more than 500 years. This privately owned and run hotel is the ideal place for walking and enjoying the breathtaking view ('one of the goodliest views in England') from British Camp, the Iron Age hill fort and ancient earthworks which stand opposite the hotel. An oak-panelled lounge bar with open log fire offers excellent bar food and a good selection of real ales. Nightingales Restaurant provides traditional rustic English cuisine complemented by a comprehensive wine list to suit all tastes. Open all year. 👑👑👑👑 *Commended, AA/RAC ***.

CHEQUERS INN,
Chequers Lane, Fladbury, Pershore,
Worcestershire WR10 2PZ

Tel: 01386 860276/860527
Fax: 01386 861286

*8 bedrooms, all with private bathroom; Free House with real ale; Historic interest;
Bar and restaurant meals; Evesham 3 miles; S££££, D££.*

A perfect example of the traditional English hostelry, the Chequers Inn stands at the end of a quiet lane in this delightful village in the Vale of Evesham. Those seeking accommodation will find beautifully kept en suite guest rooms, some with balconies, some with open rural views, and all well equipped with colour television, radio, telephone and tea trays. Even if time precludes one staying a while in this charmed area, the Chequers is still worth a flying visit for its fine fare. A carvery is provided Thursday, Friday and Saturday evenings and Sunday lunchtime; bar meals and an à la carte menu are available daily. Golf Breaks – details on request. 👑👑👑 *Commended*. **See also Colour Advertisement on page 6.**

HOLDFAST COTTAGE HOTEL,
Little Malvern, Near Malvern,
Worcestershire WR13 6NA

Tel: 01684 310288
Fax: 01684 311117

8 bedrooms, all with private bathroom; Historic interest; Children and pets welcome;
Restaurant evenings only; Non-smoking areas; Malvern 4 miles; S£££, D£££.

Surrounded by orchards and open farmland, this is a gem of a retreat – peaceful, friendly and within a short distance of the Victorian spa town of Malvern and the Severn and Wye Valleys. Personally run by proprietors, Stephen and Jane Knowles, the homely hotel, originally a 17th century cottage, exhibits many individual thoughtful touches. One may seek relaxation in a cosy Victorian-style bar or in the comfortable deep-cushioned lounge before a log fire. The four-course dinner offers quality ingredients prepared with both care and flair, featuring home-baked rolls, home-made ice creams and herbs from the hotel's own herb garden. *ETC Silver Award, AA Two Rosettes, RAC Merit Awards.*

THE OLD MILL INN,
Mill Lane, Elmley Castle, Near Pershore,
Worcestershire WR10 3HP

Tel: 01386 710407
Fax: 01386 710066

Bedrooms with private bathroom; Free House; Restaurant meals; Evesham 4 miles.

The Old Mill is a traditional free house steeped in history, standing tucked away at the far corner of the village cricket green in the beautiful village of Elmley. Proprietors, Tim and Nicole Burrows, have added a fine Garden Room restaurant with a touch of France, and charmingly furnished en suite accommodation with four-poster rooms. This is an ideal base for golfers, walkers and sightseers. *ETC* ◆◆◆

East Yorkshire

THE STAR INN,
Warter Road, North Dalton,
East Yorkshire YO25 9UX

Tel: 01377 217688

Fax: 01377 217791

7 bedrooms, all with private bathroom; Real ale; Well-behaved dogs and children welcome;
Bar and restaurant meals; Driffield 6 miles.

Set in the heart of the Yorkshire Wolds and nestling beside the village pond, this Georgian inn enjoys an idyllic setting. Located within easy reach of York, Beverley and the East Coast, it makes the ideal base. Whether your interests are history, nature or just relaxing in front of a nice log fire, this is the place for you. The inn has seven en suite rooms, all with remote-control colour television, tea and coffee making facilities and direct-dial telephone. Meals are available in the cosy, open-fired bar and in the award-winning à la carte restaurant. Special rates are available. For a brochure just call and ask for Keith or Jo. 👑👑👑👑. **See also Colour Advertisement on page 8.**

The **£** symbol when appearing at the end of the italic section of an entry shows the anticipated price, during 2000, for full Bed and Breakfast.

Normal Bed & Breakfast rate per person
(in single room)

Normal Bed & Breakfast rate per person
(sharing double/twin room)

PRICE RANGE	CATEGORY	PRICE RANGE	CATEGORY
Under £25	S£	**Under £25**	D£
£26-£35	S££	**£26-£35**	D££
£36-£45	S£££	**£36-£45**	D£££
Over £45	S££££	**Over £45**	D££££

This is meant as an indication only and does not show prices for Special Breaks, Weekends, etc. Guests are therefore advised to verify all prices on enquiring or booking.

North Yorkshire

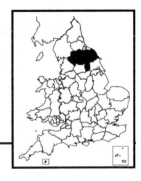

THE BUCK INN,
Thornton Watlass, Near Bedale, Ripon, North Yorkshire HG4 4AH

Tel: 01677 422461
Fax: 01677 422447

7 bedrooms, 5 with private facilities; Free House with real ale; Children welcome; Bar food and dining area; Non-smoking areas; Ripon 11 miles, Northallerton 9; S£££, D££.

Friendly country inn overlooking the delightful cricket green in a peaceful village just five minutes away from the A1. Newly refurbished bedrooms, most with en suite facilities, ensure that a stay at The Buck is both comfortable and relaxing. Delicious freshly cooked meals are served lunchtimes and evenings in the cosy bar and dining area. On Sundays a traditional roast with Yorkshire pudding is on the menu. Excellent hand-pulled Theakstons, John Smiths, Black Sheep and Tetley cask beer is available, as is a regular guest ale. This is an ideal centre for exploring Herriot country. There is a children's playground in the secluded beer garden where quoits are also played. Private fly fishing available on River Ure and five golf courses within 20 minutes' drive. 👑👑👑 *Commended, Good Pub Guide, AA*, CAMRA Good Pub Food Guide, British Cheese Board Recommended, Room at the Inn.* **See also Colour Advertisement on page 8.**

CROWN INN,
Roecliffe, Boroughbridge, North Yorkshire YO51 9LY

Tel: 01423 322578
Fax: 01423 324060

11 bedrooms, all with private bathroom; Free House with real ale; Historic interest; Children welcome; Bar and restaurant meals; Ripon 8 miles; S££, D££.

In a quiet rural village just a short walk from the banks of the River Ure, this attractive building dates from the 16th century and much of its original character remains, epitomised by its oak beams and welcoming log fires. Conveniently placed for the Yorkshire Dales and countless places of historical interest, the old hostelry is well worth visiting for its delicious and plentiful food, subject of an AA Rosette Award, and its selection of hand-pulled real ales. Thanks to stylish and contemporary comforts, this is a recommended touring base, all bedrooms having en suite facilities, remote-control satellite television, direct-dial telephone and tea and coffee-makers. First-class Yorkshire hospitality. 👑👑👑👑, *AA Rosette 1997/98.*

NEW INN HOTEL,
Clapham, Yorkshire Dales National Park,
North Yorkshire LA2 8HH

Tel: 015242 51203
Fax: 015242 51496

15 bedrooms, all with private bathroom; Free House with of real ale; Historic interest;
Bar and restaurant meals; Non-smoking areas; Kendal 21 miles, Skipton 21; Settle 6; S££, D££.

Keith and Barbara Mannion invite you to their friendly eighteenth century residential coaching inn in the picturesque Dales village of Clapham. Ideal centre for walking the three peaks of Ingleborough, Pen-y-Ghent and Whernside. All rooms have full en suite facilities, colour television and tea/coffee facilities. Enjoy good wholesome Yorkshire food in our restaurant, or bar meals in either of our two bars. Dogs welcome. Ring Barbara for details of special mid-week breaks. ♚♚♚ *Commended.* **See also Colour Advertisement on page 7.**

DUKE OF WELLINGTON INN,
West Lane, Danby, Near Whitby,
North Yorkshire YO21 2LY

Tel: 01287 660351
website: www.dukeofwellington.co.uk
e-mail: landlord@dukeofwellington.freeserve.co.uk

8 bedrooms, 7 with private bathroom; Free House with real ale; Historic interest; Children and
pets welcome; Bar meals, restaurant evenings only; Non-smoking areas; Whitby 12 miles; S££, D££.

With hosts, Tony and Liz Woods, presenting a wide choice of home-cooked starters, fish dishes, grills and desserts to beguile would-be diners (including vegetarians and children), this fine, 18th century coaching inn attracts visitors to the tranquil village of Danby in the heart of the North York Moors. Apart from the popularity of the local bar with its selection of real ales and the restaurant, restoration and renovation has provided several splendidly furnished guest rooms with en suite facilities, central heating, colour television and tea and coffee makers, accommodation keenly sought after by those wishing to spend time in an area of outstanding natural beauty. *ETC* ★★★, *CAMRA.*

THE GEORGE AT EASINGWOLD,
Market Place, Easingwold, York,
North Yorkshire YO61 3AD

Tel: 01347 821698
Fax: 01347 823448
e-mail: georgehotel.easingwold@tesco.net

15 bedrooms, all with private bathroom; Free House with real ale; Historic interest; Children welcome; Bar meals, restaurant evenings only; Non-smoking areas; York 12 miles; S£££££, D££.

An 18th century coaching inn of character, with open fires and a wealth of beams and horse brasses, the friendly, family-run George stands in the cobbled square of the pretty market town of Easingwold, where the architecture, appropriately enough, is mainly Georgian. Just off the A19, this is a splendid base for exploring an area full of interest – the North York Moors, Howardian Hills and the dales and hamlets of Herriot Country. Imposing Castle Howard of *Brideshead Revisited* fame is close by and the coast may be reached in under an hour. York with its many historic attractions is only a short drive away. Good food and drink, including local ale pulled straight from the cask and fine wines, are served in both the Courtyard Bar and the oak-beamed restaurant, where there is a choice of table d'hôte and à la carte fare. Fresh Whitby fish is always available and the chefs "specials board" is changed daily. The traditional Sunday lunch is a popular feature. Practice makes perfect, and the hospitality at the George is honed by 200 years' experience. Today, the accommodation matches up to the most exacting modern standards. Bedrooms all have en suite facilities, colour television, radio, direct-dial telephone and tea and coffee-makers. Parties and other social functions are expertly catered for. AA**, Johansens.

TENNANT ARMS
Kilnsey, Near Grassington,
North Yorkshire BD23 5PS

Tel: 01756 752301

10 bedrooms, all with private bathroom; Free House with real ale; Historic interest;
Children welcome; Bar and restaurant meals; Grassington 3 miles; S££, D£.

Friendly 17th century country inn hotel nestling under the famous Kilnsey Crag in the heart of Wharfedale, between the picturesque villages of Grassington and Kettlewell. All ten bedrooms are en suite. The cosy bars with log fires and beams serve delicious, individually prepared bar meals and hand-pulled ales; or dine in the beautiful pine-panelled non-smoking dining room and choose from our extensive à la carte menu. Ideal for exploring the Dales. Proprietors, Mr and Mrs N. Dean will give you a warm welcome. ♛♛♛ *Commended.*

ROYAL OAK HOTEL,
Great Ayton,
North Yorkshire TS9 6BW

Tel: 01642 722361
Fax: 01642 724047

5 bedrooms, all with private bathroom; Real ale; Historic interest; Children welcome;
Bar and restaurant meals; Thirsk 23 miles, Middlesbrough 9; £££/££££.

The extensive dinner menu at the Royal Oak is not one for the indecisive. Ditherers will find themselves at closing time still unable to choose from delicious fillet dijon with its mustard and cream sauce, or perhaps pan-fried pork fillet with hot green peppers and cream. I would recommend speeding up the procedure by the tossing of coins—for whatever one selects one may be sure of the deepest satisfaction. Food is also available in the tastefully decorated, comfortably rustic bars, and guest bedrooms provide well appointed overnight accommodation, all being en suite, with central heating, colour television and tea-making facilities.

THE PHEASANT HOTEL,
Harome, Helmsley,
North Yorkshire YO62 5JG

Tel: 01439 771241
Fax: 01439 771744

12bedrooms, all with private bathroom; Free House; Children over 12 years and pets welcome,
Bar lunches, restaurant evenings only; Non-smoking areas; Helmsley 3 miles; S£££, D£££.

Guest accommodation at this charming, family-run hotel is provided in twelve comfortable en suite bedrooms, some overlooking the village pond and millrace, some facing the courtyard and walled garden, and all enjoying the facilities of colour television, radio, telephone and beverage makers. An added attraction is the heated indoor swimming pool. Tasty snacks are served at lunchtime in the oak-beamed bar, kept cosy by a cheerful log fire, and a fine dinner menu is presented nightly in the dining room which looks out on to the stone-flagged terrace. Less than three miles from the market town of Helmsley, Harome is a fine example of an unspoilt Yorkshire village. *AA, RAC.*

FEVERSHAM ARMS HOTEL,
Helmsley,
North Yorkshire YO62 5AG

Tel: 01439 770766
Fax: 01439 770346

18 bedrooms, all with private bathroom; Free House; Historic interest; Children and pets welcome; Bar and restaurant meals; Non-smoking areas; Thirsk 12 miles; S££££, D£££.

Rebuilt in warm Yorkshire stone in 1855 on the site of an older hostelry, the Feversham Arms, with its open fires, retains the charm and character of an old coaching inn although, since being purchased in 1967 by the Aragues family, it has acquired the comforts and amenities of a modern hotel. It is fitting that the Richard Bar, the Annabel Lounge and the Rosalind Bar are named after the Aragues children. Decorated with style and even panache, the hotel still remains an inn at heart, even if guest accommodation could fairly be described as being of the multi-starred variety. Central heating is installed and some rooms have four-poster beds as well as luxurious bathrooms; six are located on the ground floor and are convenient for those with walking difficulties. The elegant Goya Restaurant is renowned for its good food, specialising in shellfish and game in season, and dining here by candlelight is a very special experience. The award-winning wine list is both extensive and selective. This welcoming venue stands in beautiful gardens in which there is an all-weather tennis court and an attractive heated swimming pool. The hotel stands at the gateway of the scenic North York Moors National Park and there are numerous sporting opportunities within strolling distance. Also close at hand is the North York Moors Railway which offers a delightful 18-mile ride through picturesque valleys inaccessible by road. *AA*** and Rosette, RAC*** and Restaurant Award.*

YE OLDE RED LION HOTEL,
Old Road, Holme-on-Spalding Moor,
North Yorkshire YO4 4AD

Tel: 01430 860220
Fax: 01430 861471

8 bedrooms, all with private bathroom; Free House with real ale; Bar and restaurant meals; Market Weighton 5 miles; S££, D££.

On the edge of the Yorkshire Wolds and within easy reach of York, Hull, Beverley, Leeds, Sheffield and the East Yorkshire coastal resorts, this charming, 17th century coaching inn is a little bit of history still vibrant with life. Low-beamed ceilings, oak panelling and roaring log fires are visual reminders of unhurried days gone by. However, ancient meets modern by way of the well-appointed cottage-style accommodation built in the grounds of the hotel. Warm and comfortable en suite bedrooms have remote-control television, direct-dial telephone and hospitality tray. During the summer months, the patio area is ablaze with the colours of hanging baskets, tubs and terracotta pots surrounding a central well stocked with koi and ghost carp. Sandra and Brian Walsh have been effective hosts since 1986 judging by the fact that guests find it imperative to return again and again to experience the bonhomie of two spruce bars dispensing a full range of hand-drawn real ales, wines, light meals and 'daily specials' cooked to order. For a memorable night out, the candlelit, oak-panelled restaurant is renowned for its 'Holme' cooked food, the menus including such specialities as locally-caught fish, poultry and prime beef. It is little wonder that this well-run establishment is also a popular venue for conferences and business meetings for which relevant equipment is provided. *ETC* ★★

THE WHITE ROSE HOTEL,
Bedale Road, Leeming Bar, Northallerton,
North Yorkshire DL7 9AY

Tel: 01677 424941/422707
Fax: 01677 425123

18 bedrooms, all with private bathroom; Free House; Children and pets welcome; Restaurant and bar meals; Non-smoking areas; Northallerton 6 miles, Bedale 2; S£££, D£.

Ideally situated between two National Parks, from where you can explore the Yorkshire Dales, the resorts of the East Coast, or even visit the Lake District. Both Herriot Country in the heart of North Yorkshire and the spectacular scenery of Heartbeat Country in the North Yorks Moors are just a short drive away. All our rooms have private bathroom, colour television, radio, tea/coffee making facilities, hairdryer, trouser press and private telephone. Spend an enjoyable time using our own friendly hotel as your base. ♛♛♛ *Commended, AA/RAC* **.

THE WHEATSHEAF,
Carperby, Leyburn,
North Yorkshire DL8 4DF

Tel: 01969 663216
Fax: 01969 663019
e-mail: wheatsheaf@paulmit.globalnet.co.uk

8 bedrooms, all with private bathroom; Free House with real ale; Historic interest; Children and pets welcome; Bar meals, restaurant evenings only; Non-smoking areas; Aysgarth 1 mile; S££, D££.

Set in the heart of the Yorkshire Dales, The Wheatsheaf is famous as the inn where vet-cum-writer James Herriot and his wife spent their honeymoon. Visitors today will still find the same warm hospitality – indeed little has changed, except for the unobtrusive upgrading of facilities to provide all the comforts expected by today's traveller. The beautifully appointed centrally heated bedrooms all have private bathrooms, colour television and tea/coffee making facilities; four-poster rooms are available for those wishing an extra touch of luxury. The comfortable dining room offers the best of local produce, including traditional specialities of the area, with a carefully selected wine list to provide the perfect accompaniment to one's choice. This delightful area is well worth exploring, with sport and leisure amenities to suit all interests. *ETC* ★★★, *AA**, Les Routiers.*

THE BUCK HOTEL,
Reeth, Swaledale,
North Yorkshire DL11 6SW

Tel: 01748 884210; Fax: 01748 884802
website: www.yorkshirenet.co.uk/accgde/buckhotel
e-mail: buckhtl@aol.com

10 bedrooms, all with private bathroom; Free House with real ale; Children and pets welcome; Bar meals; Richmond 9 miles; S££, D££.

One of the last unspoilt corners of the English landscape, the magnificent Yorkshire Dales attract walkers and visitors from far and near, drawn by the area's rugged dales and fells, tumbling rivers and waterfalls, historic castles and abbeys, peaceful villages and bustling market towns. The Buck Hotel stands overlooking the village green of the neat little hamlet of Reeth, which lies just nine miles west of Richmond in the heart of Herriot country. After a busy day exploring the many places of interest within comfortable driving distance, what finer prospect than a cheering glass of one's favourite tipple, and then a tasty selection from the menus of good traditional cooking available both in the bar and in the restaurant. Spacious en suite bedrooms offer a full range of amenities. 👑👑👑 *Commended.*

THE BULL INN,
Church Street, West Tanfield, Ripon,
North Yorkshire HG4 5JQ

Tel and Fax: 01677 470678
e-mail: ewba@bullin.demon.co.uk

5 bedrooms, all with private bathroom; Free House with real ale; Children and pets welcome; Bar meals; Ripon 5 miles; S£££, D££.

Dating in its present form from the 17th century, the Bull Inn has had a long and fascinating history. Accommodation is available in five en suite bedrooms, all with satellite television, radio alarm, tea and coffee making facilities and trouser press. The inn serves traditional food and the riverside garden offers barbecues in the summer months. There are many places of interest in the area such as Fountains Abbey, Ripley Castle, brewery visitor centres and markets; the village has tennis, crown green bowling, snooker and fishing (in season). *Les Routiers Casserole Award.*

THE GANTON GREYHOUND,
Ganton, Near Scarborough,
North Yorkshire YO12 4NX

Tel: 01944 710116
Fax: 01944 710738

18 bedrooms, 16 with private bathroom; Free House with real ale; Children welcome;
Bar and restaurant meals; Non-smoking areas; Filey 8 miles; S£, D£.

Hosts, Terry and Margaret Bennett, are deservedly proud of their excellent reputation for providing good hospitality, good food, and a warm, friendly atmosphere. En suite bedrooms (double, twin, family and disabled) are tastefully furnished, with tea/coffee facilities and colour television, and there is a lounge for the exclusive use of guests. Drinks and meals can be enjoyed in the pleasant bar, where large open fireplaces and oak beams add to the welcoming ambience; meals are also available in the light and airy conservatory restaurant. Its location on the main A64 York to Scarborough road is ideal for exploring this scenic area; the North Yorkshire moors and several golf courses, including Ganton Championship Course, are within easy reach.

VINTAGE HOTEL & RESTAURANT,
Scotch Corner,
North Yorkshire DL10 6NP

Tel: 01748 824424/822961
Fax: 01748 826272

8 bedrooms,5 with private bathroom; Free House; Children welcome; Bar and restaurant meals;
Non-smoking areas; Richmond 4 miles; S££, D££.

Very conveniently situated for a meal/overnight stop on A66, just 150 yards from Scotch Corner Junction(A1). Family-run with rustic Spanish-style Bar and Restaurant with picture windows overlooking open countryside. All bedrooms with central heating, double glazing, television, telephone and tea and coffee making facilities. Local attractions include historic town of Richmond (three miles), Catterick Racecourse (two miles) Croft Motor Racing Circuit (six miles), Yorkshire Dales within easy reach. Open all year except Christmas, New Year and Sunday evenings. *ETC/AA/RAC* ◆◆◆
See also Colour Advertisement on page 7.

WHITE LION INN,
Cray, Buckden, Near Skipton,
North Yorkshire BD23 5JB

Tel: 01756 760262

8 bedrooms,all with private bathroom; Free House with real ale; Historic interest;
Children and pets welcome; Bar and restaurant meals; Hawes 9 miles.

Nestling beneath Buckden Pike at the head of Wharfedale, the White Lion Inn has been tastefully restored to offer eight en suite bedrooms, while retaining its original beams, open log fires and stone-flagged floors. Traditional English fare is served in the bar or cosy dining room; children's menu available. The Inn provides a good choice of beers and spirits, including traditional hand-pulled ales, which in fine weather can be enjoyed in the beer garden. Parents can relax while children enjoy themselves in safety in the enclosed play area. The Inn is on the path of many recognised walks in the very heart of the Yorkshire Dales and makes an ideal base for touring and walking. The thriving market town of Skipton and Aysgarth with its famous falls are both less than half an hour away. There are also many sporting activities locally, including pony trekking, rock climbing, pot holing and golf. Pets welcome if well-behaved. Open all year. *CAMRA Pub of the Season 1991 for District.*

FOX AND HOUNDS,
Starbotton, Skipton,
North Yorkshire BD23 5HY

Tel: 01756 760269

Fax: 01756 760862

2 bedrooms, all with private bathroom; Free House with real ale; Children and pets welcome; Bar meals; Non-smoking areas; Skipton 15 miles; S££, D££.

In beautiful Upper Wharfedale in the heart of the Yorkshire Dales National Park, an area known for its spectacular walks, the stone-built Fox and Hounds is a welcoming sight. A pub for over 160 years, although the original building dates back some 400 years, this warm and homely hostelry has all the visual aids to appeal to tradition seekers – a cosy bar with a large stone fireplace, oak beams, a flagstone floor and walls decorated with old prints. Just off the main bar, where your host Jimmy McFadyen holds sway, is a small dining room where Hilary McFadyen's considerable prowess as a cook is becoming known to an ever-growing band of discerning diners. The bar meals, main courses and sweets offer plenty of variety.

NAG'S HEAD COUNTRY INN,
Pickhill, Near Thirsk,
North Yorkshire YO7 4JG

Tel: 01845 567391

Fax: 01845 567212

17 bedrooms, all with private bathroom; Free House with real ale; Historic interest; Children and pets welcome; Bar and restaurant meals; Non-smoking areas; Leeming 5 miles; S£££, D££.

Since the days when it provided rest and refreshment for stagecoach travellers between London and Edinburgh, facilities at this fine old inn have been considerably updated. Hosts, Raymond and Edward Boynton, have every reason to be justifiably proud of the reputation the 'Nag's Head' has acquired over recent years for the quality of its traditional ales and freshly prepared food. Although the inn still retains the historic character, guests are bound to be impressed by the attractively decorated accommodation; all rooms have en suite facilities, colour television, direct-dial telephone and tea and coffee-makers, making this an ideal base for exploring Herriot Country and the moors and dales of Yorkshire. *AA/RAC**, CAMRA.*

GOLDEN FLEECE HOTEL,
Market Place, Thirsk,
North Yorkshire YO7 1LL

Tel: 01845 523108

Fax: 01845 523996

Children and pets welcome; Northallerton 8 miles.

Set in the heart of Herriot Country, the Golden Fleece Hotel is a 300-year-old coaching inn. This season's special "Mini Break" will provide you with local information on what to see and where to go around this delightful part of North Yorkshire. The Break is a dinner, bed and breakfast package and further information and current prices can be obtained by contacting the reception team at the hotel. *ETC* ★★

LONG ASHES INN,
Threshfield, Near Skipton,
North Yorkshire BD23 5PN

Tel: 01756 752434

Fax: 01756 752937

website: www.longashesinn.co.uk

5 bedrooms, all with private bathroom; Real ale; Children welcome; Bar food and restaurant; Non-smoking areas; Skipton 9 miles, Grassington 3; S££££, D£££.

You will receive a warm welcome and personal attention in this charming traditional old Dales inn, set in picturesque Wharfedale in the Yorkshire Dales National Park. A tranquil retreat in an idyllic setting, perfect for relaxing or as a base from which to enjoy everything the Yorkshire Dales have to offer at any time of the year. The de luxe accommodation includes en suite bathrooms, central heating, tea/coffee making facilities and television, and there is also a honeymoon suite. There is a wide range of hand-pulled ales and freshly prepared food served in the restaurant, as well as a heated indoor pool, sauna, squash courts etc. adjacent, which are available for use by residents. Children's play area. ♨♨♨ *Highly Commended, AA QQQQ Selected*

THE FLASK INN,
Fylingdales, Near Robin Hood's Bay, Whitby, North Yorkshire YO22 4QH

Tel: 01947 880305
Fax: 01947 880592

6 bedrooms, all en suite; Free House with real ale; Historic interest; Children welcome; Bar meals; Non-smoking area; Whitby 7 miles; S££, D£.

A family-run inn with good food, fine ales and comfortable accommodation, this former 17th century monks' hostelry is set in the glorious North York Moors National Park, centrally located for visiting Whitby, Scarborough, Robin Hood's Bay and "Heartbeat" Country. Bedrooms are all en suite and offer colour television, tea and coffee making facilities, hairdryers and central heating. Special Three/Four night Winter Breaks are available from October to March inclusive – stay three nights and fourth night is free. *AA* ◆◆◆.

THE SHIP INN
Port Mulgrave, Hinderwell, Near Whitby, North Yorkshire TS13 5JZ

Tel: 01947 840303

4 bedrooms; Real ales; Children and pets welcome; Bar and restaurant meals; Non-smoking areas; Whitby 10 miles; S£, D£.

The Ship Inn is a traditional family-run pub, set in a little hamlet close to the sea. It is small but comfortable, with two open fires in colder weather and a pleasant beer garden for warmer days. Approximately 10 miles north of Whitby, it is easily accessible by public transport. Traditional cask ales and other beers and lagers are available, and good home-cooked meals are served daily, including vegetarian meals and a selection for children. A recently opened non-smoking restaurant offers a more extensive menu. Accommodation comprises two double/family rooms and two single rooms, each with colour television and tea/coffee facilities. Children are welcome and a cot is available on request. Please telephone for further information.

JEFFERSON ARMS,
Main Street, Thorganby, York, North Yorkshire YO19 6DA

Tel: 01904 448316

5 bedrooms, all with private bathroom; Free House with real ale; Historic interest; Children and pets welcome; Bar and restaurant meals; Non-smoking areas; Selby 7 miles; S££, D££.

This 300 year old building stands quietly in the village of Thorganby, ideally placed for visiting York, the Moors and Dales, the East Coast and many historic houses and places of interest. Food is available either in the bar or, more formally, in the elegant restaurant; whatever one's choice, a varied menu featuring the freshest ingredients is assured. Bedrooms are decorated in cottage style, with features such as trouser presses, hairdryers and colour television to pamper the overnight guest. The attractive gardens with rockery, pond and waterfall can all be enjoyed while breakfasting in the rustic surroundings of the conservatory.

THE NEW INN MOTEL,
Main Street, Huby, York, North Yorkshire YO6 1HQ

Tel: 01347 810219

8 rooms, all en suite, with shower; Restaurant meals; Non-smoking areas; York 9 miles; S££, D£.

Nine miles north of York in the village of Huby in the Vale of York, the Motel is an ideal base for a couple of nights away to visit York (15 minutes to the nearest long-stay car park), or a longer stay to visit the East Coast of Yorkshire, the Dales, the Yorkshire Moors, Herriot Country, Harrogate and Ripon. The Motel is situated behind the New Inn (a separate business) which, contrary to its name, is a 500-year old hostelry, originally an old coaching inn, and full of character. All rooms are en suite (singles, doubles, twin and family rooms), and have colour television and tea-making facilities. Good home cooking is served, including vegetarian meals, and a full English breakfast is a speciality. PETS ARE WELCOME. The accommodation is suitable for the disabled. Licensed. Special three-day breaks always available. Telephone for brochure. *AA* ◆◆◆.

THE BLACK SWAN INN,
Oldstead, Coxwold, York,
North Yorkshire YO61 4BL

Tel: 01347 868387

Bedrooms with private bathroom; Real ales; Pets wecome; Bar and restaurant meals;
Non-smoking areas; York 20 miles, Kilburn 2; S£££, D££..

This charming, family-run 18th century inn is set in the stunning scenery of the North York Moors National Park, ideal walking country and enjoying magnificent views. Accommodation is available in superb chalet-style en suite rooms with colour television, central heating and tea/coffee making facilities. Guests can enjoy Yorkshire farmhouse cooking, either from the bar meals menu or in the à la carte restaurant. Vegetarian meals are a speciality and there is a selection of fine wines. Brochure available on request.

SHIP INN,
Acaster Malbis, York,
North Yorkshire YO23 2UH

Tel: 01904 705609/703888
Fax: 01904 705971

8 bedrooms, all with private facilities; Free House with real ale, Historic interest; Children welcome;
Bar and restaurant meals; Leeds 17 miles, York 3; S££, D££.

This attractive and well-run hostelry on the banks of the Ouse is only a short distance from the magnificence of York, the United Kingdom's second most popular tourist attraction. Offering first-class fare and spruce accommodation, including one four-poster bedroom and a family room, the inn makes a superb holiday headquarters and is equally popular with boating enthusiasts and businessmen. Excellent lunches and evening snacks may be enjoyed in the friendly Riverside Bar. The inn now boasts a conservatory with water fountains, tropical plants and river views and has its own moorings for residents and visitors, as well as fishing rights. Further afield, the Yorkshire Dales beckon and the coast may be reached in less than an hour. *Tourist Board Listed Commended, AA Listed.*

SCOTLAND

Aberdeenshire, Banff & Moray

INVER HOTEL,
Crathie, By Balmoral,
Aberdeenshire AB35 5UL

Tel: 013397 42345
Fax: 013397 42009

9 bedrooms, all with private bathroom; Free House; Historic interest; Children and pets welcome;
Bar and restaurant meals; Non-smoking areas; Ballater 9 miles, Braemar 9; S£, D£.

It is hardly surprising that walkers, climbers, skiers – in fact outdoor types of all persuasions – find their way to this delightful little inn, set as it is amid the hills of the Upper Deeside Valley, just a short drive from two of the main ski centres. Those of a less active inclination are drawn here too by the breathtaking scenery, the area's royal associations, and, perhaps, by the attractions of Scotland's national drink (Royal Lochnagar distillery is a mere two miles away). Completely renovated and with all modern amenities, the inn nevertheless retains its traditional character and offers all that is finest in food and comfort, featuring the best local produce and genuine personal service.

FIFE ARMS HOTEL,
The Square, Dufftown, Near Keith,
Banffshire AB55 4AD

Tel: 01340 820220

Fax: 01340 821137

7 bedrooms, 6 with private bathroom; Free House; Children and pets welcome;
Bar and restaurant meals; Elgin 16 miles; S££, D£.

Welcome to Dufftown, the malt whisky capital of the land of distilleries where, in the centre of the village, the convivial bar of this family-run hotel is a popular meeting place. A range of tempting dishes is on offer in the lounge, including such unusual specialities as Ostrich, Bison and Buffalo Steaks. Reasonably priced bed and breakfast accommodation is available in en suite chalets at the rear of the hotel; all are attractively furnished in pine and are equipped with television and tea and coffee-makers. Good facilities exist for children and disabled guests. *STB ★ Hotel.*

MINMORE HOUSE HOTEL,
Glenlivet, Ballindalloch,
Banffshire AB37 9DB

Tel: 01807 590378

Fax: 01807 590472

website: www.SmoothHound.co.uk/hotels/minmore.html

10 bedrooms, all with private bathroom; Free House with real ale; Historic interest; Children and pets
welcome; Bar lunches and restaurant meals; Non-smoking areas; Tomintoul 6 miles; S£££, D£££.

In the lee of the magnificent Cairngorms and sheltered by four acres of gardens, this hospitable hotel was once the home of George Smith, founder of Glenlivet whisky. It is only fitting, therefore, that there should be such an impressive array of single malt whiskies displayed in the oak-panelled bar. After a hearty breakfast, days may be filled with a wide spectrum of activities: walking, fishing, bird watching, playing golf, horse riding; visiting art galleries, museums, historic castles or setting out on the famous Whisky Trail. 'At home' moments may be spent playing tennis or croquet in the grounds or swimming in the outdoor pool. Always there is the promise of a sumptuous five-course dinner to round off a perfect day. *STB ★★★ Hotel, Taste of Scotland.*

The **£** symbol when appearing at the end of the italic section of an entry shows the anticipated price, during 2000, for full Bed and Breakfast.

Normal Bed & Breakfast rate per person (in single room)		Normal Bed & Breakfast rate per person (sharing double/twin room)	
PRICE RANGE	CATEGORY	PRICE RANGE	CATEGORY
Under £25	S£	**Under £25**	D£
£26-£35	S££	**£26-£35**	D££
£36-£45	S£££	**£36-£45**	D£££
Over £45	S££££	**Over £45**	D££££

This is meant as an indication only and does not show prices for Special Breaks, Weekends, etc. Guests are therefore advised to verify all prices on enquiring or booking.

Key to Tourist Board Ratings
Scotland and Wales

The Scottish Tourist Board Star Grading System. This easy-to-understand system tells you at a glance the quality standard you can expect. The gradings range from ★ (Fair and acceptable) to ★★★★★ (Exceptional, world-class) and will also include the type of accommodation eg ★★★ Self-catering or ★★ Hotel.

The Wales Tourist Board also operates the above system for serviced accommodation only. Self-catering properties will continue to show the **Dragon Award Grading** from **One** to **Five** depending on quality and facilities.

Argyll & Bute

GALLEY OF LORNE INN,
Ardfern, By Lochgilphead,
Argyll PA31 8QN

Tel: 01852 500284

7 bedrooms, all with private bathroom; Free House; Historic interest; Children and dogs welcome;
Bar meals, restaurant evenings only; Lochgilphead 12 miles; S£££, D££.

Beautifully situated overlooking Loch Craignish, this warmly welcoming free house is particularly noted for its restaurant which offers excellent menus featuring Scottish specialities, charcoal-grilled steaks and seafood fresh from the loch; a substantial range of bar meals is also available, along with a good selection of malt whiskies. Those seeking accommodation will find spick-and-span, nicely furnished guest rooms, all with private bathrooms, colour television, and tea and coffee facilities; most have stunning views of the loch. A wide range of sporting and leisure activities in this area make this an ideal base for a Highland holiday at any time. *STB ★★★ Inn.*

INVERORAN HOTEL,
Bridge of Orchy,
Argyll PA36 4AQ

Tel: 01838 400220
Fax: 01838 400399
website: www.loch-awe/hotels.htm

8 bedrooms, one with private bathroom; Historic interest; Children and pets welcome; Bar meals
and snacks, restaurant evenings only; Non-smoking areas; Tyndrum 6 miles; S££, D££.

Well worth the trouble of turning off the beaten track (in this case off the main A82 at Bridge of Orchy onto the A8005), this secluded little hotel offers real peace and quiet in an area unrivalled for its scenic beauty at the head of Loch Tulla. As a base for a walking holiday it can surely have few equals – the West Highland Way and General Wade's Road pass the door, a variety of routes can be followed in the area at levels to suit all abilities, and the hotel itself has drying facilities and can provide packed lunches on request. Skiers and fishermen are well catered for too – White Corries and Aonach Mor are within easy reach, and salmon and trout can be caught by arrangement on private water. Whether you are actively inclined or are seeking an escape from the hustle and bustle of modern day living, you will find here a warm welcome and comfortable accommodation in centrally heated bedrooms, all with washbasins and tea and coffee making facilities. The hotel is open all year except Christmas, and on request guests can be met at the local rail station. *STB ★ Inn*

CAIRNDOW STAGECOACH INN,
Cairndow,
Argyll PA26 8BN

Tel: 01499 600286
Fax: 01499 600220

12 bedrooms, all en suite; Free House with real ale; Historic interest; Children welcome; Bar and restaurant meals; Non-smoking areas; Arrochar 12 miles, Inveraray 10; S££, D££.

Amidst the beautiful scenery which characterises the upper reaches of Loch Fyne, this historic stagecoach inn enjoys a spectacular sheltered position. In the delightful restaurant one may dine well by candlelight from the table d'hôte and à la carte menus; bar meals are served all day. There is also a new functions bar and games room. Bedrooms are centrally heated, with radio, television, direct-dial telephone, baby listening, and tea-making facilities. There are two de luxe rooms with two-person spa baths, king-size beds and 20" television! This is an ideal spot for touring Oban, the Western Highlands, Glencoe, the Trossachs, the Cowal Peninsula, Kintyre and Campbeltown. The inn is under the personal supervision of hosts Mr and Mrs Douglas Fraser, and the area offers opportunities for many outdoor pursuits and visits. Lochside beer garden, exercise room, sauna and solarium.

INSHAIG PARK HOTEL,
Easdale, Seil Island, By Oban,
Argyll PA34 4RF

Tel and Fax: 01852 300256

6 bedrooms, all with private bathroom; Free House; Bar and restaurant meals; Non-smoking areas; Oban 16 miles; S£££, D££.

The famous eighteenth century "Bridge over the Atlantic" takes one onto Seil Island and Easdale where you will find this comfortable Victorian hotel, set in its own grounds overlooking the sea and the scattered islands of the Inner Hebrides. This family-run hotel has six comfortable bedrooms, all with central heating, colour television and tea-making facilities. Meals can be taken either in Slaters Bar and Bistro (over 40 malt whiskies to sample) or in the Victorian dining room overlooking the sea. Fresh local seafood is a speciality. An ideal place to stay for an "away from it all" holiday. Open all year. STB ★★★ Hotel, Les Routiers Casserole Award 1997 and Silver Key Award 1998.

Borders

THE HORSESHOE INN,
Eddleston,
Peeblesshire EH45 8QP

Tel: 01721 730225/306
Fax: 01721 730268
website: www.horseshoeinn.com

8 bedrooms, all with private bathroom; Free House; Historic interest; Children welcome, pets by arrangement; Bar and restaurant meals; Non-smoking areas; Peebles 4 miles.

This privately owned traditional country inn offers good food, wine, and ale, either in the relaxed atmosphere of the comfortable lounge bar or in the more formal ambience of the charming restaurant. Bedrooms are situated in a separate building at the rear of the inn; all are en suite, with television and tea/coffee making facilities. Only an hour from Glasgow and half an hour from Edinburgh, the inn is ideally placed for a day in the country or for a longer break. Special activity breaks – details on request. Leisure activities include salmon and trout fishing, shooting, golf, walking and cycling. *Les Routiers.*

TRAQUAIR ARMS,
Traquair Road, Innerleithen,
Peeblesshire EH44 6PD

Tel: 01896 830229
Fax: 01896 830260

10 bedrooms, all with private bathroom; Free House with real ale; Children and pets welcome; Bar and restaurant meals; Non-smoking areas; Peebles 6 miles; S£££. D££.

A solidly constructed traditional 19th century Scottish inn, just 40 minutes from Edinburgh and 10 minutes from Peebles, in a delightful Borders valley. Hugh and Marian Anderson run it as a relaxing, friendly, family-run hotel with genuine concern for the comfort of their guests. Imaginative menus utilise the best local produce, and in appropriate weather can be enjoyed beside a blazing log fire in the dining room or al fresco in the secluded garden. The bar prides itself on its real ales. Egon Ronay's Good Pub Guide says "Bed and breakfast is recommended, particularly the handsome Scottish meal complete with superb kippers". *STB ★★★, Taste of Scotland, CAMRA, Best Breakfast in Britain 1990, "In Britain" Scottish Finalist 1993, 'Best Bar Food' Winner 1997.*

THE WHEATSHEAF AT SWINTON,
Swinton, Duns,
Berwickshire TD11 3JJ

Tel: 01890 860257
Fax: 01890 860688

6 bedrooms, all with private bathroom; Free House with real ale; Children and pets welcome; Bar and restaurant meals; Non-smoking areas; Kelso 12 miles; S£££££, D£££.

First-class food is one of the principal attractions of this appealing little 'restaurant with rooms' on the green, with fresh Scottish game and seafood specialities from an extensive menu on which fresh local produce figures prominently. There is also invariably a tempting array of daily 'blackboard specials'. Run by chef/owner, Alan Reid and his wife, Julie, the hotel boasts six well-appointed bedrooms, all of which have en suite facilities. The hotel is close to the River Tweed and the coast and is an excellent base for touring the fertile Border Country. Please note the 'Wheatsheaf' is closed all day Monday. *STB ★★★★ Restaurant with Rooms, AA, Good Pub Guide 'Dining Pub of the Year'.*

Dumfries & Galloway

ANNANDALE ARMS HOTEL,
High Street, Moffat,
Dumfriesshire DG10 9HF

Tel: 01683 220013
e-mail: reception@AnnandaleArmsHotel.co.uk
website: www.AnnandaleArmsHotel.co.uk

16 bedrooms, many with private bathroom; Bar and restaurant meals; Children and pets welcome; Dumfries 19 miles.

This fine old Coaching Hotel stands in the centre of the beautiful spa town of Moffat, amidst wonderful scenery. The hotel offers excellent accommodation in 16 bedrooms, many of which have private facilities. Fine food is served in the restaurant each evening and in the comfortable panelled bar lunchtimes and evenings. The hotel is just a few minutes from Moffat Golf Club, where visitors are welcome. One hour Edinburgh/Glasgow to the North or Carlisle to the South, and easily found one mile off Junction 15 A74(M6). Pets and children are welcome. *STB ★★★ Hotel, Les Routiers Silver Key Award 1998/1999.*

FHG PUBLICATIONS

publish a large range of well-known accommodation guides. We will be happy to send you details or you can use the order form at the back of this book.

Edinburgh & Lothians

YE OLDE ORIGINAL ROSLIN INN,
Main Street, Roslin,
Midlothian EH25 9LE

Tel: 0131-440 2384
Fax: 0131-440 2514

6 bedrooms, all with private bathroom; Free House; Historic interest; Children and pets welcome; Bar meals, restaurant evenings only; Non-smoking areas; Edinburgh 7 miles; S£££, D££.

The 'Old Original' was in former times a temperance hotel but those seeking refreshment today may be assured that all four bars are well stocked with good beers, spirits and an interesting selection of fine wines. Substantial lunches are served in the comfortable lounge bar and the a la carte dinner menu attracts locals as well as tourists to a dining room graced by an absorbing collection of antiques and here one may dine memorably by candlelight. Six centrally heated, en suite bedrooms are available for letting, including two honeymoon suites; all have pleasing decor, television and tea and coffee-making facilities. Edinburgh is only seven miles away and there is a new leisure centre with a swimming pool nearby in Loanhead. *AA, Les Routiers.*

HELP IMPROVE BRITISH TOURIST STANDARDS

You are choosing holiday accommodation from our very popular FHG Publications.

Whether it be a hotel, guest house, farmhouse or self-catering accommodation, we think you will find it hospitable, comfortable and clean, and your host and hostess friendly and helpful.

Why not write and tell us about it?

As a recognition of the generally well-run and excellent holiday accommodation reviewed in our publications, we at FHG Publications Ltd. present a diploma to proprietors who receive the highest recommendation from their guests who are also readers of our Guides. If you care to write to us praising the holiday you have booked through FHG Publications Ltd. – whether this be board, self-catering accommodation, a sporting or a caravan holiday, what you say will be evaluated and the proprietors who reach our final list will be contacted.

The winning proprietor will receive an attractive framed diploma to display on his premises as recognition of a high standard of comfort, amenity and hospitality. FHG Publications Ltd. offer this diploma as a contribution towards the improvement of standards in tourist accommodation in Britain. Help your excellent host or hostess to win it!

FHG DIPLOMA

We nominate ....

....

Because

Name ....

Address ....

Telephone No...

Highlands

NETHER LOCHABER HOTEL,
Onich, Fort William,
Inverness-shire PH33 6SE

Tel: 01855 821235
Fax: 01855 821545

5 bedrooms; Free House; Historic interest; Bar and restaurant meals;
Non-smoking areas; Edinburgh 121 miles, Glasgow 91, Oban 48, Fort William 10; S££, D££.

An ideal centre from which to explore Lochaber, the Ardnamurchan Peninsula and Glencoe. Traditional home cooking goes hand in hand with homely service, comfortable accommodation and private facilities. The inn stands on the shores of beautiful Loch Linnhe at Corran Ferry.

LOCH LEVEN HOTEL,
Onich, Fort William,
Inverness-shire PH33 6SA

Tel: 01855 821236/459
Fax: 01855 821550

All bedrooms with private bathrooms; Bar and restaurant meals; Children welcome;
Non-smoking areas; Fort William 10 miles.

This small, family-run hotel is situated on the shores of Loch Leven, ideal for touring the surrounding area which is rich in natural beauty and historical connections. The Great Glen, Loch Ness and Oban are all within easy reach, as are the ski slopes of White Corries and Nevis Range. All bedrooms are en suite, with tea/coffee facilities, television, hairdryers etc, and there is a large comfortable lounge, a lively local bar with occasional entertainment, a residents' lounge, a family room and a pleasant dining room. Relax and dine in style from the à la carte menu, or choose from the bar meals menu and enjoy the loch and mountain views. Children of all ages are welcome in the family and games room, where there are video games and two pool tables.

THE OLD INN,
Gairloch,
Ross-shire IV21 2BD

Tel: 01445 712006
Fax: 01445 712445
website: www.theoldinn.co.uk

14 bedrooms, all with private bathroom; Free House with real ale; Historic interest; Bar and restaurant meals; Non-smoking areas; Inverness 71 miles, Ullapool 56; S££, D££.

Traditional West Highland Coaching Inn with comfortable en suite rooms. Featured on TV's top holiday programme "Wish You Were Here". Emphasis on real ales, real food, real fires, real Highland hospitality. Locally caught seafood and Scottish game products are house specialities. Colour television, beverage makers, direct-dial telephones and child/baby listening facilities are provided in each guest room. Picturesque location; walking, climbing, fishing, diving, golf, pony trekking all close by. Real value-for-money special 'room only' rates are available from £35.00 (double or twin) with breakfast from £3.50. *STB ★★★ Inn, AA/RAC**.*

LOCHCARRON HOTEL,
Main Street, Lochcarron,
Wester Ross IV54 8YS

Tel: 01520 722226/722204
Fax: 01520 722612

10 bedrooms, all with private bathroom; Free House; Historic interest; Children and pets welcome; Bar meals, restaurant evenings only; Non-smoking areas; Achnasheen 21 miles; S£/£££, D£/£££.

A Highland inn of long standing, this fine establishment on the shores of Loch Carron and surrounded by the rugged grandeur of Wester Ross, has acquired and developed hotel facilities of high calibre. The bar still exudes a time-hallowed ambience in which to consider an impressive stock of draught beers and malt whiskies and, in common with the delightful dining room, a spacious seating area commands panoramic loch and mountain views. The outstanding cuisine includes several local specialities with seafood figuring prominently. Tastefully furnished en suite bedrooms serve discerning guests choosing this splendid hotel as their holiday base. *STB ★★ Hotel, AA, RAC.*

PORTLAND ARMS,
Lybster,
Caithness KW3 6BS

Tel: 01593 721208/721255
Fax: 01593 721722
e-mail: portland.arms@btconnect. com

20 bedrooms, all with private bathroom; Free House; Historic interest; Children welcome; Bar lunches, restaurant meals; Wick 12 miles; £££.

As sturdy and enduring as the cliffs of this northern corner, the Portland was built in the early 1800s as a staging post on the new parliamentary road. Enlarged and upgraded to a high standard, accommodation today comprises 20 beautifully furnished guest rooms, all with private bath or shower, electric blanket, telephone, colour television, and tea and coffee facilities; some with four poster or half-tester bed. The traditional Scottish meal of High Tea is served in the restaurant from 5pm to 6.30pm, as an alternative to the fine table d'hôte dinner, and bar snacks ranging from soups, sandwiches and baked potatoes to baked sole, sirloin and gammon steaks. *Taste of Scotland.*

FHG PUBLICATIONS

publish a large range of well-known accommodation guides. We will be happy to send you details or you can use the order form at the back of this book.

Lanarkshire

THE CROOK INN,
Tweedsmuir, Biggar,
Lanarkshire ML12 6QN

Tel: 01899 880272
Fax: 01899 880294

7 bedrooms, all with private bathroom; Free House with real ale; Historic interest;
Children and pets welcome; Bar meals; Non-smoking areas; Edinburgh 37 miles; S££, D££.

Robert Burns wrote his poem *Willie Wastle's Wife* in the kitchen of this inspiring hostelry, which has played host to Covenanter and cattle reiver as well as poet in its four-hundred-year history. Situated in attractive gardens in the upper Tweed Valley, seven guest bedrooms cater for those who would stay to savour the peace of this once-violent countryside. All have en suite facilities and are furnished comfortably and with charm, and a good breakfast is included in the accommodation charge. A varied and pleasing bar menu is presented at lunchtime and substantial evening dinners are served. The name, please note, refers to the shepherd's staff, not a member of the criminal classes. *RAC/AA***.

The **£** symbol when appearing at the end of the italic section of an entry shows the anticipated price, during 2000, for full Bed and Breakfast.

Normal Bed & Breakfast rate per person *(in single room)*		*Normal Bed & Breakfast rate per person* *(sharing double/twin room)*	
PRICE RANGE	CATEGORY	PRICE RANGE	CATEGORY
Under £25	S£	**Under £25**	D£
£26-£35	S££	**£26-£35**	D££
£36-£45	S£££	**£36-£45**	D£££
Over £45	S££££	**Over £45**	D££££

This is meant as an indication only and does not show prices for Special Breaks, Weekends, etc. Guests are therefore advised to verify all prices on enquiring or booking.

Perth & Kinross

KENMORE HOTEL,
Kenmore,
Perthshire PH15 2NU

Tel: 01887 830205
Fax: 01887 830262

40 bedrooms, all with private bathroom; Free House; Historic interest; Children and pets welcome;
Bar meals, restaurant evenings only; Non-smoking areas; Aberfeldy 6 miles; S£££, D£££.

Though one of the principal attractions of this delightful waterside hotel is the fishing and golfing breaks it promotes, being of sporting inclination is by no means a prerequisite of a stay in beautiful Kenmore, so beloved of Robert Burns that he wrote a few lines in its praise on a visit here. They can be seen in the hotel's Poet's Parlour, where one may toast oneself in front of a roaring fire while experiencing the inner warmth of good malt whisky. Local produce is heavily relied upon in the Kenmore's kitchen – little wonder in an area which boasts fine fresh salmon from the River Tay, seasonal game and the best of meat and poultry. Guest accommodation is provided in single, twin and double bedrooms, all furnished with discreet good taste and equipped with colour television and private bathroom. The Verandah Room bestows an extra touch of luxury with its own private terrace and conservatory and expansive river views. Leisure facilities including swimming pool and sauna are available nearby for the use of hotel residents, and the hotel has its own golf course set in parkland surrounding Taymouth Castle. *STB ★★★ Hotel, RAC, Les Routiers.*

PALACE HOTEL,
Breadalbane Terrace, Aberfeldy,
Perthshire PH15 2AG

Tel: 01887 820359
e-mail: clair@aberfeldypalace.co.uk

15 bedrooms, all with private bathroom; Free House with real ale; Historic interest; Children welcome;
Bar and restaurant meals; Non-smoking areas; Pitlochry 8 miles; S££, D££.

Outdoor activities, natural history, and local folklore are the order of the day. Try the challenging Taymouth Castle Golf Course, enjoy a Landrover off-road safari, and immerse yourself in local history, folklore and legends – you may even be lucky enough to see pine marten, eagles and capercaillie. Visit Loch Tay's prehistoric loch dwelling, or simply sample the delights of the local distillery. This owner-managed quality hotel offers three-day breaks in a beautiful location.

Please mention
Recommended WAYSIDE & COUNTRY INNS
when seeking refreshment or accommodation
at a Hotel mentioned in these pages.

Scottish Islands

ORASAY INN
Lochcarnan,
South Uist

Tel: 01870 610298
Fax: 01870 610390
e-mail: orasayinn@btinternet.com

Set in an area of outstanding natural beauty. Centrally placed for exploring the Uists, Orasay Inn is a privately owned hotel which serves some of the finest food in the Western Isles. Isobel is a 'Natural Cooking of Scotland' trainer and uses locally sourced products in the preparation of food. All meals are served in our tastefully appointed dining room which affords superb views across The Minch and mountains of South Uist. All rooms have en suite facilities. We serve full Scottish or Continental breakfast whenever required. Please contact Alan and Isobel Graham for details. *STB ★★★ Inn, Taste of Scotland.*

The
GOLF
GUIDE
Where to Play
Where to Stay
2000

Available from most bookshops, the 2000 edition of **THE GOLF GUIDE** covers details of every UK golf course – well over 2500 entries – for holiday or business golf. Hundreds of hotel entries offer convenient accommodation, accompanying details of the courses – the 'pro', par score, length etc.

In association with 'Golf Monthly' and including the Ryder Cup Report as well as Holiday Golf in Ireland, France, Portugal, Spain, The USA and Thailand .

£9.95 from bookshops or £10.50 including postage (UK only) from FHG Publications, Abbey Mill Business Centre, Paisley PAI ITJ

WALES

Anglesey & Gwynedd

PENHELIG ARMS HOTEL,
Terrace Road, Aberdyfi,
Gwynedd LL35 0LT

Tel: 01654 767215
Fax: 01654 767690
e-mail: penheligarms@saqnet.co.uk

10 bedrooms, all with private bathroom; Free House with real ale; Children and pets welcome;
Bar and restaurant meals; Non-smoking areas; Machynlleth 9 miles; S£££, D£££.

This bright and friendly establishment takes in superb views of the Dyfi estuary and in fine weather, visitors can sit by the sea wall and enjoy a drink or an excellent meal, the hotel's reputation for first-class food well supported by a highly commended and interesting wine list. The charmingly appointed (non-smoking) bedrooms have wonderful views of the sea and mountains beyond and amenities such as en suite facilities, colour television, radio and direct-dial telephone ensure that a stay here is truly relaxing. Set on the seaward fringe of the Snowdonia National Park, Aberdyfi is an ideal centre for touring North and mid-Wales and where better to stay than this comfortable and informal hotel. *WTB* ★★★ *Hotel, AA 'Seafood Pub of the Year Wales and the Marches', Welsh Rarebits.*

North Wales

WHEATSHEAF INN,
Betws-yn-Rhos, Abergele,
North Wales LL22 8AW

Tel: 01492 680218

Fax: 01492 680666

4 bedrooms, all en suite; Free House with real ale; Historic interest; Children welcome; Bar and restaurant meals; Non-smoking areas; Abergele 4 miles; S££, D£.

An ale house in the 13th century and licensed as a coaching inn in the 17th century, this fascinating hostelry retains several attractive features including brass-strewn oak beams, stone pillars and an original hayloft ladder. The warm atmosphere of the olde-worlde lounge bar is well in keeping with the mood, and dining by candlelight in the intimate restaurant is a rewarding experience. Beautifully placed in a picturesque village a little way inland from the main North Wales coastal resorts, the inn is popular with locals and visitors alike. Accommodation is available in comfortable bedrooms (single, double and family), all with colour television and tea/coffee facilities. *WTB* ★★.

THE HAWK AND BUCKLE INN,
Llannefydd, Near Denbigh,
North Wales LL16 5ED

Tel: 01745 540249

Fax: 01745 540316

10 bedrooms, all with private bathroom; Free House; Historic interest;
Bar lunches and restaurant meals; Non-smoking areas; Colwyn Bay 7 miles; S£££, D££.

Every 20th century comfort is to be found at this welcoming seventeenth century village inn. All the en suite guest rooms in the tasteful extensions are equipped with telephones, tea/coffee making facilities and televisions; trouser press and hairdryer available. Furnishings are comfortable and pleasing to the eye. Local game, pork, lamb and freshly caught salmon and trout are imaginatively served in the inn's popular restaurant, and varied and substantial bar snacks are offered at lunchtimes and evenings. Closed lunchtimes (except Wednesday and weekends) between October 1st and May 1st. Hosts Robert and Barbara Pearson will happily supply a wealth of information on the area. Visa and Mastercard accepted. *WTB* ★★★ *Inn, Egon Ronay, Ashley Courtenay.* **See also Colour Advertisement on page 8.**

GOLDEN PHEASANT HOTEL,
Glyn Ceiriog, Near Llangollen,
North Wales LL20 7BB

Tel: 01691 718281

Fax: 01691 718479

19 bedrooms, all with private bathroom; Free House; Children and pets welcome;
Bar and restaurant meals; Non-smoking areas; Llangollen 3 miles; S££, D££.

The Golden Pheasant has been described as a "home-from-home" – but that presupposes one's home enjoys the ultimate in comfort, breathtaking hill and valley views, and such facilities as whirlpool bath, four-poster bed and an attentive and willing staff! All guest accommodation is appointed to a high standard with tea and coffee facilities, colour television and bathroom en suite, and public rooms throughout combine charm and elegance with sumptuous comfort. The romantic split-level restaurant provides a lovely setting for the imaginative menus presented nightly. This scenic area offers many attractions and special rates for short breaks make an extended stay a particularly appealing prospect. *WTB* ★★★, *AA* ***.

BRITANNIA INN,
Horseshoe Pass, Llangollen,
North Wales LL20 8DW

Tel and Fax: 01978 860144
e-mail: brit@globalnet.co.uk
website: www.users.globalnet.co.uk/~brit

5 bedrooms, all with private bathroom; Free House with real ale; Historic interest; Children and pets welcome; Bar meals, restaurant evenings only; Non-smoking areas; Wrexham 9 miles; S££, D£.

The Britannia Inn can trace its origins back to the 15th century, and great care was taken during refurbishment to preserve its original character while providing up-to-date facilities. Whether stopping off on a day out exploring the lovely countryside around Llangollen or staying for a short break or extended holiday, patrons will be delighted by the excellent range of food and refreshments on offer, and by the warm welcome which greets all. Four-poster or half-tester beds come as standard in all the pretty, cottage-style en suite bedrooms, along with modern amenities such as colour television and tea/coffee making facilities. *WTB ★★★ Inn, Wales in Bloom Award Winner.*

The **£** symbol when appearing at the end of the italic section of an entry shows the anticipated price, during 2000, for full Bed and Breakfast.

Normal Bed & Breakfast rate per person (in single room)		Normal Bed & Breakfast rate per person (sharing double/twin room)	
PRICE RANGE	CATEGORY	PRICE RANGE	CATEGORY
Under £25	S£	**Under £25**	D£
£26-£35	S££	**£26-£35**	D££
£36-£45	S£££	**£36-£45**	D£££
Over £45	S££££	**Over £45**	D££££

This is meant as an indication only and does not show prices for Special Breaks, Weekends, etc. Guests are therefore advised to verify all prices on enquiring or booking.

FHG PUBLICATIONS

publish a large range of well-known accommodation guides. We will be happy to send you details or you can use the order form at the back of this book.

Cardiganshire

GEORGE BORROW HOTEL,
Ponterwyd, Aberystwyth,
Cardiganshire SY23 3AD

Tel: 01970 890230; Fax: 01970 890587
e-mail: georgeborrow@clara.net
website: www.george-borrow.co.uk

9 bedrooms,all en suite; Free House with real ale; Historic interest; Children welcome,
pets by prior arrangement; Bar meals, restaurant evenings only; Devil's Bridge 3 miles;S£, D£.

Nestling in the foothills of the Cambrian Mountains, close to the source of the River Severn and the famous Devil's Bridge, this comfortable hostelry has two pleasant bars serving fine ale and home-cooked food whilst, for more formal dining, the 40-seater restaurant presents an interesting à la carte menu featuring local specialities and vegetarian meals. Antique furniture and log fires add to the homely ambience and for those wishing to extend their stay in an area of dramatic scenery, the hotel has a number of well-appointed bedrooms. Perched on the edge of the Rheidol Gorge, the hotel enjoys stunning views, emphasising that this is a splendid venue for walking, fishing and bird watching. *WTB* ★★ *Hotel.*

WEBLEY WATERFRONT HOTEL,
Poppit Sands, St Dogmaels,
Cardiganshire SA43 3LN

Tel and Fax: 01239 612085

8 bedrooms, 4 with private bathroom; Free House with real ale; Historic interest; Children welcome;
Bar and restaurant meals; Non-smoking areas; Cardigan 2 miles; S££, D£.

The only hotel at the northern eand of the Pembrokeshire Coastal Path, this fine and friendly spot buzzes with vitality and is a popular rendezvous for dinghy sailors, yachtsmen, wind surfers and local dry-bobs alike. In a picturesque setting on the shores of the Teifi estuary, the hotel also attracts walkers, bird watchers and naturalists; horse riding, pony trekking and golf may be arranged. All are assured of good home-cooked food and draught ales to go with the convivial company. The lovely little village of St.Dogmaels with its 12th century abbey remains is only a mile away. The hotel has several en suite rooms overlooking the estuary and there is also a residents' television lounge and non-smoking dining area. *AA.*

Key to Tourist Board Ratings
Scotland and Wales

The Scottish Tourist Board Star Grading System. This easy-to-understand system tells you at a glance the quality standard you can expect. The gradings range from ★ (Fair and acceptable) to ★★★★★ (Exceptional, world-class) and will also include the type of accommodation eg ★★★ Self-catering or ★★ Hotel.

The Wales Tourist Board also operates the above system for serviced accommodation only. Self-catering properties will continue to show the **Dragon Award Grading** from **One** to **Five** depending on quality and facilities.

Carmarthenshire

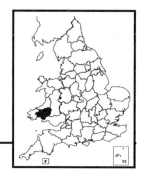

ANGEL INN,
Salem, Llandeilo,
Carmarthenshire SA19 7LY

Tel: 01558 823394
Fax: 01558 823371

3 bedrooms, all with private bathroom; Free House with real ale; Children and pets welcome; Bar and restaurant meals (weekday evenings only); Non-smoking areas; Carmarthen 14 miles; S££, D£.

Hosts, Bernard and Mary Kindred, welcome all who crave peace and plenty in surroundings of unspoiled natural beauty, although there are numerous diversions, apart from walking, to enjoy in this lovely area – golf, horse riding, fishing, swimming and bowls to name but a few. A bar lounge with a log fire is a convivial meeting place and the restaurant is widely acknowledged for its superb fare. Bar and restaurant meals are available in the evening and there is a carvery for Sunday lunch. A large garden with a safe play area is an attraction for children, and those seeking to linger longer in this tranquil part of Wales have excellent en suite accommodation at their disposal. *AA* ◆◆◆◆

THE ROYAL OAK INN,
Rhandirmwyn, Llandovery,
Carmarthenshire SA20 0NY

Tel: 01550 760201, Fax: 01550 760332
e-mail: royaloak@globalnet.co.uk

5 bedrooms, 3 with private bathroom; Free House with real ale; Bar and restaurant meals; Llandovery 7 miles; ££.

We know from the comments in our Visitors' Book that we are friendly, efficient and courteous, the most frequent remarks being "home from home" and "We'll be back". Our spacious rooms offer comfort and most have colour television and private facilities; all have tea and coffee making. The very full menu caters for most tastes, including vegetarian, and is complemented by a good range of wines and real ales. Within easy reach are visitor attractions to suit all, including some fine walking, riding and fishing. *AA Listed, Les Routiers Approved.*

NOTE

All the information in this book is given in good faith in the belief that it is correct. However, the publishers cannot guarantee the facts given in these pages, neither are they responsible for changes in policy, ownership or terms that may take place after the date of going to press. Readers should always satisfy themselves that the facilities they require are available and that the terms, if quoted, still apply.

Powys

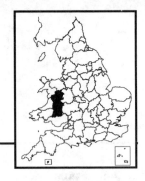

SEVERN ARMS HOTEL,
Penybont, Llandrindod Wells,
Powys LD1 5UA

Tel: 01597 851224/851344

Fax: 01597 851693

10 bedrooms, all with private bathroom; Free House with real ale; Historic interest; Children and pets welcome; Bar meals, restaurant evenings only plus Sunday lunch; Llandrindod Wells 4 miles; S££, D£.

A handsome early Victorian coaching inn, the Severn Arms enjoys an enviable reputation for first-class service and hospitality at reasonable prices — a reputation which the friendly proprietors are determined to maintain. Olde worlde bars provide tasty and wholesome snacks and meals, while the à la carte restaurant is a most pleasant setting for the enjoyment of the fine cuisine offered there. Cosy bedrooms, all with private bathrooms and colour television, provide overnight accommodation, and the inn's position on the A44 makes it a perfect stop for travellers and tourists visiting the many attractions in the Welsh heartland. *WTB ★★ Hotel, Les Routiers, CAMRA, Egon Ronay.*

DOLFORWYN HALL HOTEL,
Abermule, Montgomery,
Powys SY15 6JG

Tel: 01686 630221; Fax: 01686 630360

e-mail: kandcgalvin@dolforwynhall.freeserve.co.uk

8 bedrooms, all with private bathroom; Free House with real ale; Historic interest; Children welcome; Bar meals, restaurant evenings only; Non-smoking areas; Newtown 4 miles; S£££, D££.

Dolforwyn Hall, a fully licensed country hotel, is ideally situated for exploring Mid-Wales and the Borders. This picturesque Grade II listed building enjoys a tranquil setting in four acres of wooded grounds, overlooking the scenic Severn Valley. All eight bedrooms are non-smoking, have private facilities, colour television, telephone and beverage trays. The restaurant, situated in the oldest part of the house, offers traditional country cooking, using fresh local and home-grown produce whenever possible. The spacious lounge bar with winter log fires, has an extensive bar menu for lunches and informal dining and a choice of real Welsh ales. *WTB ★★★ Country Hotel.*

THE HARP INN,
Old Radnor, Presteigne,
Powys LD8 2RH

Tel and Fax: 01544 350655

4 bedrooms, 2 with private bath; Free House with real ale; Historic interest;
Well-behaved children and pets welcome; Bar meals, restaurant evenings only;
Non-smoking areas; Hereford 24 miles, Kington 4; S££, D£.

Peacefully situated amidst the dramatic splendour of the Welsh Marches with unrivalled views over Radnor Valley, this fine 15th century country inn offers a tranquil and most comfortable base away from the bustle of modern life. After a peaceful night's sleep and a hearty Welsh breakfast, what could be more relaxing than a stroll across the village green to inspect the architectural splendours of St Stephen's Church, with its ancient organ screen and font. Those actively inclined will find plenty to occupy them, and at various times of the year sheepdog trials, Eisteddfods, trotting races and even rodeos attract locals and visitors alike. Slate-flagged floors, exposed beams and stone walls and interesting antiques enhance the period charm of the interior, where good food and ale are dispensed with friendly and professional ease. *Egon Ronay, Good Pub Guide, CAMRA Good Beer Guide.*

FOR THE MUTUAL GUIDANCE OF GUEST AND HOST

Every year literally thousands of holidays, short breaks and overnight stops are arranged through our guides, the vast majority without any problems at all. In a handful of cases, however, difficulties do arise about bookings, which often could have been prevented from the outset.

It is important to remember that when accommodation has been booked, both parties – guests and hosts – have entered into a form of contract. We hope that the following points will provide helpful guidance.

GUESTS: When enquiring about accommodation, be as precise as possible. Give exact dates, numbers in your party and the ages of any children. State the number and type of rooms wanted and also what catering you require – bed and breakfast, full board etc. Make sure that the position about evening meals is clear – and about pets, reductions for children or any other special points.

Read our reviews carefully to ensure that the proprietors you are going to contact can supply what you want. Ask for a letter confirming all arrangements, if possible.

If you have to cancel, do so as soon as possible. Proprietors do have the right to retain deposits and under certain circumstances to charge for cancelled holidays if adequate notice is not given and they cannot re-let the accommodation.

HOSTS: Give details about your facilities and about any special conditions. Explain your deposit system clearly and arrangements for cancellations, charges etc. and whether or not your terms include VAT.

If for any reason you are unable to fulfil an agreed booking without adequate notice, you may be under an obligation to arrange suitable alternative accommodation or to make some form of compensation.

While every effort is made to ensure accuracy, we regret that FHG Publications cannot accept responsibility for errors, omissions or misrepresentations in our entries or any consequences thereof.

Prices in particular should be checked because we go to press early. We will follow up complaints but cannot act as arbiters or agents for either party.

South Wales

SLOOP INN,
Llandogo, Near Monmouth,
South Wales NP5 4TW

Tel: 01594 530291
Fax: 01594 530935

4 bedrooms, all with private bathroom; Free House with real ale; Historic interest; Children and pets welcome; Bar and restaurant meals; Chepstow 6 miles; S££, D££££.

Named after the barges which once traded between Bristol and Llandogo, the 18th century Sloop Inn is a delectable little retreat overlooking the lovely River Wye. Here one may find a captivating amalgam of traditional and modern facilities that offer outstanding value for money. Each charming guest room has a bathroom or shower en suite, colour television and tea and coffee-maker. Terms include a full English breakfast; other meals, including bar snacks, vegetarian dishes and full steak dinners, are served in attractive surroundings during normal opening hours. Seeking a touch (or more) of romance? Then a suite with a large four-poster bed and a private balcony with a fine view of the river could well be the answer. *AA* ◆◆◆.

ROYAL GEORGE HOTEL,
Tintern, Near Chepstow,
South Wales NP6 6SF

Tel: 01291 689205
Fax: 01291 689448

16 bedrooms, all with private bathroom; Free House; Historic interest; Children and pets welcome; Bar and restaurant meals; Non-smoking areas; Chepstow 4 miles; S££££, D£££.

In a sheltered position at the foot of a thickly wooded hillside, this 17th century hotel sits amidst its own gardens on the banks of a trout stream, and is just a pleasant stroll from Tintern Abbey. Sixteen spacious, well-appointed bedrooms provide guests with every comfort desirable, including private bathroom, colour television, radio, tea and coffee facilities and direct-dial telephone, and some have balconies offering superb views across the valley. Courteous, efficient service will be found in the Angiddy Room Restaurant, as light and attractive as the name suggests, and inspired table d'hôte menus are presented for luncheon and dinner, offering a good choice for all courses and featuring local seasonal produce and several Welsh speciality dishes. *WTB* ★★★ *Hotel, AA** and Rosette.*

The 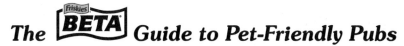 Guide to Pet-Friendly Pubs

Whenever you visit one of our public houses or hotels listed within the Beta Guide to Pet-Friendly Pubs you can be sure your four-legged friend will be more than welcome. He will find a fresh bowl of water, provided by the landlord to quench his thirst, and it's likely he will meet other canine visitors.

Beta Complete Dog Food
the best nutritional care at home and on holiday...

BERKSHIRE

THE GREYHOUND (known locally as 'The Dog')
The Walk, Eton Wick, Berkshire (01753 863925).
Dogs allowed throughout the pub.
Pet Regulars: Harvey (Retriever), retrieves anything, including Beer mats. KIA - German Shepherd.

THE SWAN
9 Mill Lane, Clewer, Windsor, Berkshire (01753 862069).
Dogs allowed throughout the pub.
Pet Regulars: Ziggy and her family, Simba, Thumper and Cassy (Bichon Prise) – useful for keeping your lap warm; Taffy, who has a very waggy tail and who curls up and sleeps under a chair until closing time; Ben, a very friendly Alsatian who enjoys a drop or two of London Pride; Rupert, another Bichon, who calls in after his walks; Ben, the latest addition, a playful Springer Spaniel puppy.

THE TWO BREWERS
Park Street, Windsor, Berkshire (01753 855426).
Dogs allowed, public and saloon bars.
Pet Regulars: Jack (Labrador), Chef feeds him sausages. Harry (Pyrenean) and his mate Molly (Newfoundland) take up the whole bar. Newcomer - 'Bear' - Black Labrador.

BUCKINGHAMSHIRE

WHITE HORSE
Village Lane, Hedgerley, Buckinghamshire SL2 3UY (01753 643225).
Dogs allowed at tables on pub frontage, beer garden (on leads), public bar.

CAMBRIDGESHIRE

YE OLD WHITE HART
Main Street, Ufford, Peterborough, Cambridgeshire (01780 740250).
Dogs allowed in non-food areas.

CHESHIRE

JACKSONS BOAT
Rifle Road, Sale, Cheshire (0161 973 3208).
Dogs allowed throughout on lead with the exception of the dining area.

CORNWALL

DRIFTWOOD SPARS HOTEL
Trevaunance Cove, St Agnes, Cornwall (01872 552428).
Dogs allowed everywhere except the restaurant.
Pet Regulars: Buster (Cornish Labrador cross) - devours anything.

JUBILEE INN
Pelynt, Near Looe, Cornwall PL13 2JZ (01503 220312).
Dogs allowed in all areas except restaurant; accommodation for guests with dogs.

THE MILL HOUSE INN
Trebarwith Strand, Tintagel, Cornwall PL34 0HD (01840 770200).
Pet Friendly.

THE MOLESWORTH ARMS HOTEL
Molesworth Street, Wadebridge, Cornwall PL27 7DP (01208 812055).
Dogs allowed in all public areas and in hotel rooms.
Pet Regulars: Thomson Cassidy (Black Lab) and his mate Ozzie who is partial to a bit of cheese on a Sunday.

THE WHITE HART
Chilsworthy, Near Gunnislake, Cornwall (01822 832307).
Dogs allowed in non-food bar, car park tables, beer garden.
Pet Regulars: Kai, Ben and Lawson (German Shepherds).

WELLINGTON HOTEL,
The Harbour, Boscastle, Cornwall (01840 250202).
Dogs allowed in bedrooms and on lead in pub.
Pet Regulars: Too many to mention. Own private 10-acre woodland walk. Dogs welcome free of charge.

CUMBRIA

THE BRITANNIA INN
Elterwater, Ambleside, Cumbria LA22 9HP (015394 37210).
Dogs allowed in all areas except dining room.
Pet Regulars: Bonnie (Collie cross) meat-only scrounger with his own chair.

THE MORTAL MAN HOTEL
Troutbeck, Windermere, Cumbria LA23 1PL (015394 33193).
Dogs allowed throughout and in guest rooms.

STAG INN
Dufton, Appleby, Cumbria (017683 51608).
Dogs allowed in non-food bar, beer garden, village green plus B&B.
Pet Regulars: Kirk (Dachshund), carries out tour of inspection unaccompanied – but wearing lead; Kim (Weimaraner), best bitter drinker; Buster (Jack Russell), enjoys a quiet evening.

WATERMILL INN
School Lane, Ings, Near Staveley, Kendal, Cumbria (01539 821309).
Dogs allowed in beer garden, Wrynose bottom bar.
Pet Regulars: Smudge (sheepdog); Gowan (Westie) and Scruffy (mongrel). All enjoy a range of crisps and snacks. Scruffy regularly drinks Blacksheep special. Pub dogs Misty (Beardie). Owners cannot walk dogs past pub, without being dragged in!

DERBYSHIRE

JINGLERS/FOX & HOUNDS
(A517) Belper Road, Bradley, Ashbourne, Derbyshire (01335 370855).
Dogs allowed in non-food bars, beer garden, accommodation for guests with dogs.
Pet Regulars: Benson (Springer), Hamlet (Pointer/Lab) – pedigree drinkers and Walkers crisps crunchers.

THE GEORGE HOTEL
Commercial Road, Tideswell, Near Buxton, Derbyshire SK17 8NU (01298 871382).
Dogs allowed in snug and around the bar, water bowls provided.

DOG AND PARTRIDGE COUNTRY INN & MOTEL
Swinscoe, Ashbourne, Derbyshire (01335 343183).
Dogs allowed throughout, except restaurant.
Pet Regulars: Include Mitsy (57); Rusty (Cairn); Spider (Collie/GSD) and Rex (GSD).

DEVONSHIRE ARMS
Peak Forest, Near Buxton, Derbyshire SK17 8EJ (01298 23875)
Dogs allowed in bar.
Pet Regulars: Fergie (Collie-cross), known as "The Fireguard".

WHITE HART
Station Road, West Hallam, Derbyshire DE7 6GW (0115 932 6069).
Dogs allowed in all non-food areas.
Pet Regulars: Archie, Chester and Brewser. Four cats: Itsy, Bitsy, Jasper and Bertie.

DEVON

THE SHIP INN
Axmouth, Devon EX12 4AF (01297 21838).
A predominantly catering pub, so dogs on a lead and on the floor please.
Pet Regulars: Cassie, Charlie, Digby and Beamish. Also resident Tawny Owls.

BRENDON HOUSE HOTEL
Brendon, Lynton, North Devon EX35 6PS (01598 741206).
Dogs very welcome and allowed in tea gardens, guest bedrooms by arrangement.
Pet Regulars: Jasmine (cat), self appointed cream tea receptionist. Years of practice have perfected dirty looks at visiting dogs.

THE BULLERS ARMS
Chagford, Newton Abbot, Devon (01647 432348).
Dogs allowed throughout pub, except dining room/kitchen. "More than welcome".

CROWN AND SCEPTRE
2 Petitor Road, Torquay, Devon TQ1 4QA (01803 328290).
Dogs allowed in non-food bar, family room, lounge.
Pet Regulars: Samantha (Labrador), opens, consumes and returns empties when offered crisp packets; Max (Collie), Bar dancer; Buddy & Jessie (Collies), beer-mat frisbee experts; Cassie (Collie), scrounging.

THE DEVONSHIRE INN
Sticklepath, Near Okehampton, Devon EX20 2NW (01837 840626).
Dogs allowed in non-food bar, car park, beer garden, family room, guest rooms.
Pet Regulars: Bess (Labrador), 'minds' owner; Annie (Shihtzu), snoring a speciality; Daisy (Collie), accompanies folk singers.

THE JOURNEY'S END INN
Ringmore, Near Kingsbridge, South Devon TQ7 4HL (01548 810205).
Dogs allowed throughout the pub except in the dining room.

PALK ARMS INN
Hennock, Bovey Tracey, Devon TQ13 9QS (01626 836584).
Pets welcome.

THE ROYAL OAK INN
Dunsford, Near Exeter, Devon EX6 7DA (01647 252256).
Dogs allowed in non-food bars, beer garden, accommodation for guests with dogs.
Pet Regulars: Cleo

THE SEA TROUT INN
Staverton, Near Totnes, Devon TQ9 6PA (01803 762274).
Dogs allowed in lounge and public bar, car park tables, beer garden, owners' rooms (but not on beds).
Pet Regulars: Billy (Labrador-cross), partial to drip trays; Curnow (Poodle), brings a blanket.

THE WHITE HART HOTEL
Moretonhampstead, Newton Abbot, Devon TQ13 8NF (01647 440406).
Dogs allowed throughout, except restaurant.
Pet Regulars: Twiggers and Demi.

DORSET

THE ANVIL HOTEL
Sailsbury Road, Pimperne, Blandford, Dorset DT11 8UQ (01258 453431).
Pets allowed in bar, lounge and bedrooms.

DURHAM

MOORCOCK INN
Hill Top, Eggleston, Teesdale, County Durham DL12 9AU (01833 650395).
Pet Regulars: Thor, the in-house hound dog, and Raymond, the resident hack, welcome all equine travellers.

TAP AND SPILE
27 Front Street, Framwellgate Moor, Durham DH1 5EE (0191 386 5451).
Dogs allowed throughout the pub.

ESSEX

THE OLD SHIP
Heybridge Basin, Heybridge, Maldon, Essex (01621 854150).
Dogs allowed throughout pub.

GLOUCESTERSHIRE

THE CROWN INN
Frampton Mansell, Stroud, Gloucestershire GL6 8JG (01285 760601).
Well behaved pooches welcome in our comfortable hotel.
Pet Regulars: Buster (Sheepdog) rounds up all the beer-mats and gathers them in a pile in the corner.

THE OLD STOCKS HOTEL
The Square, Stow on the Wold, Gloucestershire GL54 1AF (01451 830666).
Dogs allowed in the beer garden, accommodation for dogs and their owners also available.
Pet Regulars: Ben (Labrador) enjoys bitter from the drip trays and Oscar (Doberman) often gets carried out as he refuses to leave.

GREATER LONDON
THE PHOENIX
28 Thames Street, Sunbury on Thames, Middlesex (01932 789163).
Dogs allowed in non-food bar, beer garden, family room.
Pet Regulars: "Olly" (57 variety).

THE TIDE END COTTAGE
Ferry Road, Teddington, Middlesex (0208 977 7762).
Dogs allowed throughout the pub.
Pet Regulars: Chester, Golder Retriever – eats anything.

HAMPSHIRE
HIGH CORNER INN
Linwood, Near Ringwood, Hampshire BH24 3QY (01425 473973).
Dogs, horses and even goats are catered for here.

THE CHEQUERS
Ridgeway Lane, Lower Pennington, Lymington, Hants (01590 673415).
Dogs allowed in non-food bar, outdoor barbecue area (away from food).
Pet Regulars: Otto (Hungarian Vizsla), eats beer-mats and paper napkins. Likes beer but not often indulged.

THE VICTORY
High Street, Hamble-le-Rice, Southampton, Hampshire (023 8045 3105).
Dogs allowed.
Pet Regulars: Sefton (Labrador), his 'usual' chew bars are kept especially.

HEREFORDSHIRE
THE GREEN MAN INN
Fownhope, Hereford, Herefordshire HR1 4PE (01432 860243).
Dogs welcome, but not in the restaurant.

THE INN ON THE WYE
Kerne Bridge, Goodrich, Near Ross-on-Wye, Hereforshire
Pets welcome.

HERTFORDSHIRE
THE BLACK HORSE
Chorley Wood Common, Dog Kennel Lane, Rickmansworth, Herts (01923 282252).
Dogs very welcome and allowed throughout the pub.

THE ROBIN HOOD AND LITTLE JOHN
Rabley Heath, near Codicote, Hertfordshire (01438 812361).
Dogs allowed in non-food bar, car park tables, beer garden.
Pet Regulars: Bonnie (Labrador), beer-mat catcher. The locals of the pub have close to 50 dogs between them, most of which visit from time to time. The team includes a two Labrador search squad dispatched by one regular's wife to indicate time's up. When they arrive he has five minutes' drinking up time before all three leave together.

KENT

KENTISH HORSE
Cow Lane, Mark Beech, Edenbridge, Kent (01342 850493).
Dogs allowed.

THE OLD NEPTUNE
Marine Terrace, Whitstable, Kent CT5 1EJ (01227 272262).
Dogs allowed in non-food bar and beach frontage.
Pet Regulars: Josh (mongrel), solo visits, serves himself from pub water-bowl. Poppy and Fred (mongrel and GSD), soft touch and dedicated vocalist – barks at anything that runs away.

PRINCE ALBERT
38 High Street, Broadstairs, Kent CT10 1LH (01843 861937).
Dogs allowed in non-food bar.

THE SWANN INN
Little Chart, Kent TN27 OQB (01233 840702).
Dogs allowed - everywhere except restaurant.
Pet Regulars: Tramp – cross Lurcher – chases rabbits; Duster (Retriever?), places his order – for crisps – with one soft bark for the landlady.

UNCLE TOM'S CABIN
Lavender Hill, Tonbridge, Kent (01628 483339).
Dogs allowed throughout.
Pet Regulars: Flossie, Pipa, Rusty. 10pm is dog biscuit time!

LANCASHIRE

ABBEYLEE
Abbeyhills Road, Oldham, Lancashire (0161 678 8795).
Dogs allowed throughout.
Pet Regulars: Include Susie (Boxer), so fond of pork scratchings they are now used by her owners as a reward in the show ring.

MALT'N HOPS
50 Friday Street, Chorley, Lancashire PR6 0AH (01257 260967).
Dogs allowed throughout pub.
Pet Regulars: Abbie (GSD), under-seat sleeper; Brandy (Rhodesian Ridgeback), at the sound of a bag of crisps opening will lean on eater until guest's legs go numb or he is offered a share; Toby (Labrador), valued customer in his own right, due to amount of crisps he eats, also retrieves empty bags; Mork – says please for bag of crisps.

LEICESTERSHIRE

CHEQUERS INN
1 Gilmorton Road, Ashby Magna, Near Lutterworth, Leicestershire (01455 209523).
Dogs allowed in bar.
Pet Regulars: Suki – talking Samoyed.

LINCOLNSHIRE

THE HAVEN INN
Ferry Road, Barrow Haven, North Lincolnshire DN19 7EX (01469 530247).
Dogs allowed in the public bar, beer garden, and bedrooms on their own bed/blanket.
Pet Regulars: Moby, the one-eyed Jack Russell, and Jester the Collie.

THE BLUE DOG INN
Main Street, Sewstern, Grantham, Lincs NG33 5QR (01476 860097).
Dogs allowed in bar.
Pet Regulars: The Guv'nor (Great Dane), best draught-excluder in history; Jenny (Westie) shares biscuits with pub cats; Jemma (98% Collie), atmosphere lapper-upper. Spud and Nelson – Terriers.

MERSEYSIDE

AMBASSADOR PRIVATE HOTEL
13 Bath Street, Southport, Merseyside PR9 0DP (01704 543998).
Dogs allowed in non-food bar, lounge, guest bedrooms.

THE SCOTCH PIPER
Southport Road, Lydiate, Merseyside (0151 526 0503).
Dogs allowed throughout the pub.

MIDLANDS

AWENTSBURY HOTEL
21 Serpentine Road, Selly Park, Birmingham B29 7HU (0121 472 1258).
Dogs allowed.

NORFOLK

THE SPREAD EAGLE COUNTRY INN
Barton Bendish, Norfolk PE33 9DP (01366 347295).
Pet Regulars: Dirty Gertie and Little Urn.

MARINE HOTEL
10 St Edmunds Terrace, Hunstanton, Norfolk PE36 5EH (01485 533310).
Dogs allowed throughout, except dining room.
Pet Regulars: Many dogs have returned with their owners year after year to stay at The Marine Bar.

THE OLD RAILWAY TAVERN
Eccles Road, Quidenham, Norwich, Norfolk NR16 2JG (01953 888223).
Dogs allowed in non-food bar, beer garden.
Pet Regulars: Maggie (Clumber Spaniel); Soshie (GSD); Annie (Labrador); and pub dog Elsa (GSD). Elsa is so fond of sitting, motionless, on her own window ledge that new customers often think she's stuffed!

THE ROSE AND CROWN
Nethergate Street, Harpley, King's Lynn, Norfolk (01485 520577).
Dogs allowed in non-food bar, car park tables.
Pet Regulars: A merry bunch with shared interests – Duffy (mongrel); Tammy (Airedale); Bertie & Pru (Standard Poodles), all enjoy pub garden romps during summer and fireside seats in winter.

OXFORDSHIRE

THE BELL INN
High Street, Adderbury, Oxon (01295 810338).
Dogs allowed throughout the pub.
Owner's dogs; Bess and Elsa (Black Labradors).

SHROPSHIRE

THE TRAVELLERS REST INN
Church Stretton, Shropshire (01694 781275).
Well-mannered pets welcome - but beware of the cats!

LONGMYND HOTEL

Cunnery Road, Church Stretton, Shropshire SY6 6AG (01694 722244).

Dogs allowed in owners' hotel bedrooms but not in public areas.

Pet Regulars: Sox (Collie/Labrador), occasional drinker and regular customer greeter; Sadie (Retriever), self appointed fire-guard; and owner's dogs, Sam and Sailor.

REDFERN HOTEL

Cleobury Mortimer, Shropshire SY14 8AA (01299 270395).

Dogs allowed in reception area and in guests' bedrooms.

SOMERSET

CASTLE OF COMFORT HOTEL

Dodington, Nether Stowey, Bridgwater, Somerset TA5 1LE (01278 741264).

Pet Friendly.

THE BUTCHERS ARMS

Carhampton, Somerset (01643 821333).

Dogs allowed in bar.

Pet Regulars: Lobo and Chera (Samoyeds), eating ice cubes and drinking; Emma (Spaniel), a whisky drinker; Benji (Spaniel-cross), self-appointed rug. Jimmy, a pony, also occasionally drops in for a drink.

HALFWAY HOUSE

Pitney, Langport, Somerset TA10 9AB (01458 252513).

Dogs allowed.

Pet Regulars: Sam (Collie), Barnaby (Retriever), Joe (Cocker Spaniel).

HOOD ARMS

Kilve, Somerset TA5 1EA (01278 741210)

Pets welcome.

THE SHIP INN

High Street, Porlock, Somerset (01643 862507).

Dogs allowed throughout and in guests' rooms.

Pet Regulars: Include Buster, Hardy and Crackers (Jack Russells), terrorists from London; Bijoux (Peke), while on holiday at The Ship enjoys Chicken Supreme cooked to order every evening.

THE SPARKFORD INN

High Street, Sparkford, Somerset BA22 7JN (01963 440218).

Dogs allowed in bar areas but not in restaurant; safe garden and car park.

Pet Regulars: Holly (Jack Russell) and Stoner (Grizzly Bear)!

SUFFOLK

SIX BELLS AT BARDWELL

The Green, Bardwell, Bury St Edmunds IP31 1AW (01359 250820).

Dogs allowed in guest bedrooms and garden but not allowed in bar and restaurant.

THE COMPASSES INN

Wenhaston, Near Southwold, Suffolk IP19 9EF (01502 478319).

Dogs allowed throughout the pub and B&B (but not on the beds!). Bar open evenings only Monday to Saturday, and Sunday lunchtimes.

Pet Regulars: Raffles (ex racing Greyhound) who loves all visiting dogs and crisps; Penny (Collie) and Cisco (young Doberman) who like to stand up at the bar.

SURREY

THE CRICKETERS
12 Oxenden Road, Tongham, Farnham, Surrey (01252 333262).
Dogs allowed in beer garden.

SUSSEX

CHARCOAL BURNER
Weald Drive, Furnace Green, Crawley, West Sussex RH10 6NY (01293 653981).
Dogs allowed in non-food bar areas and front and back patios.
Pet Regulars: Lucy (Irish Setter), dedicated to cheese snips.

THE FORESTERS ARMS
High Street, Fairwarp, Near Uckfield, East Sussex TN22 3BP (01825 712808).
Dogs allowed in the beer garden and at car park tables, also inside.
Owner's Dogs: Rascal and Sophie (Springer Spaniels).

THE INN IN THE PARK (CHEF & BREWER)
Tilgate Park, Tilgate, Crawley, West Sussex RH10 5PQ (01293 545324).
Dogs allowed in Patio area.
Owner's dogs; "Mia".

THE PLOUGH
Crowhurst, Near Battle, East Sussex TN33 9AY (01424 830310).
Dogs allowed in non-food bar, car park tables, beer garden.
Pet Regulars: Kai (Belgian Shepherd), drinks halves of Websters; Poppy and Cassie (Springer Spaniels), divided between the lure of crisps and fireside.

THE PRESTONVILLE ARMS
64 Hamilton Road, Brighton, East Sussex (01273 701007).
Dogs allowed in beer garden, throughout the pub (Pet Friendly).

QUEENS HEAD
Village Green, Sedlescombe, East Sussex (01424 870228).
Dogs allowed throughout the pub.

THE SLOOP INN
Freshfield Lock, Haywards Heath, West Sussex RH17 7NP (01444 831219).
Dogs allowed in public bar and garden.

THE SMUGGLERS' ROOST
125 Sea Lane, Rustington, West Sussex BN16 2SG (01903 785714).
Dogs allowed in non-food bar, at car park tables, in beer garden, family room.
Pet Regulars: Moffat (Border Terrier), beer makes him sneeze; Leo (Border Terrier), forms instant affections with anyone who notices him; Tim (King Charles Spaniel), quite prepared to guard his corner when food appears. The landlord owns a Great Dane and an Alsatian.

THE SPORTSMAN'S ARMS
Rackham Road, Amberley, Near Arundel, West Sussex BN18 9NR (01798 831787).
Dogs allowed throughout the pub.
Pet Regulars: Pippin, Spud, Mollie, Nell; Tess, the Landlord's dog will not venture into the cellar which is haunted by the ghost of a young girl.

WELLDIGGERS ARMS
Lowheath, Petworth, West Sussex GU28 0HG (01798 342287).
Dogs allowed throughout the pub.

WILTSHIRE

THE HORSE AND GROOM
The Street, Charlton, Near Malmesbury, Wiltshire (01666 823904).
Pet Regulars: P.D. (Pub Dog – Labrador).

THE PETERBOROUGH ARMS
Dauntsey Lock, Near Chippenham, Wiltshire SN15 4HD (01249 890409).
Dogs allowed in non-food bar, at car park tables, in beer garden, family room (when non-food).
Pet Regulars: Include Winston (Jack Russell), will wait for command before eating a biscuit placed on his nose; Waddi (GSD), can grab a bowling ball before it hits the skittle pins.

THE THREE HORSESHOES
High Street, Chapmanslade, Near Westbury, Wiltshire (01373 832280).
Dogs allowed in non-food bar and beer garden.
Pet Regulars: Include Clieo (Golden Retriever), possibly the youngest 'regular' in the land - his first trip to the pub was at eight weeks. Westbury and District Canine Society repair to the Three Horseshoes after training nights (Monday/Wednesday). Six cats and two dogs in residence.

WAGGON AND HORSES
High Street, Wootton Bassett, Swindon, Wiltshire (01793 850617).
Dogs allowed throughout.
Pet Regulars: Include Gemma, a very irregular Whippet/Border collie cross. She likes to balance beer-mats on her nose, then flip them over and catch them, opens and shuts doors on command, walks on her hind legs and returns empty crisp bags. She is limited to one glass of Guinness a night.

NORTH AND EAST YORKSHIRE

BARNES WALLIS INN
North Howden, Howden, East Yorkshire (01430 430639).
Guide dogs only
Pet Regulars: A healthy cross-section of mongrels, Collies and Labradors. One of the most popular pastimes is giving the pub cat a bit of a run for his money.

KINGS HEAD INN
Barmby on the Marsh, East Yorkshire DN14 7HL (01757 638357).
Dogs allowed in non-food bar.
Pet Regulars: Many and varied!

THE FORESTERS ARMS
Kilburn, North Yorkshire YO6 4AH (01347 868386).
Dogs allowed throughout, except restaurant.
Pet Regulars: Ainsley (Black Labrador)..

THE GREENE DRAGON INN
Hardraw, Hawes, North Yorkshire DL8 3LZ (01969 667392).
Dogs allowed in bar, at car park tables, in beer garden, family room but not dining room or restaurant.

NEW INN HOTEL
Clapham, Near Settle, North Yorkshire LA2 8HH (015242 51203).
Dogs allowed in non-food bar, beer garden, family room.
Owner's dog: Time, (Rhodesian Ridgeback).

PREMIER HOTEL
66 Esplanade, South Cliff, Scarborough, North Yorkshire YO11 2UZ (01723 501062).
Dogs allowed throughout in non-food areas of hotel.

SIMONSTONE HALL
Hawes, North Yorkshire DL8 3LY (01969 667255).

Dogs allowed except dining area.

Pet Regulars: account for 2,000 nights per annum. More than 50% of guests are accompanied by their dogs, from Pekes to an Anatolian Shepherd (the size of a small Shetland pony!) Two dogs have stayed, with their owners, on 23 separate occasions.

SOUTH YORKSHIRE

THE SPINNEY
Forest Rise, Balby, Doncaster, South Yorkshire DN4 9HQ (01302 852033).

Dogs allowed throughout the pub.

Pet Regulars: Shamus (Irish Setter), pub thief. Fair game includes pool balls, beer mats, crisps, beer, coats, hats. Recently jumped 15 feet off pub roof with no ill effect. Josh; (Labrador) a guide dog. Indi and Jacques.

THE ROCKINGHAM ARMS
8 Main Street, Wentworth, Rotherham, South Yorkshire S62 7LO (01226 742075).

Dogs allowed throughout pub.

Pet Regulars: Sheeba (Springer Spaniel), Charlie and Gypsy (Black Labradors). Kate and Rags (Airedale and cross-breed), prefer lager to coffee; Holly (terrier and pub dog), dubbed 'the flying squirrel', likes everyone, whether they like it or not!

THE GOLDEN FLEECE
Lindley Road, Blackley, near Huddersfield, West Yorkshire (01422 372704).

Dogs allowed in non-food bar, at outside tables.

Pet Regulars: "Holly", (Border Collie).

WALES

ANGLESEY & GWYNEDD

THE GRAPES HOTEL
Maentwrog, Blaenau Ffestiniog, Gwynedd LL41 4HN (01766 590365).

Pet Friendly.

PLAS YR EIFL HOTEL
Trefor, Caernarfon, Gwynedd LL54 5NA (01286 660781).

Pet Regulars: We have both dogs and cats

THE BUCKLEY HOTEL
Castle Street, Beaumaris, Isle of Anglesey LL58 8AW (01248 810415).

Dogs allowed throughout the pub, except in the dining room and bistro.

Pet Regulars: Cassie (Springer Spaniel) and Rex (mongrel), dedicated 'companion' dogs, also Charlie (Spaniel).

NORTH WALES

THE WEST ARMS HOTEL
Llanarmon Dyffryn Ceiriog, Llangollen, North Wales LL20 7LD (01691 600665).

Welcome Pets.

POWYS

SEVERN ARMS HOTEL
Penybont, Llandrindod Wells, Powys LD1 5UA (01597 851224).

Dogs allowed in the bar, but not the restaurant, and in the rooms - but not on the beds.

SCOTLAND

ABERDEENSHIRE, BANFF & MORAY

THE CLIFTON BAR

Clifton Road, Lossiemouth, Moray (01343 812100).

Dogs allowed throughout pub.

Pet Regulars: Include Zoe (Westie), has her own seat and is served coffee with two lumps; Milo (Jack Russel), Bob (Collie) and Holly.

ROYAL OAK

Station Road, Urquhart, Elgin, Moray (01343 842607).

Dogs allowed throughout pub.

Pet Regulars: Mollie (Staffordshire Bull Terrier) – food bin. Biscuits (from the landlady), Maltesers (from the landlord), sausages and burgers (from the barbecue).

ARGYLL & BUTE

CAIRNDOW STAGECOACH INN

Cairndow, Argyll PA26 8BN (01499 600286).

Pet Regulars: Our own dog Rocky is a Golden Labrador.

THE BALLACHULISH HOTEL

Ballachulish, Argyll PA39 4JY (01855 811606).

Dogs allowed in the lounge, beer garden and guests' bedrooms, excluding food areas.

Pet Regulars: Thumper (Border Collie/GSD-cross), devoted to his owner and follows him everywhere.

BORDERS

CULGRUFF HOUSE HOTEL

Crossmichael, Castle Douglas, Kirkcudbrightshire DG7 3BB (01556 670230).

Dogs allowed in family room, guest bedrooms, but must be kept on leads outside.

Pet Regulars: A cross-section of canine visitors.

HIGHLANDS

ARISAIG HOTEL

Arisaig, Inverness-shire (01687 450210).

Dogs welcome.

Pet Regulars. Regulars in the public bar include Luar (Lurcher), Cindy (Collie), Whisky (Terrier).

PERTH & KINROSS

FOUR SEASONS HOTEL

St Fillans, Perthshire (01764 685333).

Dogs allowed in all non-food areas.

Pet Regulars: Regulars are few but passing trade frequent and welcome. Previous owner's dog was a renowned water-skier.

CHANNEL ISLANDS

JERSEY

LA PULENTE INN

La Pulente, St Brelade, Jersey (01534 44487).

Dogs allowed in public bar.

Pet Regulars: Dusty (Old English Sheepdog).

"FAMILY FRIENDLY"
Pubs, Inns and Hotels

These are establishments which make an extra effort to cater for parents and children. The majority provide a separate children's menu or they may be willing to serve small portions of main course dishes on request; there are often separate outdoor or indoor play areas where the junior members of the family can let off steam while Mum and Dad unwind over a drink.

ENGLAND

CAMBRIDGESHIRE

THE NAG'S HEAD HOTEL, Eynesbury, St Neots (01480 4768112). Half portions; high chairs and family room; garden.

CHESHIRE

THE EGERTON AT ASTBURY, Astbury Village, Near Congleton (01260 273946). Children's menu and half portions; high chairs and family room; garden.

CHURCH HOUSE INN, Bollington, Macclesfield (01625 574014). Children's menu and half portions; high chairs.

CORNWALL

THE HALZEPHRON INN, Gunwalloe, Helston (01326 240406). Children's menu and half portions; high chairs, family room and baby changing facilities; garden.

TREWELLARD ARMS HOTEL, Pendeen, Near Penzance (01736 788634). Children's menu and half portions; high chairs, family room and baby changing facilities; garden.

CRUMPLEHORN MILL, Polperro (01503 272348). Children's menu; high chairs and family room.

THE CROOKED INN, Trematon, Saltash (01752 848177). Children's menu; high chairs and family room; garden.

THE WENDRON NEW INN, Wendron (01326 572683). Half portions; garden.

CUMBRIA

THE THREE SHIRES INN, Ambleside (015394 37215). Children's menu and half portions, high chairs and garden.

QUEEN' ARMS INN & MOTEL, Warwick-on-Eden, Carlisle (021228 560699). Children's menu and half portions; high chair and family room; garden.

SHEPHERD'S ARMS HOTEL, Ennerdale Bridge, Cleator (Tel & Fax: 01946 861249). Children's menu and half portions; family room; garden.

GRASMERE RED LION HOTEL, Grasmere (015394 35456). Children's menu; high chairs; family room.

COLEDALE INN, Braithwaite, Near Keswick (017687 78272). Children's menu; outdoor play area; high chairs; family room.

QUEEN' HEAD INN, Tirril, Near Penrith (01768 963219). Children's menu and half portions; high chairs.

RUSLAND POOL HOTEL, Haverthwaite, Ulverston (01229 861384). Children's menu and half portions; high chairs; garden.

MORTAL MAN HOTEL, Troutbeck, Windermere (015394 33193). Children's menu and half portions, high chairs.

DERBYSHIRE

BENTLEY BROOK INN & FENNY'S RESTAURANT, Fenny Bentley, Ashbourne (01335 350278). Children's menu; high chairs and family room; garden.

THE WHEATSHEAF, Baslow (01246 582240). Children's menu and half portions; high chairs; garden.

STRINES INN, Bradfield Dale, Sheffield (0114-285 11247). Half portions; garden.

THE CASTLE HOTEL, Castleton (01433 620578). Children's menu, half portions, high chairs, baby changing facilities.

MILLSTONE INN, Hathersage (01433 650258). Children's menu; high chairs.

DEVON

THE SWAN, Bampton (01398 331257). Children's menu and half portions.

THE PALK ARMS INN, Hennock, Bovey Tracey (01626 836584). Children's menu and half portions; family room; garden.

THE DREWE ARMS, Drewsteignton, Exeter (01647 281224). Children's menu and half portions.

THE GISSONS ARMS, Kennford, Exeter (01392 832444). Children's menu; high chairs; garden.

MONKTON COURT, Monkton, Near Honiton (01404 42300). Children's menu and half portions; high chairs and family room.

THE KING'S ARMS, Stockland, Near Honiton (01404 881361). Children's menu and half portions; garden.

OLD SAWMILL INN, Watermouth, Ilfracombe (01271 882259). Children's menu and half portions; high chairs and family room; garden.

DOLPHIN INN, Kingston, Near Bigbury (01548 810314). Children's menu and half portions; family room; garden.

GEORGE HOTEL, South Molton (Tel & Fax: 01769 572514). Children's menu and half portions; high chairs and family room; baby changing facilities; play room.

STAG INN, Rackenford, Near Tiverton (01884 881369). Children's menu.

THE DURANT ARMS, Ashprington, Totnes (01803 732240/732471). Children's menus and half portions, high chairs.

THE CHURCH HOUSE INN, Harberton, Near Totnes (01803 863707). Children's menu and half portions; high chairs and family room.

THE CRIDFORD INN, Trusham, Newton Abbot (Tel & Fax: 01626 853694). Children's menu; family room; garden.

DORSET

ACORN INN, Evershot, Dorchester (01935 83228). Half portions; high chairs.

KING'S ARMS INN, Near Gillingham (01747 838325). Half portions; high chair; garden.

SCOTT ARMS, Kingston, Corfe Castle (01929 480270). High chairs, family room, garden.

ANTELOPE HOTEL, Greenhill, Sherborne (01935 812077). children's menu, half portions, high chairs, family room; baby changing facilities.

THE BANKES ARMS COUNTRY INN, Studland, Near Swanage (01929 450225). Children over five years. Children's menu and half portions; family room; garden.

SWAN INN, Sturminster Newton (01258 472208). Half portions; high chairs; garden.

SMUGGLERS INN, Osmington Mills, Near Weymouth (01305 833125). Children's menu; high chairs and family room; garden.

ESSEX

YE OLDE WHITE HART HOTEL, Burnham on Crouch (01621 782106). Limited children's menu, half portions, high chair, family rooms and garden.

THE CRICKETERS, Clavering, Near Saffron Walden (01799 550442). Children's menu and half portions; high chairs and family room; garden.

RED LION HOTEL, Colchester (01206 577986). Half portions; high chairs and baby changing facilities; family room.

GLOUCESTERSHIRE

THE OLD NEW INN, Bourton-on-the-Water (01451 820467). Children's menu and half portions; high chairs, family room and baby changing facilities; garden.

FOSSEBRIDGE INN, Fossebridge, Near Cheltenham (01285 720721). Children's menu, half portions; high chairs; garden.

ROSE & CROWN INN, Nympsfield, Stonehouse (01453 860240). Children's menu, high chairs; family room; garden.

FALCON INN, Painswick (01452 814222). Half portions, high chairs and family room.

YE OLDE MALT SHOVEL INN, Ruardean (01594 543028). Half portions.

AMBERLEY INN, Near Stroud (01453 872565). Children's menu and half portions; high chairs and family room; garden.

HAMPSHIRE

JACK RUSSELL INN, Faccombe (01264 737315). Children welcome in the conservatory and there is play equipment in the garden.

THE JOLLY MILLER, North Warnborough, Hook (01256 701085). Children's menu; family room and garden.

WELLINGTON ARMS HOTEL, Stratfield Turgis, Hook (01256 882214). Children's menu and half portions; high chairs; garden.

YE OLDE GEORGE INN, East Meon, Near Petersfield (01730 823481). Half portions; garden.

HEREFORDSHIRE

THE GREEN MAN, Fownhope (Children's menu, high chairs; family room; outdoor play area with swing.

THE NEW INN, St Owen's Cross, Near Ross-on-Wye (01989 730274). Children's menu; high chairs; garden.

THE MILL RACE INN & RESTAURANT, Walford, Ross-on-Wye (01989 562891). Children's menu and half portions; high chairs and baby changing facilities; garden.

ISLE OF WIGHT

CLARENDON HOTEL & WIGHT MOUSE INN, Chale (01983 730431). Children's menu and family room; outdoor play area; pony rides; high chairs; baby changing facilities.

THE NEW INN, Shalfleet (01983 531314). Children's menu and high chairs; garden.

THE BUGLE HOTEL, Yarmouth (01983 760272). Children's menu; high chairs and family room; garden.

KENT

THE BULL INN HOTEL, Sevenoaks ((01732 789800/789819). Half portions and high chairs; baby changing facilities.

THE ROYAL OAK INN, Charing, Near Ashford (01233 7112612). Half portions; family room.

LANCASHIRE

THE BLUE ANCHOR, Bolton-le-Sands, Carnforth (01524 823241). Children's menu, high chairs and garden.

SCALE HALL FARMHOUSE TAVERN, Lancaster (01524 69255). Children's menu and half portions, high chairs; family room, baby changing facilities and garden.

CARTFORD COUNTRY INN, Little Eccleston (01995 670166). Children's menu, half portions, high chairs; family room; baby changing facilities; play area.

LEICESTERSHIRE

THE BRANT INN, The Brantings, Near Groby (0116-287 2703). Children's menu; high chairs and family room; garden.

THE GEORGE INN, Great Oxendon, Market Harborough (01858 465205). Half portions and high chairs; family room; garden.

THE NEVILL ARMS, Medbourne (01858 565288). Children's menu and half portions; high chairs.

KINGS ARMS INN, Wing (01572 737634). Children's menu and half portions; high chairs and family room; garden.

EXETER ARMS, Wakerley (01572 747817). Children's menu, half portions; high chairs; family room; garden.

LINCOLNSHIRE

LEA GATE INN, Coningsby (01526 342370). Children's menu; high chairs and baby changing facilities; garden.

MARQUIS OF GRANBY, Wellingore, Lincoln (01522 810442). Children's menu and half portions; high chairs and family room; garden.

SKIPWORTH ARMS, Moortown, Market Rasen (01472 851770). Half portions; high chairs and family room.

FINCH HATTON ARMS HOTEL, Ewerby, Sleaford (01529 460363). Half portions, high chairs; family room and garden.

THE OLDE FARMHOUSE HOTEL, Stallingborough (01469 560159). Children's menu and half portions; high chairs and family room.

NORFOLK

FEATHERS HOTEL, Dersingham (01485 540207). Children's menu and half portions; high chairs and family room; garden.

THE HALF MOON INN, Rushall, Near Diss (Tel & Fax: 01379 740493). Children's menu; high chairs and family room; garden.

THE PLOUGH INN, Marsham (01263 735000). Children's menu and half portions; high chairs and family room; garden.

CROWN HOTEL, Mundford, Thetford (01842 878233). Half portions and high chairs.

NORTHUMBERLAND

VICTORIA HOTEL, Bamburgh (01668 214431). Children's menu, half portions; high chairs, family room and baby changing facilities; garden.

THE COTTAGE INN, Dunstan, Craster (01665 576658). Children's menu, high chairs, garden.

COOK & BARKER INN, Newton-on-the-Moor, Felton, Morpeth (01665 575234). Half portions and high chairs; garden.

NOTTINGHAMSHIRE

THE HOLE IN THE WALL, Underwood (01773 713936). Children's menu; high chairs; baby changing facilities.

OXFORDSHIRE

THE DOG HOUSE HOTEL, Frilford Heath, Abingdon (01865 390830). Children's men and half portions; high chairs; garden.

THE INN FOR ALL SEASONS, The Barringtons, Burford (01451 84432). Children's menu, half portions, high chairs; baby changing facilities; garden.

THE WHITE HORSE, Woolstone, Near Faringdon (01367 820726). Children's menu, high chairs; garden.

SHEPHERDS HALL INN, Freeland (01993 881256). Children's menu and family room; high chairs; indoor and outdoor play areas.

THE TOLLGATE INN & RESTAURANT, Kingham (01608 658389). Children's menu and half portions; family room; garden.

THE CRAZY BEAR HOTEL, Stadhampton (01865 890714). High chairs and baby changing facilities.

BLOWING STONE INN, Kingston Lisle, Wantage (Tel & Fax: 01367 820288). Children's menu, half portions and high chairs; garden.

ROSE REVIVED INN, Newbridge, Near Witney (01865 300221). Children's menu and high chairs; baby changing facilities; garden.

KILLINGWORTH CASTLE INN, Woodstock (Tel & Fax: 01993 811401). Family room, garden.

SHROPSHIRE

THE KING' ARMS, Cleobury Mortimer (01299 270252). Children's menus and half portions; high chairs.

BEAR HOTEL & COUNTRY INN, Hadnet, Near Market Drayton (01630 685214). Children's menu and half portions; high chairs and family room; garden.

THE CHURCH INN, Buttercross, Ludlow (01584 872174). Children welcome. High chairs and family room.

GASKELL ARMS HOTEL, Much Wenlock (01952 727212). Children's menu, half portions, high chairs; family room; baby changing facilities; garden.

LONGVILLE ARMS, Longville-in-the-Dale, Much Wenlock (01694 771206). Children's menu and half portions; high chairs; garden.

SOMERSET

KINGS ARMS, Litton, Near Bath (01761 241301). Children's menu; high chairs, family room; garden.

BLACK SMOCK INN, Stathe, Near Burrowbridge (01823 698352). Half portions and high chairs; garden.

THE MALT SHOVEL INN, Cannington, Bridgwater (01278 653432). Childrens menus; high chairs and family room with toy corner.

LION HOTEL, Dulverton (01398 323444). Children's menu and half portions; high chair; family rooms, baby changing facilities.

THE FULL MOON AT RUDGE, Frome (01373 8340936). Children's menu and high chairs; garden.

HOOD INN, Kilve (01278 741210). Children's menu and half portions; high chairs, family room, garden.

OLD POUND INN, Aller, Langport (01458 250469). Children's menu, half portions; high chairs; family room; baby changing facilities; garden.

HALF MOON INN, Horsington, Templecombe (01963 370140). Children's menu and half portions; baby changing facilities; garden.

SPARKFORD INN, Sparkford, Yeovil (01963 440218). Indoor play area, enclosed garden, adventure trail.

SUFFOLK

PEACOCK INN, Chelsworth, Near Lavenham (01449 740758). Children's menu and high chairs; garden.

THE FOUR HORSESHOES, Thornham Magna, Near Eye (01379 678777). Children's menu, high chairs, garden.

SIBTON WHITE HORSE, Sibton, Near Saxmundham (01728 660337). Children's menu, half portions and high chairs; garden.

THE BELL INN, Walberswick, Southwold (01502 723109). Children's menu; high chairs and baby changing facilities; family room; garden.

THE FROIZE INN, Chillesford, Woodbridge (01394 450282). Children's menu; baby changing facilities; garden.

SURREY

CHASE LODGE HOTEL, Hampton Wick, Kingston-upon-Thames (0181-943 1862). Children's menu and half portions; high chairs and family room.

WEST SUSSEX

THE HORSE GUARDS INN, Petworth (01798 342332). Children welcome for lunches or dinner and accommodation; high chairs.

WARWICKSHIRE

THE OLDE COACH HOUSE INN, Ashby St Ledgers, Near Rugby (01788 890349). Children's menu and half portions; high chairs; family room and baby changing facilities; garden.

THE HOUNDSHILL, Ettington (01789 740267). Children's menu; high chairs; garden.

HOWARD ARMS, Ilmington, Near Shipston-on-Stour (Tel & Fax: 01608 682226). Half portions and high chair; garden.

WILTSHIRE

THE NEELD ARMS INN, Near Castle Combe (Tel & Fax: 01249 782470). Children's menu, high chairs and family room.

OLD BELL HOTEL, Malmesbury (01666 822344). Children's menu and half portions; high chairs; family room; baby changing facilities; garden.

CROWN & ANCHOR, Ham, Near Marlborough (01488 668242). Children's menu and high chairs.

WORCESTERSHIRE

TALBOT HOTEL, Knightwick (01886 821235). Half portions and high chairs.

HOLDFAST COTTAGE HOTEL, Little Malvern, Near Malvern (01684 310288). Half portions; high chairs, family room and baby changing facilities; garden.

NORTH YORKSHIRE

BUCK INN, Thornton Watlass, Near Bedale (01677 422461). Children's menu; outdoor play area; high chairs.

CROWN INN, Roecliffe, Boroughbridge (01423 322578). Children's menu, half portions, high chairs and family room.

DUKE OF WELLINGTON INN, Danby, Near Whitby (01287 660351). Children's menu and half portions; high chairs and family room.

THE GEORGE AT EASINGWOLD, Easingwold, York (01347 821698). Children welcome; high chairs and family room.

GANTON GREYHOUND, Ganton, Near Scarborough (01944 710116). Children's menu, half portions; high chairs, family room, baby changing facilities; garden.

FEVERSHAM ARMS HOTEL, Helmsley (01439 770766). Children's menu and half portions; high chairs and family room; garden.

THE WHEATSHEAF, Carperby, Leyburn (01969 663216). Children's menu, high chairs, garden.

VINTAGE HOTEL & RESTAURANT, Scotch Corner (01748 824424). Half portions; garden.

THE FOX AND HOUNDS, Starbotton, Skipton (01756 760269). Children's menu and half portions.

THE BUCK HOTEL, Reeth, Swaledale (01748 884210). Children's menu and half portions; high chairs, family room.

NAG'S HEAD COUNTRY INN, Pickhill, Near Thirsk (01845 567391). Half portions, high chairs and garden.

SCOTLAND

ABERDEEN, BANFF AND MORAY

INVER HOTEL, Crathie, By Balmoral (013397 42345). Half portions; high chairs and family room; garden.

MINMORE HOUSE HOTEL, Glenlivet, Ballindalloch (01807 590378). Children's menu and half portions; high chairs; garden.

FIFE ARMS HOTEL, Dufftown (01340 820220). Children's menu; high chairs and family room; garden.

ARGYLL & BUTE

GALLEY OF LORNE INN, Ardfern, By Lochgilphead (01852 500284). Children's menu, half portions, high chairs; garden.

INVERORAN HOTEL, Bridge of Orchy (01838 400220). Half portions; family room.

BORDERS

THE WHEATSHEAF AT SWINTON, Swinton, Duns (01890 860257). Half portions, high chairs; baby changing facilities; garden.

EDINBURGH AND LOTHIANS

YE OLDE ORIGINAL ROSLIN INN, Roslin (0131-440 2384). Children's menu and half portions; high chairs, family room and baby changing facilities; garden.

LOCHCARRON HOTEL, Lochcarron (01520 722260). Children's menu; high chairs; family room.

PERTH AND KINROSS

PALACE HOTEL, Aberfeldy (01887 820359). Children's menu and half portions; high chairs, family room and baby changing facilities.

KENMORE HOTEL, Kenmore (01887 830205). Half portions, high chairs and family room.

WALES

ANGLESEY AND GWYNEDD

PENHELIG ARMS HOTEL, Aberdyfi (01654 767215). Half portions, high chairs and family room.

NORTH WALES

WHEATSHEAF INN, Betws yn Rhos, Abergele (01492 680218). Children's menu, half portions, high chairs; garden.

BRITANNIA INN, Llangollen (01978 860144). Children's menu, half portions, high chairs; garden.

GOLDEN PHEASANT, Glyn Ceiriog, Near Llangollen (01691 718281). Children's menu, half portions; high chairs; family room.

CARDIGANSHIRE

WEBLEY WATERFRONT HOTEL, St Dogmaels (01239 612085). Children's menu and high chairs; garden.

CARMARTHENSHIRE

ANGEL INN, Salem, Llandeilo (01558 823394). Children's menu and half portions. High chairs, family room, garden.

SOUTH WALES

THE ROYAL GEORGE HOTEL, Tintern, Near Chepstow (01291 689205). Children's menu and half portions; high chairs, family room and baby changing facilities; garden.

DOLFORWYN HALL HOTEL, Abermule, Montgomery (01686 630221). Children's menu and half portions; high chairs and family room; garden.

FHG PUBLICATIONS

publish a large range of well-known accommodation guides. We will be happy to send you details or you can use the order form at the back of this book.

ONE FOR YOUR FRIEND 2000

FHG Publications have a large range of attractive holiday accommodation guides for all kinds of holiday opportunities throughout Britain. They also make useful gifts at any time of year. Our guides are available in most bookshops and larger newsagents but we will be happy to post you a copy direct if you have any difficulty. We will also post abroad but have to charge separately for post or freight. *The inclusive cost of posting and packing the guides to you or your friends in the UK is as follows:*

FARM HOLIDAY GUIDE
England, Scotland, Wales and Channel Islands.
Board, Self-catering, Caravans/
Camping, Activity Holidays.
£5.60 inc p&p

BED AND BREAKFAST STOPS.
Over 1000 friendly and comfortable overnight stops.
Non-smoking, Disabled and Special Diets Supplements.
£5.60 inc p&p.

BRITAIN'S BEST HOLIDAYS
A quick-reference general guide for all kinds of holidays.
£4.20 inc p&p.

SELF-CATERING HOLIDAYS
in Britain
Over 1000 addresses throughout for Self-catering and caravans in Britain.
£5.00 inc p&p.

Recommended
WAYSIDE AND COUNTRY INNS
of Britain
Pubs, Inns and small hotels.
£5.00 inc p&p

Recommended
COUNTRY HOTELS OF BRITAIN
Including Country Houses, for the discriminating
£5.00 inc p&p

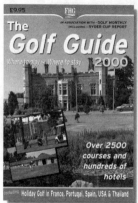  

GOLF GUIDE –
Where to play. Where to stay.
In association with GOLF
MONTHLY.Over 2500 golf courses
in Britain with convenient
accommodation. Holiday Golf in
France, Portugal, Spain,USA and
Thailand.
£10.50 inc p&p.

The FHG Guide to CARAVAN &
CAMPING HOLIDAYS
Caravans for hire, sites and
holiday parks and centres.
£4.30 inc p&p.

BED AND BREAKFAST
in Britain
Over 1000 choices for touring
and holidays throughout Britain.
Airports and Ferries Supplement.
£4.20 inc p&p.

CHILDREN WELCOME! Family Holidays and Attractions guide.
Family holidays with details of amenities for children and babies.   £5.00 inc p&p.

PETS WELCOME!
The unique guide for holidays for pet owners and their pets.   £5.60 inc p&p.

Tick your choice and send your order and payment to

FHG PUBLICATIONS, ABBEY MILL BUSINESS CENTRE,
SEEDHILL, PAISLEY PA1 1TJ
(TEL: 0141-887 0428; FAX: 0141-889 7204).
Deduct 10% for 2/3 titles or copies; 20% for 4 or more.

FHG

Send to: NAME...

            ADDRESS ....

            ....

            ....

            POST CODE ....

I enclose Cheque/Postal Order for £...

            SIGNATURE ....DATE ....

Please complete the following to help us improve the service we provide. How did
you find out about our guides?:

☐Press   ☐Magazines   ☐TV/Radio   ☐Family/Friend   ☐Other

Map 7

0 10 20 30 40 50 Kilometres
0 10 20 30 Miles
Grid interval is 30 miles

SHETLAND ISLANDS

	A	B	C	D	E	F		

1

ORKNEY ISLANDS
MAINLAND
Stromness
Kirkwall
HOY
YELL
MAINLAND

2

Lerwick
Sumburgh

3

LEWIS
WESTERN ISLES

Durness
Bettyhill
Tongue
Thurso
John o'Groats
Wick
Scourie
Lochinver

4

Gairloch
Poolewe
Ullapool
Lairg
Golspie
Bonar Bridge
Dornoch
Tain
Helmsdale

HIGHLAND

Portree
SKYE
Dingwall
Rosemarkie
Elgin
Cullen
Banff
Fraserburgh
Fochabers
Fortrose
Nairn
Forres
Keith
Turriff
Peterhead
Beauly
Croy
Kilravock Castle
MORAY
Huntly
Inverness
Daviot
Grantown-on-Spey
Tomintoul
Inverurie
CITY OF ABERDEEN
Broadford
Kyle of Lochalsh
Dornie
Kyleakin
Carrbridge
Aviemore
Aberdeen

5

Mallaig
Fort Augustus
Kingussie
ABERDEENSHIRE
Braemar
Banchory
Stonehaven

6

INNER HEBRIDES

Fort William
Kinlochleven
Glencoe
Ballachulish
Kinloch Rannoch
Pitlochry
ANGUS
Brechin
Aberfeldy
Dunkeld
Forfar
Montrose
Tobermory
MULL
Taynuilt
Oban
Killin
Lochearnhead
PERTH & KINROSS
Blairgowrie
Monifieth
Arbroath
Carnoustie
Dalmally
Crianlarich
Strathyre
Crieff
Perth
Dundee
Inveraray
Callander
Auchterarder
Cupar
St Andrews
Arrochar
Tarbet
Aberfoyle
Kinross
FIFE

7

ARGYLL & BUTE
JURA
Lochgilphead
Luss
Drymen
Stirling
STIRLING
Kirkcaldy
North Berwick
Ardrishaig
Dunoon
Gourock
Balloch
Dumbarton
Dunfermline
EDINBURGH
Dunbar
Tarbert
Rothesay
Greenock
Paisley
Glasgow
Dalkeith
Haddington
Eyemouth
Largs
Beith
Hamilton
Lanark
Chirnside
Berwick upon Tweed
ISLAY
KINTYRE
NORTH AYRSHIRE
Ardrossan
Fenwick
SOUTH LANARKSHIRE
Biggar
Lauder
Duns
Coldstream
Cornhill-on-Tweed
Irvine
Kilmarnock
Peebles
Galashiels
Bamburgh
Brodick
Troon
EAST AYRSHIRE
Abington
SCOTTISH BORDERS
Selkirk
Kelso
Wooler
Seahouses
Lamlash
Prestwick
Ayr
Hawick
Jedburgh
Campbeltown
ARRAN
Maybole
New Cumnock
Moffat
Beattock
Alnwick

8

9

10

8. INVERCLYDE
9. RENFREWSHIRE
10. WEST DUNBARTONSHIRE
11. EAST DUNBARTONSHIRE
12. NORTH LANARKSHIRE
13. CITY OF GLASGOW
14. EAST RENFREWSHIRE

SOUTH AYRSHIRE
Girvan
Langholm
NORTHUMBERLAND
Bellingham
Morpeth

DUMFRIES & GALLOWAY
New Galloway
Crocketford
Dumfries
Gretna
Longtown
Newcastle-upon-Tyne
Whitley Bay
Stranraer
Newton Stewart
Castle Douglas
Annan
Greenhead
Hexham
Corbridge
Portpatrick
Wigtown
Gatehouse of Fleet
Kirkcudbright
Silloth
Carlisle
Greenhead
CUMBRIA
Alston
Durham
Port William
Bassenthwaite
Penrith

11

1. CITY OF DUNDEE
2. CLACKMANNANSHIRE
3. FALKIRK
4. WEST LOTHIAN
5. CITY OF EDINBURGH
6. MIDLOTHIAN
7. EAST LOTHIAN

A	B	C	D	E	F	G

© GEOprojects (U.K.) Ltd
Crown Copyright Reserved

Map 1

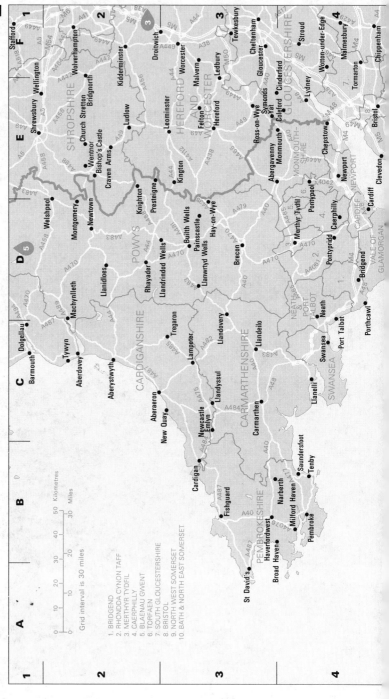

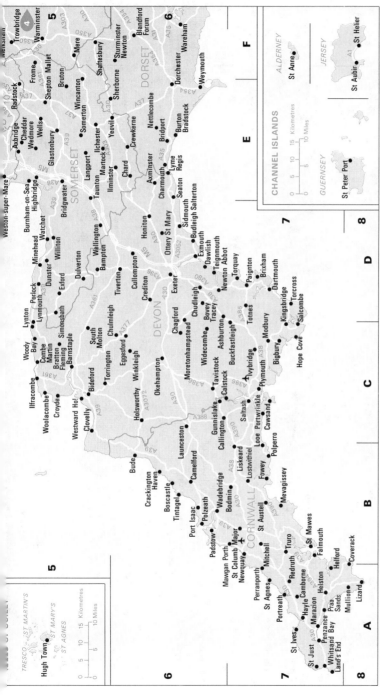

Map 2

CHANNEL ISLANDS

ALDERNEY
St Anne

GUERNEY
St Peter Port

JERSEY
St Aubin • St Helier

0 5 10 15 Kilometres
0 5 10 Miles

TRESCO • ST MARTIN'S
ST MARY'S
Hugh Town • ST AGNES

0 5 10 15 Kilometres
0 5 10 Miles

GEOprojects (U.K.) Ltd
Crown Copyright Reserved

Place names

Trowbridge, Warminster, Mere, Sturminster Newton, Blandford Forum, Wareham, Weymouth, Dorchester, Sherborne, Shaftesbury, Wincanton, Bruton, Frome, Radstock, Shepton Mallet, Axbridge, Cheddar, Wedmore, Wells, Bradstock, Burton, Bridport, Nettlecombe, Crewkerne, Yeovil, Ilchester, Somerton, Glastonbury, Langport, Martock, Chard, Ilminster, Taunton, Wellington, Axminster, Charmouth, Lyme Regis, Seaton, Sidmouth, Budleigh Salterton, Exmouth, Dawlish, Teignmouth, Torquay, Paignton, Brixham, Dartmouth, Torcross, Salcombe, Kingsbridge, Hope Cove, Bigbury, Modbury, Ivybridge, Plymouth, Totnes, Ashburton, Buckfastleigh, Bovey Tracey, Widecombe, Chagford, Moretonhampstead, Chudleigh, Exeter, Crediton, Tiverton, Cullompton, Honiton, Ottery St Mary, Bampton, Dulverton, Exford, Dunster, Williton, Watchet, Minehead, Porlock, Lynmouth, Lynton, Woody Bay, Combe Martin, Ilfracombe, Woolacombe, Croyde, Braunton, Fleming, Barnstaple, South Molton, Chulmleigh, Eggesford, Winkleigh, Torrington, Bideford, Westward Ho!, Clovelly, Bude, Crackington Haven, Boscastle, Tintagel, Port Isaac, Polzeath, Padstow, Wadebridge, Bodmin, Camelford, Launceston, Okehampton, Holsworthy, Simonsbath, Tavistock, Calstock, Gunnislake, Callington, Saltash, Liskeard, Lostwithiel, Fowey, Loe, Polperro, Portwrinkle, Cawsand, Mevagissey, St Austell, St Mawes, Truro, Falmouth, Helford, Coverack, Lizard, Mullion, Helston, Marazion, Praa Sands, Penzance, Land's End, Whitsand Bay, St Just, St Ives, Portreath, St Agnes, Perranporth, Newquay, Mawgan Porth, St Columb Major, Mitchell, Redruth, Camborne, Hayle, Weston-super-Mare, Burnham-on-Sea, Highbridge, Bridgwater, Nailsea

DORSET, SOMERSET, DEVON, CORNWALL

Map 3

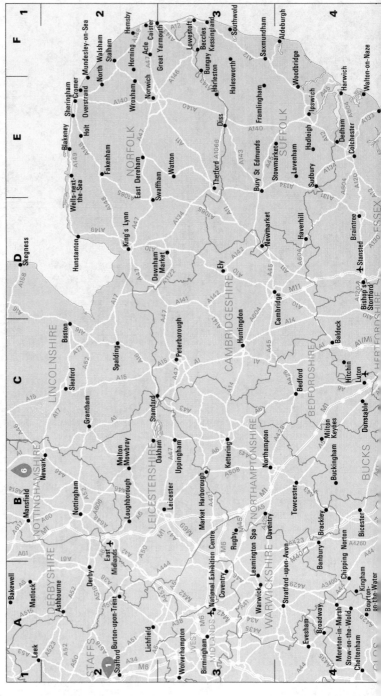

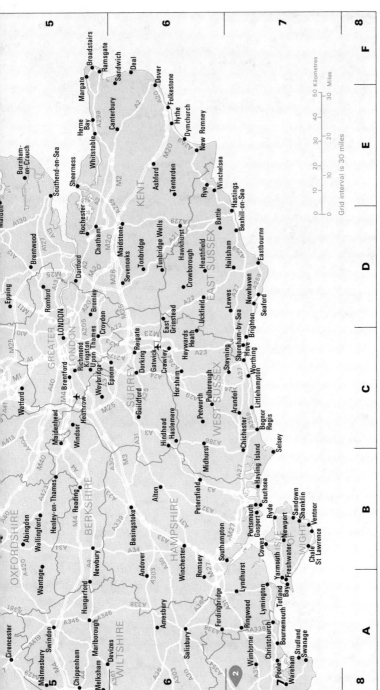

Map 4

© GEOprojects (U.K.) Ltd.
Crown Copyright Reserved

Grid interval is 30 miles

Kilometres
Miles

OXFORDSHIRE
WILTSHIRE
BERKSHIRE
HAMPSHIRE
GREATER LONDON
SURREY
WEST SUSSEX
EAST SUSSEX
KENT
ISLE OF WIGHT

Cirencester
Malmesbury
Swindon
Chippenham
Melksham
Devizes
Marlborough
Hungerford
Wantage
Abingdon
Wallingford
Henley-on-Thames
Reading
Newbury
Andover
Basingstoke
Winchester
Romsey
Southampton
Lyndhurst
Lymington
Salisbury
Amesbury
Fordingbridge
Ringwood
Wimborne
Poole
Wareham
Studland
Swanage
Christchurch
Bournemouth
Totland Bay
Freshwater
Yarmouth
Cowes
Newport
Chale
St Lawrence
Ventnor
Shanklin
Sandown
Ryde
Portsmouth
Gosport
Southsea
Havling Island
Petersfield
Alton
Midhurst
Haslemere
Hindhead
Petworth
Chichester
Bognor Regis
Selsey
Arundel
Littlehampton
Worthing
Steyning
Shoreham-by-Sea
Hove
Brighton
Newhaven
Seaford
Lewes
Pulborough
Horsham
Crawley
Gatwick
Haywards Heath
Uckfield
Guildford
Dorking
Reigate
East Grinstead
Epsom
Weybridge
Windsor
Maidenhead
Heathrow
Brentford
Kingston Upon Thames
Richmond
Croydon
Bromley
Watford
Epping
Brentwood
Romford
Dartford
Sevenoaks
Tonbridge
Tunbridge Wells
Crowborough
Heathfield
Hawkhurst
Maidstone
Chatham
Rochester
Sheerness
Southend-on-Sea
Burnham-on-Crouch
Whitstable
Herne Bay
Margate
Broadstairs
Ramsgate
Sandwich
Deal
Canterbury
Dover
Folkestone
Hythe
Dymchurch
New Romney
Ashford
Tenterden
Rye
Winchelsea
Hastings
Battle
Bexhill-on-Sea
Eastbourne
Hailsham

Map 5

© GEOprojects (U.K.) Ltd
Crown Copyright Reserved

1

A B C 7 D

Girvan

DUMFRIES AND GALLOWAY

Langholm Bellingh NORTH

New Galloway

2

Newton Stewart Dumfries Annan Gretna Longtown Greenhead

Castle Douglas Brampton A69

Wigtown Gatehouse of Fleet Silloth Carlisle

Kirkcudbright Alston

Port William Wigton

A596

3

Maryport Bassenthwaite Penrith

Cockermouth Brampton

Workington Keswick Appleby

Whitehaven Ennerdale Bridge Ullswater Shap Kirkby Stephen

CUMBRIA Rydal Ambleside

Gosforth Little Langdale Hawkshead Windermere

Seascale Coniston Kendal Sedbergh

Newby Bridge Kirkby Lonsdal

Broughton-in-Furness Ulverston Arnside Ingletc

Millom Grange-over-Sands

Ramsey Barrow-in-Furness Settle

Peel Morecambe

ISLE OF MAN Lancaster

Port Erin Douglas

Castletown Fleetwood

Port St Mary Clitheroe

4

Blackpool LANCASHIRE

Lytham St Annes Preston Blackburn

5

Southport Chorley

Formby Bolton

Wigan GREATER MANCHEST

MERSEYSIDE Manches

Amlwch Hoylake Liverpool

ANGLESEY Birkenhead

Holyhead Llanerchymedd Llandudno Colwyn Bay Rhyl Prestatyn Knutsford

Menai Beaumaris Northwich

Llangefni Bridge Conwy Abergele Holywell Chester CHESHIRE

6

Bangor ABERCONWY & COLWYN FLINT SHIRE Nannerch

Caernarvon Llanrwst Denbigh Nantwich

Llanberis Ruthin DENBIGH-SHIRE Newcastle-under-Ly

Betws-y-Coed Corwen Wrexham WREXHAM Wem

GWYNEDD Llangollen Market Drayton

Nefyn Portmadoc Ffestiniog Bala Oswestry Wellington

Criccieth Penrhyndeudraeth SHROPSHIRE

Pwllheli Harlech Shrewsbury

Llanbedrog

Abersoch Dolgellau

7

Aberdaron Barmouth Welshpool 1

POWYS

Tywyn Machynlleth

A B C D

Map 6

E   F   G   H   1

UMBERLAND
Morpeth
Whitley Bay
Tynemouth
Corbridge   Newcastle upon-Tyne   South Shields
Hexham   TYNE AND WEAR   Sunderland

2

0   10   20   30   40   50 Kilometres
0   10   20   30   Miles
Grid interval is 30 miles

1. STOCKTON-ON-TEES
2. MIDDLESBROUGH
3. KINGSTON UPON HULL
4. NORTH EAST LINCOLNSHIRE

Durham
DURHAM   HARTLEPOOL
Bishop Auckland   Redcar
Middleton-in-Teesdale   Middlesbrough   Saltburn-by-the-Sea
Barnard Castle   Darlington   REDCAR & CLEVELAND
Stokesley   Guisborough   Whitby

3

Richmond
Leyburn   Northallerton
Middleham   Thirsk   Helmsley   Pickering   Scarborough
Ayton   Cayton Bay
Filey
NORTH YORKSHIRE
Ripon   Castle Howard   Malton   Flamborough
Grassington   Huby   Sledmere   Bridlington
Driffield

4

Skipton   Harrogate
Keighley   Ilkley   York
Bingley   EAST RIDING OF YORKSHIRE   Hornsea
Bradford   Leeds   YORK   Beverley
Heptonstall   WEST   Selby
Halifax   YORKSHIRE   Hull   Withernsea
Goole
Huddersfield   NORTH LINCOLNSHIRE
Barnsley   Scunthorpe   Grimsby
Glossop   Doncaster   Cleethorpes
SOUTH YORKSHIRE

5

Sheffield   Gainsborough   Louth
Buxton   Worksop   Mablethorpe
cclesfield   Bakewell   Chesterfield   Alford
ngleton   Matlock   Lincoln   Horncastle
Leek   Mansfield   LINCOLNSHIRE   Skegness
oke-on-Trent   Ashbourne   DERBYSHIRE   NOTTINGHAM-SHIRE   Newark   Sleaford   Boston
Derby   Nottingham   Grantham

6

TAFFORDSHIRE   East Midlands   Melton Mowbray   Spalding
Stafford   Loughborough
Burton-upon-Trent
Lichfield   LEICESTERSHIRE   Stamford
Oakham   Peterborough
Leicester   Uppingham

7

E   F   G   H

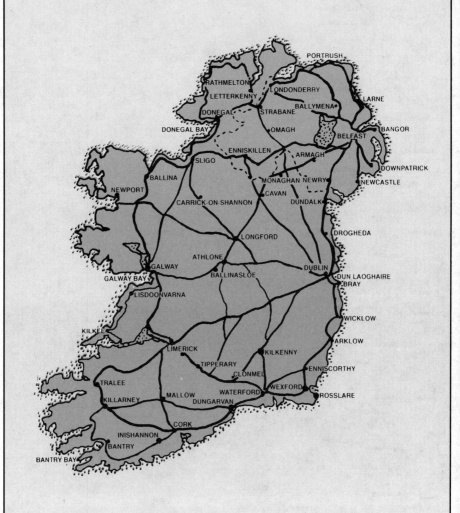